MULTIPLE MODERNITIES
AND POSTSECULAR SOCIETIES

Global Connections

Series Editor: Robert Holton, Trinity College, Dublin

Global Connections builds on the multi-dimensional and continuously expanding interest in Globalization. The main objective of the series is to focus on 'connectedness' and provide readable case studies across a broad range of areas such as social and cultural life, economic, political and technological activities.

The series aims to move beyond abstract generalities and stereotypes: 'Global' is considered in the broadest sense of the word, embracing connections between different nations, regions and localities, including activities that are trans-national, and trans-local in scope; 'Connections' refers to movements of people, ideas, resources, and all forms of communication as well as the opportunities and constraints faced in making, engaging with, and sometimes resisting globalization.

The series is interdisciplinary in focus and publishes monographs and collections of essays by new and established scholars. It fills a niche in the market for books that make the study of globalization more concrete and accessible.

Also published in this series:

Legitimization in World Society
Edited by Aldo Mascareño and Kathya Araujo
ISBN 978-1-4094-4088-8

Global Islamophobia
Muslims and Moral Panic in the West
Edited by George Morgan and Scott Poynting
ISBN 978-1-4094-3119-0

Managing Cultural Change
Reclaiming Synchronicity in a Mobile World
Melissa Butcher
ISBN 978-1-4094-2510-6

Decolonizing European Sociology
Transdisciplinary Approaches
Edited by Encarnación Gutiérrez Rodríguez,
Manuela Boatca and Sérgio Costa
ISBN 978-0-7546-7872-4

Multiple Modernities
and Postsecular Societies

Edited by

MASSIMO ROSATI
University of Rome Tor Vergata, Italy

KRISTINA STOECKL
University of Vienna, Austria

ASHGATE

Published by
Ashgate Publishing Limited
Wey Court East
Union Road
Farnham
Surrey, GU9 7PT
England

Ashgate Publishing Company
110 Cherry Street
Suite 3-1
Burlington, VT 05401-3818
USA

www.ashgate.com

British Library Cataloguing in Publication Data
Multiple modernities and postsecular societies. -- (Global
    connections)
    1. Civilization, Modern--21st century--Philosophy.
    2. Civilization, Secular--Case studies. 3. Religion and
    sociology. 4. Postsecularism.
    I. Series II. Rosati, Massimo, 1969- III. Stoeckl,
    Kristina.
    306.6'0905-dc23

Library of Congress Cataloging-in-Publication Data
Rosati, Massimo, 1969-
    Multiple modernities and postsecular societies / by Massimo Rosati and Kristina Stoeckl.
        p. cm. -- (Global connections)
    Includes bibliographical references and index.
    ISBN 978-1-4094-4412-1 (hardback) -- ISBN 978-1-4094-4413-8 (ebook) 1. Secularism-
-History. 2. Social history. I. Stoeckl, Kristina. II. Title.
    BL2752.R67 2012
    301--dc23

                                                                        2012022164

ISBN 9781409444121 (hbk)
ISBN 9781409444138 (ebk – PDF)
ISBN 9781409472384 (ebk – ePUB)

Printed and bound in Great Britain by the
MPG Books Group, UK.

Contents

List of Figures   *vii*
List of Tables   *ix*
Notes on Contributors   *xi*

Introduction   1
Massimo Rosati and Kristina Stoeckl

1   From Multiple Modernities to Multiple Democracies   17
    Alessandro Ferrara

2   Multifaceted or Fragmented Public Spheres in Turkey and Iran   41
    Uğur Kömeçoğlu

3   The Turkish Laboratory:
    Local Modernity and the Postsecular in Turkey   61
    Massimo Rosati

4   Russia's 'Cursed Issues', Post-Soviet Religion,
    and the Endurance of Secular Modernity   79
    Alexander Agadjanian

5   European Integration and Russian Orthodoxy:
    Two Multiple Modernities Perspectives   97
    Kristina Stoeckl

6   A State Goddess in the New Secular Nepal:
    Reflections on the Kumari Case at the Supreme Court   115
    Chiara Letizia

7   Big Man of the Big God:
    Nigeria as a Laboratory for Multiple Modernities   143
    Enzo Pace

8   The Modernity of New Societies:
       South Africa, Brazil and the Prospect of a World-Sociology   163
       Peter Wagner

Index   *181*

List of Figures

3.1   Relationships between modernity and religions   72

6.1   Kathmandu Durbar Square, September 2009.
       Kumari Jatra Festival.   123
6.2   Kathmandu Durbar Square, September 2009.
       Kumari Jatra Festival.   124

7.1   The Federation of Nigeria with its 36 States   146
7.2   The waves of Christianity in Nigeria   148
7.3   The multiple creativity of the charismatic profile of leadership   152

List of Tables

7.1   Religions in Nigeria   147
7.2   The four types of Pentecostal leadership   154

Notes on Contributors

Alexander Agadjanian is Professor at the Center for the Study of Religion at the Russian State University for Humanities, Moscow. He earned his PhD from the Institute of Oriental Studies, Russian Academy of Sciences, worked as scholar at the same Institute and taught at Arizona State University. He is the author and editor of several books and articles on religious developments in post-Soviet Russia and Eurasia.

Alessandro Ferrara is Professor of Political Philosophy at the University of Rome Tor Vergata and former president of the Italian Association for Political Philosophy. Recently he has published *The Force of the Example. Explorations in the Paradigm of Judgment* (New York, Columbia University Press, 2008). His *The Democratic Horizon: Openness, Hyperpluralism and the Renewal of Political Liberalism* is forthcoming.

Uğur Kömeçoğlu is Associate Professor of Sociology and acting Chair of Sociology at Süleyman Şah University in Istanbul. From 2001 to 2010 he worked as a lecturer at Istanbul Bilgi University and the London School of Economics external programme. He has published articles in various journals and books on public space, social movements, gender sociability, Islamic identities, modernity, and the Ottoman public sphere. His recent works focused on popular religion in Istanbul, and on the Kurdish question from a conflict resolution perspective.

Chiara Letizia is a social anthropologist and historian of religions. She is a researcher and lecturer in cultural anthropology at the University of Milano-Bicocca and Research Associate at the Institute of Social and Cultural Anthropology, University of Oxford. She has been carrying out fieldwork on Nepalese religion and society since 1997. She is now conducting research about the understandings of secularism in Nepal and has just published an article on the subject, 'Shaping secularism in Nepal', in the *European Bulletin of Himalayan Research* 39 (2012).

Enzo Pace is Professor of Sociology and Sociology of Religion at the University of Padova, Italy. Formerly President of the International Society for the Sociology of Religion (ISSR/SISR), he was Visiting Professor at the École des Hautes Études en Sciences Sociales in 1995 and in 2000. His recent publications include 'Salvation Goods, the Gift Economy and Charismatic Concern', *Social Compass*, 2006 (47); 'Religion as Communication: the Changing Shape of Catholicism in Europe', in Nancy Ammermann (ed.), *Everyday Religion* (New York, Oxford

University Press); 'Globalization and the Conflict of Values in the Middle Eastern Societies', in P. Beyer, L. Beaman (eds), *Religion, Culture and Globalization* (Leiden, Brill, 2007); and *Religion as Communication* (Farnham, Ashgate, 2011).

Massimo Rosati, director of the CSPS (www.csps.uniroma2.it), teaches sociology at the University of Rome Tor Vergata. He is the author of *Ritual and the Sacred. A Neo-Durkheimian Analysis of Politics, Religion and the Self* (Farnham, Ashgate, 2009). He co-edited with W.S.F. Pickering *Suffering and Evil. The Durkheimian Legacy* (2008).

Kristina Stoeckl is APART Postdoctoral Research Fellow in political sciences at the University of Vienna; from 2009 until 2012 she was a Marie Curie fellow at the University of Rome Tor Vergata. She is the author of *Community After Totalitarianism: The Russian Orthodox Intellectual Tradition and the Philosophical Discourse of Political Modernity* (Frankfurt, Lang, 2008) and has published articles on the Russian Orthodox Church after communism, Russian religious philosophy, Orthodox Christianity in Europe, modernity and postsecularism. Her *The Russian Orthodox Church and Human Rights* is forthcoming.

Peter Wagner is ICREA Research Professor at the University of Barcelona and currently principal investigator of the ERC-advanced grant project 'Trajectories of modernity' (TRAMOD; 2010–2015). His main research interests are in historical and comparative sociology and in social and political theory. His recent publications include: *Modernity: Understanding the Present* (Cambridge, Polity, 2012); *Modernity as Experience and Interpretation: A New Sociology of Modernity* (Cambridge, Polity, 2008); *Varieties of World-making: Beyond Globalization*, ed. with Nathalie Karagiannis (Liverpool, Liverpool University Press, 2007).

Introduction

Massimo Rosati and Kristina Stoeckl

This volume has its origins in a workshop on 'Multiple Modernities and Postsecular Societies' held at the *Centre for the Study and Documentation of Religions and Political Institutions in Postsecular Society* (CSPS) at the University of Rome Tor Vergata in May 2011, and in several lectures on this topic at CSPS during 2011 and 2012.[1] The articles gathered in this volume bring together reflection on the paradigm of multiple modernities with recent theorizing on the postsecular and on postsecular society. The empirical perspective we have chosen for this volume is mostly non-Western – in the sense that most of the case-studies refer to non-Western experiences – but our conceptual starting point lies at the heart of a Western theoretical debate that is characterized by self-reflectivity and the deconstruction of long-held assumptions about the connection between modernity and secularism (Calhoun, Juergensmeyer and Van Antwerpen 2011). By examining non-Western experiences of modernization, secularization and religious revival, we hope to shed light on some fundamental questions that shape the current academic debate on multiple modernities and postsecularity: is the idea of multiple modernities able to grasp differences as well as similarities between different kinds of modernities and democracies? Are modernity, democracy and secularism universalistic concepts or are they, on the contrary, peculiar to Western civilization? What is really meant by the concept of the postsecular? Which kind of relationship can be established between multiple trajectories of modern development and the emergence of postsecular societies both on a regional and a global level? These are some of the questions we want to address and if possible answer in the coming pages and in the contributions to this volume.

In this introduction, we first define the key-concepts of this debate – multiple modernities and postsecular societies – before introducing the individual articles and bringing out, in a dialogue *ex-post* with our contributors, how each of the papers spells out the relationship between the paradigm of multiple modernities and the concept of the postsecular.

---

1   The editors acknowledge the financial support by the Fondazione Roma III Settore for the organization of the workshop and CSPS-lectures.

Multiple Modernities

The theory of multiple modernities, which was first formulated by Shmuel Eisenstadt, and has grown into a prolific school of thought with a long series of programmatic publications and related research-programs (see for example Eisenstadt 2003; Arnason, Eisenstadt and Wittrock 2005; Adams, Smith and Vlahov 2011), offers a contemporary theory about civilizational differences that seeks to overcome the *clash-of-civilization* type of scenarios of globalization. The multiple modernities approach holds that the Western trajectory of modernization must not be seen as the only possible pathway to modernity. Instead, we find in the world a multiplicity of continually evolving modernities, each of which realizes a particular institutional and ideological interpretation of the modern program according to specific cultural prerequisites. Religions are usually considered one element that can account for the differentiation of pathways to modernity. The specific aim of this book lies in examining more closely the interaction of religion and secularization processes in the emergence of multiple forms of modernity.

The case-studies on Turkey, Russia, Nepal, Nigeria, South Africa and Brazil gathered in this volume offer a theoretical and empirical analysis of the relationship between different religious traditions and modernity. All authors share the perception that modernity is being reinterpreted in multiple ways by different religious traditions. Whereas the Western program of modernity includes at least ideologically, as one of its principal components, secularization – with its functional differentiation, privatization of religion and decline of religious beliefs (Casanova 2001) – modernization in non-Western settings often incorporates or even thrives on religion rather than excluding or diminishing it.

Several of the contributions in this volume describe, in one way or the other, differently secular modernities. They look, on the one hand, at the role of religion in modernization processes and, on the other hand, at the impact of modernization on religious practices and religious organizations. The general picture which emerges from these studies is that religion continues to play a decisive role in modernization processes, either as a motor of modernization, as Vincenzo Pace shows in his study of Pentecostalism in Nigeria, or as an antagonistic force vis-à-vis modernization, as the case-studies on Russia in this volume partially demonstrate. Some contributions in this volume, in particular the articles by Massimo Rosati and Ugur Kömeçoglu, show, however, that there is also something else going on which can no longer adequately be explained by the dichotomy of the religious and the secular. This is the reality of contemporary modern societies which are faced with a resurgence of religion, and with new forms of religious pluralism within a secular horizon that call into question established secular institutions and practices. It is precisely these cases which the term 'postsecular' seeks to grasp both analytically and normatively.

Defining the Postsecular

'Postsecular' society has become a catchword in contemporary debates on religion in the philosophical, political and sociological sciences. The term has gained conceptual relevance as a consequence of a scrutiny of classical theories of modernization and secularization (see Davie 2007). Looking at the existing literature, one gets the feeling that the notion expresses two things at the same time: on the one hand, a general intuition that classical theories of secularization are insufficient to grasp the present state of the relationship between religions and contemporary societies and/or political arrangements, and, on the other hand, a stance that there is a need, from a normative point of view, to find more just ways of accommodating religious claims in liberal institutions. However, not much more seems clear beside such a very general intuition. This vagueness, and the empirical fragility of the concept, make authoritative voices in the social science debate sometimes sceptical about its utility (see Turner 2011). Albeit humbly, we try to suggest a possible way to push the discussion on the postsecular a step forward, offering a more sound theoretical clarification and putting it to the test empirically through the case-studies in this book.

Jürgen Habermas's definition of postsecular society can conveniently be taken as starting point for scrutinizing the double-meaning of the postsecular. According to Habermas,

> This term "postsecular society" refers not only to the fact that religion continues to assert itself in an increasingly secular environment and that society, for the time being, reckons with the continued existence of religious communities. The expression *postsecular* does not merely acknowledge publicly the functional contribution that the religious communities make to the reproduction of desired motives and attitudes. Rather, the public consciousness of postsecular society reflects a normative insight that has consequences for how believing and unbelieving citizens interact with one another politically. In postsecular society, the realization that "the modernization of public consciousness" takes hold and reflexively alters religious as well as secular mentalities in staggered phases is gaining acceptance. If together they understand the secularization of society to be a complementary learning process, both sides can, for cognitive reasons, then take seriously each other's contributions to controversial themes in the public sphere. (Habermas 2006: 258)

The key concept in the above definition is that of the *complementary learning process*. Proper to the postsecular condition is the epistemic disposition of bearers of both secular conceptions and religious worldviews to 'take seriously each other's contributions to controversial themes in the public sphere'. We take Habermas's definition as a starting point for our considerations on the postsecular, but we suggest that there are several implicit themes in this definition that deserve to be made explicit and reconsidered critically. In other words, Habermas's definition has to be unpacked and enriched.

Habermas's definition of the postsecular implicitly rests on the idea that both Western secular modernity and religious traditions are *reflective*. A process of complementary learning can be triggered and can reach a positive result only if both sides demonstrate high degrees of reflectivity, a key feature of every Axial civilization (Wittrock 2005). It would seem that from Habermas's point of view the reflectivity of religious traditions consists in their ability to embrace the language of public reason. In his paper, Rosati suggests a different understanding of religious reflectivity. Following Adam B. Seligman's suggestions and work (Seligman 2000 and 2004), he argues that the reflectivity of religious traditions is more conveniently sought in the inner resources for principled tolerance of religious traditions themselves. Good reasons for adjusting to a secular environment and to the modern 'immanent frame' (Taylor 2007) have to be articulated by religious traditions not by *giving up* their vocabulary and embracing an allegedly neutral public reason, but on the contrary by *mobilizing* their religious language and their own religious imaginary in order to respond to the modern condition. A postsecular society, from this perspective, is a society in which one can find high levels of reflectivity both on the side of secular modern society and of religious traditions, both being capable of finding from within their own imaginaries good reasons to enter into a dialectical relationship of mutual tolerance and/or recognition.

If reflectivity of both secular modernities and religious traditions is the first feature of a postsecular society, a second key feature is thus the co-presence or co-existence within the same public space of religious and secular world-views and practices. This is a crucial point: a postsecular society is not a de-secularized society, but a society where religious and secular views are called to live together, and to live together differently. Where early (Western) modernity conceived of religions as opposite to Reason and Enlightenment, contemporary modernity professes an increased consciousness that 'the relationship between the "religious" and the "secular" is dialectic and not merely oppositional' (Knott 2005: 125). In other terms, the idea of the postsecular does not mean that we are living in a non-secular environment and with non-secular institutions; rather, it 'refers to the limits of the secularization thesis' and emphasizes the interrelation between the two camps (Molendijk, Beaumont and Jedan 2010: x). As Kim Knott (2005) makes clear, *the secular and the religious are part of the same field*. The postsecular is characterized by the co-presence of religious and secular viewpoints and practices, and accordingly it is not to be confused with de-secularization. What is proper to the postsecular is that the 'dividing lines (and hence roles) of religions and science, faith and reason, tradition and innovation are no longer rigidly enforced (or indeed enforcible), and new relations of possibility are emerging' (Beaumont and Baker 2011: 2). Interpenetration – to use Nilüfer Göle's (2005) expression – between once rigidly separated borders is essential to the making (and understanding) of a postsecular society. Accordingly, the co-presence of secular and religious beliefs and practices that interact dialectically in a way that can sometimes move and reshape the dividing lines between them, also raises the possibility of new configurations both of secular and religious viewpoints and practices.

A third key element in the definition of the postsecular is the de-privatization of religion. A postsecular society is one where religion cannot be considered only as a private, strictly individualized, spiritualized, de-ritualized experience. Western modernity is not at odds with religion per se, and it can easily consider religious individualization as one of the expressions of modern individualism. Believing without belonging, religious patchworks, invisible religions, even invented religions – just to mention some of the formulae used by sociologists of religions to name contemporary forms of religiosity – are perfectly in keeping with the modern horizon and, at the end of the day, are compatible with Western modern sensitivity. Developments over the last few decades have shown a new ability of religions to become active in the public sphere (Casanova 1994, Ward and Hoelzl 2008). What is interesting about the renewed centrality of religions in the public sphere is what Jakelević has called 'collectivistic religions' (2010), by which she means religious traditions that run against Western modernity's dogmas such as free choice and individual autonomy, and that claim a public voice for traditional or newly de-privatized religions – Catholicism, Christian Orthodoxy, Islam, Judaism, and Pentecostalism. They thereby challenge the Western idea of the autonomous Self, the idea of a secular, neutral public space, and the idea of a neat discontinuity between the right and the good, religious world-views and the Law.

If reflectivity, co-existence of secular and religious viewpoints and practices, and de-privatized religions are three essential features of a postsecular society, a fourth theme is the presence of religious pluralism. A postsecular society is one in which religious pluralism, fostered by globalization and immigration, challenges the conditions of religious monopoly. A postsecular society requires an end not only of the modernist dream of the total eclipse of the sacred or of the privatization of religions, but also the end of conditions of strict religious monopoly. A truly postsecular society is a multi-religious society, where so to speak 'indigenous' traditions nowadays live side by side with diasporic religious communities. Religious pluralism is part and parcel of the sociological conditions of a postsecular society. Such a pluralism can be considered simply as a fact, perhaps a disturbing fact by some, and notwithstanding a fact that has to be tolerated; or it can be considered as a value, something that fosters the vitality of a democratic public sphere. At least in principle, religions, as both Habermas and Casanova argue, can be not only a normative source of meaning, but also a tool of social criticism. In fact, religions can challenge the self-referentiality of modern differentiated subsystems, and can exert pressure on them from a normative point of view (Casanova 1994). Accordingly, a postsecular society has to be understood as one in which a plurality of individual *and* collective religious beliefs and practices enrich and strengthen pluralism in general. A postsecular society is a society full of religious differences and particularities. It is a cosmopolitan society, but one in which cosmopolitanism has to be conceived of as rooted and not detached (Beck 2006), not bypassing and not neutralizing differences.

The last key element in the definition is that postsecular society is one where the sacred can take different forms, immanent and civic as well as transcendent. If we consider a postsecular society to be a society in which not only 'modernist' new religious movements contribute to 're-enchant' the world, but also (if not above all) traditional religions show their unexpected (by sociologists) stamina, then we must conclude that the sacred also continues to inhabit our social horizon as a transcendent and heteronomous force (Seligman 2000). Traditional religions that claim a public voice in the social and political sphere, and whose presence must be recognized as a fact if not as a shared value, do not look at this world as the final and only reality, but keep the capacity for 'beyonding', transcending the given reality in the name of a more perfect and heteronomous reality (Bellah 2011: 9).

To sum up, in our view, Habermas's idea of the postsecular as a process of complementary learning between religious and secular worldviews and practices has to be enriched in a way that includes the five features listed above. Reflectivity of both secular modernities and religious traditions, co-existence of secular and religious worldviews and practices, de-privatization of religions, religious pluralism vs. religious monopoly, and the sacred understood (also) as a heteronomous transcendent force vs. only immanent understanding of it: these are the sociological features that add empirical thickness to the philosophical and normative idea of the complementary learning process.

While Habermas's idea of the complementary learning process has a clear normative dimension, and many discussions on the postsecular, as well as on 'reflective' forms of secularism (see Calhoun, Juergensmeyer, Van Antwerpen 2011, Gorski, Kyuman, Torpey and Van Antwerpen 2012, Nynäs, Lassander, Utriainen 2012) have a normative dimension too (Ferrara, Kaul and Rasmussen 2010), what we seek to do in this book is to empirically enrich the discussion on the postsecular and, in turn, sketch a more articulate ideal-type of postsecular society. The five above-listed features and conditions of an ideal-typical postsecular society (reflectivity, co-existence of secular and religious worldviews, de-privatization of religions, religious pluralism vs. religious monopoly, and heteronomous conceptions of the sacred vs. only immanent ones) are empirical features of several societies, in the West and elsewhere. Their exact combination, and their ability to trigger processes of complementary learning – or instead their partial absence and/or ineffectiveness with regard to the making of a postsecular society – is something that cannot be addressed in the abstract, but must be analyzed in relation to specific and particular contexts. This is what the essays gathered in this volume seek to do.

Multiple Modernities, Religions and Postsecular Practices

The articles gathered in this volume offer a wide range of comparative cases to discuss multiple modernities, the idea of the postsecular and their mutual relationship. Most try to relate theoretical questions and empirical cases, while some focus on theoretical issues.

Alessandro Ferrara's paper is an exercise in reflectivity, and therefore his argument resonates with what we have called the first feature of postsecular society and the most important condition for the postsecular complementary learning process. His theoretical and conceptual argument prepares the ground for the rest of the contributions in this book. The reconstruction of the development of the multiple modernities paradigm in the first part of Ferrara's chapter is a valuable addition to our observations on modernity and religion in the beginning of this introduction. Ferrara brings out the central role of religion for theories of modernization, both in Eisenstadt, who was convinced of the significance of religion for the economic ethic of a society, and in Weber and Jasper, who both considered religion central for the explanation of Axial civilizations.

The point that religion is not merely one feature in the multiple trajectories of modernization, but indeed the most important feature is put to the test in the second part of Ferrara's chapter, where he analyses sources for democracy in different civilizational settings. Starting from the observation that in our contemporary world, 'democracy' has, on the one hand, become the political system which most countries and peoples aspire to, but, on the other hand, runs the risk of being reduced to a mere set of democratic procedures, Ferrara traces 'true democracy' back to a reconstructed 'democratic ethos' to be found in a number of diverse Western contexts, but which flourished best within radical protestant modernity. But can democracy be made applicable also to other cultural and religious contexts? Ferrara suggests that it can and argues that the idea of multiple modernities is of help in disentangling significant aspects of the 'spirit of democracy' from the original cultural seedbed in Protestantism. Having distinguished three basic elements of the 'spirit of democracy' – orientation to the common good, to equality, and to the intrinsic value of individuality – he looks for resources in support of these elements in different cultural settings. What is particularly interesting in the context of our argument on multiple modernities and religion is the fact that the cultural resources which Ferrara analyzes are all *religious* resources: religious teachings, texts and practices in Buddhism, Confucianism, Hinduism, Islam, and Judaism. He demonstrates how religious traditions can principally mobilize, from within their own semantic universe, ideas in support of democracy. At the same time, Ferrara points out, dissonances between these multiple sources for democracy and the fundamentals of the Western modern liberal democratic model persist. The two components of the 'spirit of democracy' for which it is most problematic to find equivalents in non-Western and non-Protestant cultures are the priority of rights over duties and the valuing of contestation and agonism within democratic life. However, these dissonances can trigger a self-reflective process on the side of the Western liberal mainstream. Ferrara thus demonstrates how the self-reflective mobilization of religious language for the justification of democracy can become the first element in the complementary learning process of a postsecular society, and self-critical reflection on the fundamentals of liberal democracy in the West the second element. Multiple modernities, in the light of this analysis, are a necessary condition for the emergence of postsecular societies.

Turkey and Iran are the first two countries which the authors in this volume analyze in the optic of multiple modernities and postsecularity. Uğur Kömeçoglu's and Massimo Rosati's chapters share a great deal, both in terms of empirical focus (Turkey and Iran in Kömeçoglu's case, and only Turkey in Rosati's) and theoretical frame. Both start from a reconsideration of classical modernist links between the idea of modernity as a product solely of the Western world, on the one hand, and secularization (conceived along Western lines) on the other. Both of them consider highly plausible that such reconsideration implies a close connection between the paradigms of multiple modernities and of the postsecular. Just as theories of modernity were strictly entwined with theories of secularization, multiple modernities and the postsecular are entwined with each other. Turkey and Iran, for different but also similar reasons, can be taken as good empirical examples of this new theoretical perspective.

Kömeçoglu's chapter offers a wide and colorful range of examples of the new relationship between the secular and the religious that is taking shape in Turkey and Iran. In Kömeçoglu's view, Iran is like a 'distorted mirror' of Turkey 'because it reflects the implementation of a purified official public sphere, but it is counter-reflection because Turkish secularist elites see the authoritarianism of their 'Other' in the mirror of Iran, and Turkish Sunni Islamic politicians see their sectarian Other, namely Shia fundamentalism, in Iranian Islamism' (this volume, p. 46). Furthermore, against the official (authoritarian) Kemalist secularism of Turkey, and the official (authoritarian) Islamism of Iran, both countries show 'multifaceted or fragmented' public spheres, in which the alleged homogeneity of social space depicted (and politically enforced in illiberal ways) by political elites is questioned, opened up and transformed by what we call 'postsecular social practices'.

The examples offered by Kömeçoglu show the multifaceted character of Turkish and Iranian public spheres, from Turkish neo-traditional coffeehouses to different veiling fashions and western-style shopping centers and cafes in close proximity to areas where pious people commemorate sacred events of the past in Iran. What emerges from the relevant mass of empirical examples made by Kömeçoglu is the consonance with our idea of the postsecular and its relationship with the notion of multiple modernities. Pointing out the fragmented and multifaceted character of Turkish and Iranian public spheres, where secular and religious forms of life and practices co-exist on an everyday basis, Kömeçoglu contributes to defining in conceptual and empirical terms the postsecular. First of all, he perceives Turkish and Iranian public spheres as postsecular spaces because here, more than in other contexts, the secular and the religious are clearly part of the same field (Knott 2005), rather than simply opposing one another. They are in tense and conflictual relationships, of course, but exactly because there are wide areas of 'interpenetration' (Göle 2005). As Göle has shown, it is only a sociological almost-Goffmanian approach (Göle 2011) that makes it possible to thematize those individual and collective performances that question traditional borders between the secular and the religious, private and public and so on. Secondly, and consistently with the previous point, Kömeçoglu points out how the postsecular has to do with the blurring of traditional dividing lines between the secular and the religious and, thirdly, with an increasing reflectivity and awareness on the part of social actors of the need to accommodate their religious identities within a modern horizon or, depending on the context, the other way around. Though the author does not emphasize the inner religious pluralism both of Turkey and Iran, the above mentioned elements are perfectly consistent with our definition of the elements defining the postsecular. But there is one more point that is worth stressing in Kömeçoglu's analysis, namely the idea that as much as postsecular social practices in Turkey are a tool to democratize the authoritarian official secularist and Kemalist understanding of public space, secular life-styles endorsed by young people in Iran are not simply a vector of homologation to Western or capitalistic consumption habits. On the contrary, both the Turkish and the Iranian cases, and their fragmented public spheres, show how postsecular social practices can be (in principle and in practice, though not as a matter of necessity) a tool of resistance to authoritarian ideologies, a means of transformation, and may embed emancipatory understandings of modernity.

Rosati's chapter shares a lot with Kömeçoglu's approach, not least a special emphasis on the spatial dimension and the general understanding of the present Turkish situation (in everyday flux, and consequently not easy to fix). Through a culturalist analysis of old (Mustafa Kemal Atatürk and Haghia Sophia) and new (the Turkish-Armenian journalist Hrant Dink) symbols of the Turkish imaginary and value system, Rosati discusses the shifting understandings of the Turkish idea of secularism. In contrast to many interpreters, Rosati suggests that Turkey is not simply shifting from an assertive to a passive conception of secularism, but is interesting exactly because, at least sociologically speaking, it is a laboratory of a postsecular society. From the Turkish case, he derives the list of features of the postsecular (a sort of ideal-type of the concept in Weberian terms) that we are endorsing in this introduction too. Finally, from the Turkish post-Republican history, Rosati tries also to sketch out a more general framework to organize conceptually different forms of relationships between politics and religions in modern societies. The outcome is a four-quadrant model, according to which modernity and religions can mis-recognize each other (a), modernities can take an authoritarian stance towards religions that play a democratizing role (b), modernities can domesticate paternalistically religions by instrumentalizing them (c), or finally modernities and religions can try to enter into that process of complementary learning that defines the postsecular (d). Needless to say, such a theoretical model and proposal needs to be tested on other contexts besides the Turkish one from which it has been derived.

Two further contributions – by Alexander Agadjanian and Kristina Stoeckl – are dedicated to Russia as an example for a *sui generis* modern trajectory and postsecular society. Russia's 'cursed issue' – to recall Dostoevsky's famous definition – is the question of how to catch up with modernity without losing its Orthodox Christian 'soul' or identity. In his paper, Agadjanian describes several waves of modernization in Russian history, from the reforms of Peter I to the Bolshevik modernization and the post-Soviet reforms. All of these reforms were generated and stimulated by encounters with Western European modernity; all were reactions to a perceived backwardness vis-à-vis European processes of modernization. In fact, Agadjanian writes, all of them were conceived *within* the paradigm of Western modernity. For this reason he is critical of the idea of multiple modernities when applied to the Russian case. From the Russian perspective, he argues, modernity continues to be a single project, a historically and culturally distinct phenomenon, related to the *temporal and spatial* coordinates of Western European modernity.

Agadjanian is also critical of the attempts in recent sociological theorizing to de-couple modernization and secularization. He suggests that the Russian case reveals a strong link between modernity and secularity. Modernization processes in Russian history, he argues, have always come along with an attack on religion or, in a peculiar 'pendulum logic', with its opposite, the glorification of religion. Both cases, however, implied the secularization of religion by subordinating it to an overall process of modernization and nation-building.

The problem Agadjanian addresses in his article with regard to the 'modernity' of multiple modernities can, in our view, be compared to Ferrara's argument that 'true democracy' requires a 'spirit of democracy'. Agadjanian is wary of the illusion of the complete originality of various cultural programs of modernity. Not only does such a view risk downplaying the hegemonic role of Western secular modernity, it also risks underestimating the normative importance of the secular, liberal and democratic program of modernity in those political contexts where democracy, secularity and equal justice are still to be achieved. Claims to a *sui generis* modern development may also come handy for authoritarian regimes to oppose democratic reforms and individual human rights. Hence the desire of both Agadjanian and Ferrara to pin down a 'normative threshold' that would guide us in describing a society and polity as 'truly modern' or 'truly democratic'.

The question Agadjanian asks at the end of his article is whether we can describe contemporary Russia as 'postsecular'. Russia today, he argues, is witnessing a paradoxical simultaneity of two opposite trends: the first real experience of secularism on the one hand, and the rise of the public relevance of religion on the other hand. According to the definition of the postsecular we have outlined above, the co-presence of secular and religious forces in Russian society definitely qualifies as a postsecular phenomenon. Also the fact that the Russian Orthodox Church elaborates programmatic documents in response to modern challenges can, in our view, be described as an example of postsecular reflectivity. Agadjanian himself is more critical on this point and prefers to speak about the 'implicit modernity' of the Russian Orthodox Church, which implicitly accepts the 'universal' language of human rights through an explicit refusal.

Kristina Stoeckl's article is also dedicated to the Russian Orthodox Church's confrontation with modernity in two recent programmatic documents, the Social and the Human Rights Doctrine. Her interpretation of these documents differs slightly from that of Agadjanian. Stoeckl is more inclined to read them as evidence that the Russian Orthodox Church is indeed confronting secular modern society in a postsecular learning process, and not merely succumbing to the dominant language game. She emphasizes that Russian Orthodoxy finds itself today in a situation of pluralism that puts it at the defensive both to the outside – vis-à-vis other religions and the West – as well as to the inside – vis-à-vis a rapidly modernizing and secular Russian society. The cited documents can therefore be described as both a sign for the renewed importance of Orthodox religion in Russia, and also a gesture of self-defence of the Church in trying to stake its claims in a heterogeneous and pluralist Russian and global society.

The main point of Stoeckl's paper, however, is conceptual. She looks at the example of Russian Orthodoxy and of its treatment in recent multiple-modernities-literature in order to show that the Orthodox position is not only a matter of civilizational difference, but that it also stands for a critical attitude towards modernization that may cut across civilizational borders. The modernization-critique of the Russian Orthodox Church is compatible with modernization-critiques of the Catholic Church or of conservative Protestant Churches, and it is therefore an undue reduction to think about multiple modernities in civilizational terms only. The resurgent role of religion in public debates has become a global phenomenon, and it has cast into question the liberal and secular modern mainstream. Stoeckl argues that the moment we draw together in *one* theoretical framework the idea of a confrontation of multiple modernities *and* the observation that this confrontation may lead to a re-definition of Western modernity, we are shifting from a comparative-civilizational understanding of multiple modernities to a *postsecular* understanding.

Stoeckl's argument resonates with Ferrara's observation about 'persisting dissonances' in the confrontation of different cultural programs of modernity. Her analysis of the Russian Orthodox position on human rights confirms Ferrara's observation that the Western priority of rights over duties is the most difficult aspect of the 'spirit of democracy' that non-Western and non-Protestant cultures have to confront. However, Stoeckl suggests in her concluding remarks on Habermas's notion of a 'global postsecular society' that these dissonances could become the starting point for a critical reflection on core issues of Western modernity itself. Only once such a process of self-reflectivity sets in, both on the side of the religious traditions as well as on the side of secular knowledge regimes, can we talk about a postsecular learning process.

The confrontation of a religious tradition with modernity is also the topic of the chapter by Chiara Letizia on Nepal. After the Maoist revolution, the new Nepalese Parliament proclaimed Nepal a secular state in 2006, a decision that was confirmed in 2008 by the Constituent Assembly that followed elections. However, the constitutional end of a two-century-old Hindu kingdom didn't imply the complete withdrawal of religions (Hinduism in primis) from the social and political horizon. Letizia's chapter shows how deep and diffuse the effectual and symbolic presence of religion in Nepalese life continues to be. Most importantly, she discusses a legal case against the ancient tradition of the worshiping of the Kumari, a living goddess, who in the past played the role of legitimizing the king and nowadays continues, though not without changes, to work as a symbolic legitimation for the President of the secular republic. Once again, rather than summarizing Letizia's account of the case in point, we want to emphasize reasons why, from the perspective of this book, the Kumari case, and the author's discussion of it, are of such interest for our reflections on multiple modernities and their link with the notion of the postsecular. Though previous steps had already been taken in 2002, the tradition of the Kumari has been challenged by human rights lawyers since 2005, with the argument that the condition of the Kumari violates the rights of the children selected to play this role. As Letizia maintains, 'the very fact that the powerful goddess legitimizing the kings of Nepal [and nowadays the President of the secularist Republic, editors] could thus be scrutinized in court as a human being deprived of human rights mirrors the political and symbolic transformation of the last years' (this volume, p. 126). However, even more relevant seems to be the whole process of redefinition of the place of the Kumari tradition in contemporary Nepal. The first point that is worth stressing is the highly reflective condition under which the process is conducted. The first indicators of such a reflectivity are arguments against and in defense of the Kumari tradition. In fact, there was no intention on the part of the human rights lawyer that presented the case to the Supreme Court to abolish the Kumari tradition and cult, but rather to reform it, to make it consistent with human rights, and prevent the tradition from eventually dying out. It was, in other words, a sort of immanent social criticism, already capable of joining at least part of the counterpart's sensitivity. On the other hand, the Supreme Court, in defending the legitimacy of the tradition, urged religious actors to make it consistent with the new secular horizon, and with full respect for human rights. In order to do so, the Court delegated the revision of the tradition, and a deeper reflection of the whole issue, to a committee of experts, that included both petitioners and religious actors. This is an extremely interesting point, showing how secularism in Nepal is the outcome (still far from being definitive) of a tentative process that includes religious and secular actors, envisaged as revising through common reflection their points of view in the light of others' world-views. Far from being a passive application of Western models, France-like or Anglo-Saxon like, republican or liberal, assertive or passive, the process of definition of secularism in Nepal looks like Bhargava's idea of principled distance (Bhargava 2011), or contextual secularism. This way of framing theoretically the Nepalese case is perfectly consistent with our argument on reflective secularism. Just as Turkey has been considered a laboratory of a reflective secularism (Calhoun, Juergensmeyer and Van Antwerpen 2011) –

another way to express a basic feature of a postsecular society – Letizia reveals Nepal as another key postsecular laboratory.

One more case in point for a postsecular laboratory is Nigeria, at the centre of Enzo Pace's chapter. The interest for Pace's chapter lies, among other things, in showing exactly how it is possible to be 'both fully modern and fully religious' (Davie 2007: ix). It shows how old dichotomies like tradition and modernity, or religion and modernity, are no longer appropriate for understanding for example the 'socio-cultural change occurring in sub-Saharan States' (this volume, p. 160). On the contrary, the Nigerian case is an appropriate example of how religion can be a vector of modernization. Via the resurgent power of religious imagination, notably of Pentecostal and Charismatic African churches, a reconfiguration of the relationship between modernity and religion is taking shape in Nigeria. The theoretical frame of multiple modernities offers an appropriate lens through which to understand this change. In Pace's account, in the Nigerian case *multiple* refers to the specific dimension of the Pentecostal movement. Here, Pentecostalism is able to give a new meaning to traditional religious codes 'oppressed and repressed over the past three centuries' (this volume, p. 160), not simply subsuming tradition under modernity. What we can observe in Nigeria is, he suggests, a modern religious form of believing and belonging. Crucial elements of this modern form are the individualization of believing, and the de-territorialization of belonging. In this way, new charismatic churches foster social mobility and individualism, two landmarks of the idea of modernity, while they revitalize traditional religious codes. However, in order to grasp this process and its outcomes, Pace's consideration of three elements is key, namely the importance of religious leadership, the power of the spoken word (the power of communication), and the centrality of religious spaces, three elements that are inextricably linked one another. Pentecostalism cannot be understood without studying specific ways in which Pentecostal pastors exercise the power of the spoken word, and their strategies to empower their communicative skills. The reinvention of specific liturgies (connected to traditional religious symbols) within specific spaces such as mega-churches, are key points in understanding the communicative power of these religious charismatic figures. As Pace writes,

> the liturgical space – in Durkheimian terms – works as *le fait sociale*, the social dimension of the sacred performance in which the actors are able to create a new *social images of themselves*. In the sacred space, the leaders often present themselves as successful entrepreneurs, offering themselves as a model to be followed. Their lifestyle and their material world define their public images. Their creative attempt to construct their own style is shaping a new "aesthetic of African Pentecostal Pastors" made by a perfect synthesis of spirituality and public culture. (this volume, p. 151)

Pace's sociological approach helps to understand how modernization via Pentecostalism in Nigeria happens not least through the performative effects of the communicative power of liturgical action, spoken word and shared symbols. In the context of the reflections in this volume, this is a very important element. In fact, it happens quite frequently that discussion on multiple modernities and the postsecular share (ironically) the modernist bias of the priority of beliefs over practices, and that they (ironically though unintentionally) suffer from the same cognitivist reduction of the notion of religion proper to a protestant-like modernity (Rosati 2009, Seligman 2000, Seligman et al. 2008). Pace's chapter, on the contrary, is an opportune reminder of the importance of an embedded idea of religion (that includes rituals, symbols, the body, communication in its verbal and non-verbal dimensions) as a conceptual key to the understanding both of multiple modernities and the postsecular.

The last chapter in this book by Peter Wagner does not offer any conclusions; it rather indicates an alternative approach in the panorama of contemporary debates on multiple modernities and religion, and a possible way out of some deadlocks which these debates may run into. Wagner shares with the other contributors to this book the idea that the social sciences need to look at different social and cultural constellations in a comparative and global perspective, but he remains unconvinced that multiple modernities and (post)secularism are necessarily the most fruitful keys for such an analysis. Wagner's main criticism of the multiple modernities paradigm is that, in his view, this paradigm assumes too high degrees of cultural and civilizational continuity. From a multiple modernities perspective, differences in modern trajectories are generally explained in terms of a variety of cultural and/or religious foundations. This downplays the creative role of human agency and the formative impact of historical events, in particular colonization. Wagner therefore looks at South Africa and Brazil as examples of two 'new' (settler) societies in the context of colonization, which experienced a modern development that can neither be explained in terms of civilizational continuity nor in terms of colonial 'import' of Western European modernity alone.

The chapter by Wagner not only resonates with the criticism of overtly strong assumptions about the originality of contemporary programs of modernity already voiced by Agadjanian and of the cultural-civilizational multiple modernities perspective by Stoeckl. His argument also challenges the main assumption that lies behind this book in general, namely that there is an intrinsic connection between modernity and secularism. In asking the question what role religion plays for the emergence of multiple modernities, and in hypothesizing that the changing balance between religion and the Western European secular program of modernity may lead to the emergence of postsecular societies in Europe and in other parts of the world, we have taken for granted that religion is indeed an important formative factor for modernization-processes. Wagner challenges this assumption. He suggests that conflict, human creativity and the human capacity for the re-creation of socio-political arrangements play a much more decisive role in modernization than cultural continuity and commonality. From this perspective, religion (or secularization, for that matter) do not necessarily play an important part in the emergence of multiple programs of modernity.

As editors, we welcome this challenge to our thesis at the end of a concentrated and multi-faceted conversation on multiple modernities and postsecular societies. However, we would nonetheless like to stress that understanding the role of religion is crucial for any analysis of modernization processes. We acknowledge that from Wagner's world-sociological perspective the term 'postsecular' may appear as just one more phenomenon of 'Old World' thinking that constantly looks for continuities. Indeed, the prefix *post* suggests continuity with a previous stadium, namely *secularism*. However, the nature of postsecular continuity is twofold. The Western European, Turkish or Russian examples in this volume demonstrate that postsecularism comes as a break with an earlier period of decline of religion or forced secularization, whereas postsecularism in other contexts described in this book, in particular Nigeria, South Africa, Brazil and Nepal, means that religion is part and parcel of a process of modernization continuous with religious and cultural traditions. Postsecularism in this twofold perspective is a useful conceptual tool, which has allowed us to grasp the commonalities and the transformative role of religions across a variety of multiple modernities.

References

Adams, S., Smith, K.E. and Vlahov, G. 2011. Special issue: Johann P. Arnason, Encounters and Interpretations. *European Journal of Social Theory*, 14 (1).

Arnason, J.P., Eisenstadt, S.N. and Wittrock, B. (eds) 2005. *Axial Civilizations and World History*. Leiden, Boston: Brill.

Bhargava, R. 2011. Rehabilitating Secularism. In *Rethinking Secularism*, edited by C. Calhoun, M. Juergensmeyer and Van Antwerpen, J. (eds). Oxford: Oxford University Press.

Beaumont, J. and Baker, C. 2011. *Postsecular Cities. Space, Theory and Practice*. London: Continuum.

Beck, U. 2006. *The Cosmopolitan Vision*. Cambridge: Polity Press.

Bellah, R. 2011. *Religion in Human Evolution*. Cambridge, MA: The Belknap Press of Harvard University Press.

Calhoun, C., Juergensmeyer, M. and Van Antwerpen, J. (eds) 2011. *Rethinking Secularism*. Oxford: Oxford University Press.

Casanova, J. 1994. *Public Religions in the Modern World*. Chicago: University of Chicago Press.

Casanova, J. 2001. Secularization. In *International Encyclopedia of the Social and Behavioural Sciences*, edited by N.J. Smelser and P.B. Baltes. Amsterdam, Paris et al.: Elsevier, 13786–13791.

Davie, G. 2007. *The Sociology of Religion*. London: Sage.

Eisenstadt, S.N. 2003. *Comparative Civilizations and Multiple Modernities*, 2 Vol. Leiden: Brill.

Ferrara, A., Kaul V. and Rasmussen D. 2010. *Philosophy and Social Criticism. Special Issue: Postsecularism and Multicultural Jurisdictions*, Vol. 36.

Göle, N. 2005. *Interpénétrations. L'Islam et l'Europe.* Paris: Galaade Éditions.

Göle, N. 2011. 'The Disruptive Visibility of Islam in the European Public Space: Political Issues, Theoretical Questions', paper delivered at the 'Centre for the Study and Documentation of *Religions and Political Institutions in Post-secular Society'*, University of Rome Tor Vergata, 28 April.

Gorski, P., Kyuman Kim, D., Torpey, J. and Van Antwerpen, J. 2012. *The Post-Secular in Question: Religion in Contemporary Society.* New York: New York University Press.

Habermas, J. 2006. On the Relations Between the Secular Liberal State and Religion. In *Political Theologies. Public Religions in a Post-secular World*, edited by H. de Vries and L.E. Sullivan. New York: Fordham University Press, 251–260.

Habermas, J. 2011. 'The Political': The Rational Meaning of a Questionable Inheritance of Political Theology. In *The Power of Religion in the Public Sphere*, edited by E. Mendieta and J. Van Antwerpen. New York: Columbia University Press.

Jakelevič, S. 2010. *Collectivistic Religions. Religion, Choice, and Identity in Late Modernity.* Farnham: Ashgate.

Knott, K. 2005. *The Location of Religion. A Spatial Analysis.* London: Equinox Publishing Ltd.

Molendijk, A.L., Beaumont, J. and Jedan, C. 2010. *Exploring the Postsecular. The Religious, the Political, and the Urban.* Leiden-Boston: Brill.

Nynäs, P., Lassander, M. and Utriainen, T. 2012. Post-Secular Society. New Brunswick and London: Transaction Publisher.

Rosati, M. 2009. *Ritual and the Sacred. A Neo-Durkheimian Analysis of Politics, Religion and the Self.* Farnham: Ashgate.

Seligman, A.B. 2000. *Modernity's Wager. Authority, the Self, Transcendence.* Princeton: Princeton University Press.

Seligman, A.B. 2004. *Modest Claims. Dialogues and Essays on Tolerance and Tradition.* Notre Dame: University of Notre Dame Press.

Seligman, A.B., Weller, R.P., Puett, M.J. and Simon, B. 2008. *Ritual and Its Consequences. An Essay on the Limits of Sincerity.* Oxford: Oxford University Press.

Taylor, C. 2007. *A Secular Age.* Cambridge, MA: The Belknap Press of Harvard University Press.

Turner, B.S. 2011. *Religion and Modern Society.* Cambridge: Cambridge University Press.

Ward, G. and Hoelzl, M. 2008. *The New Visibility of Religion. Studies in Religion and Cultural Hermeneutics.* London: Continuum.

Wittrock, B. 2005. The Meaning of the Axial Age. In *Axial Civilizations and World History*, edited by J.P. Arnason, S.N. Eisenstadt and B. Wittrock. Leiden, Boston: Brill, 50–85.

Chapter 1
From Multiple Modernities to Multiple Democracies

Alessandro Ferrara

Along with the idea of 'secularization', the theory of 'modernization' has been recently questioned as yet another by-product of the Enlightenment linear view of history. Drawing on Max and Alfred Weber's comparative work and on Jaspers' notion of an axial age which encompasses a plurality of ancient civilizations, Eisenstadt, Arnason, Assmann, Wittrock and a number of other leading social theorists have put forward a new framework for making sense of global history, known under the heading of 'multiple modernities'.

In this chapter, I will highlight some of the questions that the 'multiple modernities' approach can generate in the specific field of *political philosophy*. Assuming that we can distinguish formal democracy as a set of procedures that can merely ritually be paid lip service to from 'democracy with a democratic spirit', can we disentangle the 'spirit of democracy' from its original roots in the culture of radical Protestantism and envisage a plurality of 'cultures of democracy' anchored to various civilizational bedrocks? Are 'multiple democracies' genuinely viable versions of the same model of political order, or are they way-stations towards the Western modern form of liberal democracy?

From the 'Rise of Modern Rationalism' to 'Multiple Modernities' and the Rediscovery of the Axial Age

Eisenstadt is usually credited for the notion of multiple modernities and its polemical emphasis against the linear theory of modernization. His life-work encompasses the transition from a comparative version of the paradigm of modernization to the paradigm of multiple modernities. Drawing on Weber's thesis about the distinctive contribution of Calvinism to the development of a modern capitalist society, Eisenstadt began a comparative investigation of different paths to modernization. In the late 1960s, he brought together an influential volume (Eisenstadt 1968) on the 'functional equivalents' of Puritanism in a plurality of non-Western contexts – Tokugawa religion in Meiji Japan, certain sub-traditions of Islam in North Africa, Gandhi's version of Hinduism, the *santris* of East Java and countless others. The emphasis was still on explaining why some countries have gone further along the path of a modern 'economy and society' nexus, and the explanation was sought in terms of the transformative potential inherent in the 'economic ethic' (*Wirtschaftsethik*) conveyed by various strands of religiosity. Back in the 1960s, it was still a matter of 'faster' and 'slower' modernization, 'first-wave' modernization and subsequent adaptations. Quite revealing of the underlying spirit of the comparative research program is Eisenstadt's comparison of Catholic and Protestant societal contexts in Europe. The seeds of what Polany would call 'the great transformation' existed 'in most countries' of Europe; yet, Eisenstadt argues, 'in the Catholic countries – in Spain, France, and even earlier in the Italian states of the Renaissance in which modern statecraft first developed – these potentially diversifying tendencies were stifled' (1968: 12). Innovative features such as the newly emerging role of the capitalist entrepreneur, the new type of wage-labor, the banking system, even though sporadically present, could not in Catholic countries 'be freed from their dependence, in terms both of goal orientation and legitimation, on the political center' (Eisenstadt 1968: 13). From this comparative perspective, Eisenstadt examined religious cultures in terms of their potential for producing results similar to those attributed to the influence of Puritanism – i.e., in terms of their potential for leading to a rationalization of culture, of social life and of the actor's life-conduct.[1]

Forty years later, in the decade 2000–2010, this research-program in 'comparative modernization' underwent a radical change. Attention is being paid now not so much to the *convergence* of institutional, economic, social and cultural patterns towards a modern form of life originating in and epitomized by the West, but to the specific and alternative paths followed by societies rooted in different cultural-civilizational-religious contexts, when they negotiate their own *distinctive* version of the patterns of structural differentiation, urbanization, autonomization of the market, the replacement of status with contract and of ascription with achievement, and patterns of cultural and institutional reflexivity which characterize a modernity no longer prejudicially equated with its Western version. The insight underlying the paradigm of *multiple modernities* is the idea that becoming modern and becoming Westernized are two different things which need not coincide.[2]

---

1   This line of research is exemplified by Schluchter's reconstruction of Weber's 'developmental history' and, more particularly, by the implicit matrix of indicators of rationalization (extension of the class of addresses of the moral imperative, complexity of the object of moral regulation, reflexivity of the moral actor's consciousness, source of normativity for moral commands) that Schluchter traces underneath Weber's succession of still enchanted magical ethics, axial age ethics of norms, modern ethics of principle (the new quantum leap in rationalization inaugurated by Protestantism), the ethics of responsibility. See Schluchter (1981: 39–48).

2   Needless to say, ideology has its own inertia. The original Western-centric thrust of modernization theory survived in the 1980s and 1990s not only under the heading of the 'end of history' approach developed by Fukuyama in the wake of 1989, indeed a 'mission accomplished' statement that argues for the final entrenchment of the one and only version of socio-political modernity, but also in Huntington's idea that such a triumph will not be

As Sachsenmaier, Riedel and Eisenstadt (2002: 3–4) point out, earlier approaches to modernity and modernization embedded the strong assumption that the structural transformations distinctive of a modern society (again, urbanization, the rise of a market economy based on wage-labor and separated from the state, reflexivity) would spontaneously result in giving rise to a 'secular and rational world-view' and to a widespread atomistic individualism. As in Walzer's reconstruction of the 'covering-law' universalism rooted in Isaiah's prophetic voice (1990), according to modernization theorists Western modern societies have the privilege of living under patterns which others will at best come to imitate at later points in history. Current approaches couched in the paradigm of multiple modernities instead renounce this perspective, deconstruct the 'ideologically premised' unity of the Western form of modernity, by pointing to the variability of modern patterns across the Atlantic Ocean and between Northern and Southern Europe, and above all emphasize that, *pace* Fukuyama, 'although modernity has spread to most of the world, it has not given rise to *a single institutional pattern* or *a single modern civilization*' (Sachsenmaier, Riedel and Eisenstadt 2002: 4, emphasis added).[3] Rather, modernity has 'influenced the development of *several* modern civilizations, or at least civilizational patterns, i.e. of societies that share some characteristics, but have developed different ideological and institutional dynamics' (Sachsenmaier, Riedel and Eisenstadt 2002: 4).

This reorientation can be understood as a function both of a cultural dynamics associated with the decentering of reason, typical of Western high-culture after the Linguistic Turn of the early twentieth century and of globalization. What has come under attack in the decade 2000–10 is the very idea that when conceiving and institutionalizing modern patterns of sociation and political life, the West can legitimately 'draw from its internal resources while the others must be inspired solely from outside' (Sachsenmeier, Riedel and Eisenstadt 2002: 58).

The attempt to de-Westernize the notion of modernity has led to a resurgence of interest in the notion of an axial age. The term refers to a quantum leap, relatively concentrated in time when compared with the tempo of the evolution of the species and simultaneously occurring in several distinct civilizational contexts, in the reflexivity of social organization – an increase in reflexivity consisting of: a) an

---

free of contestation and will result in a 'clash of civilizations'. See Fukuyama (1992) and Huntington (1997).

3   Moreover, Western modernity has itself been the object of contested and conflicting appraisals. For one line of thinking it amounts to the liberating experience of differentiation, the institutionalization of individual freedom, the individuation of the individual, the idea of government as legitimated by the consent of the governed. For another equally Western-centric line of thinking, modernity entails the painful rendering of previously integrated communities, the rise of unbridgeable chasms or Entzweiungen among values, the rise of an unstable polytheism, rational irregimentation in the service of irrational values, techno-scientific domination over life-forms that are turned asunder, the rise of a new heteronomy oriented to the peer-group in lieu of authority. So Western modernity in a way has tormented itself, and the rest of the world, with its own self-interpretation.

'opening up of potentially universal perspectives, in contrast to the particularism of more archaic modes of thought'; b) an 'ontological distinction between higher and lower levels of reality'; and c) 'a normative subordination of the lower level to the higher' (Arnason 2005: 2). Such increased reflexivity in turn generates new dimension of agency, a perception of historicity and responsibility of human actions and institutions (Wittrock 2005: 67).

Weber was the first to notice, in his essays on Hinduism and Buddhism within his investigation on the sociology of religion, that in India a philosophical reflection on nature and religion developed in the seventh century BC, to be accompanied within the span of a few centuries by the rise of Confucianism, Greek philosophy and Judaic prophecy. Although causally unconnected, these breakthroughs in cultural evolution set the scene for the overcoming of magical, animistic and mythological world-views, and generated diverse but convergent paths to a differentiated and more reflexive social life.

Then Jaspers in his *Origin and Goal of History* formulated the idea of an axial age as a 'total spiritual phenomenon'.[4] In an attempt to decentre the Western vision of universal history, which from Augustine to Hegel had centered 'on a Christian or post-Christian axis of progress', Jaspers conceived of the 'spiritual process' of the axial age as the rise of a 'common frame of historical self-comprehension for all peoples' (quoted in Arnason 2005: 27). The substance of this 'common frame' is a shared awareness on the part of the human subject 'of Being as a whole, of himself and his limitations', as well as an experience of absoluteness 'in the depths of selfhood and in the lucidity of transcendence' (Jaspers 1953: 8). At the same time, the multifocal narrative of the axial age is one of diversity. Like in the reiterative type of universalism which Walzer understands as originating from Amos's prophecy, each and every axial breakthrough generates a historical path of its own: hence the axial age constitutes the paradigm for thinking of a multiplicity of modernities, supposedly one for each of the major civilizations where an axial breakthrough occurred.

With Eisenstadt – and also with Voegelin's work[5] – the axial age is brought into systematic relation with modernity. Axiality, as Arnason points out, introduces an unprecedented dynamism into the balancing of 'order-maintaining' and 'order-transforming' symbolic forces within each of the axial civilizations, leading to a long-term prevalence of transformation, though with different historical pace in different contexts.

---

4   Here I follow Arnason's concise reconstruction, in Arnason 2005: 19–48.

5   See Voegelin (1957, 1974) and the commentaries by Duso (1988) and Thomassen (2010: 328–30).

Democracy and the Spirit of Democracy

This perspective on axiality can be fruitful when applied to the prospects for democracy in the world we inhabit. Democracy *qua* self-government originated at the time of the first axial age, in the Western version of it which unfolded in Greece, then flourished to unprecedented levels when, during the second axial age, it was combined with the liberal idea of individual rights, with the notion of a constitution and constitutionalism, and with the modern nation state (itself a combination of a state apparatus, the rule of law, a nation with a common history and memory, and a territorially delimited market economy); now in the global world it has become a general horizon and the legitimate form of government *par excellence*. Evidence for this claim is the fact that no one, when considering the kind of polity existing in Spain, the UK, Sweden, Norway, Denmark, the Netherlands or Belgium, thinks that these polities cannot be considered democracies because technically they are monarchies – as everyone would have thought during the previous 24 centuries.

In fact, from Plato's time up to a hundred years ago, democracy had basically remained the rule of the many, as opposed to the rule of the few or the one. It is only after democracy's merging with the modern nation-state, with liberalism and constitutionalism, that all the major democratic advances have occurred: the separation of powers, universal suffrage, social rights, the protection of privacy, the ideal of publicity and transparency in administration, gender equality, cultural rights and multiculturalism, and the rights of future generations. This process, in combination with the communicative possibilities opened up by the process of globalization and the competitive economic pressures equally emanating from it, has led to a series of big waves of democratization in the last third of the twentieth century and at the beginning of the twenty-first: initially some countries in Southern Europe in the 1970s (Spain, Portugal, Greece), then the momentous wave of the democratization of Central and Eastern European countries after 1989, then the democratization of the countries of Latin America in the 1990s, and now the Arab Spring of 2011.

However, this tremendous success carries its problems. First and foremost, democracy risks becoming a vague accolade of praise that every regime in the world tries to obtain, due to the obvious advantages it procures: easier credit lines with the main global financial institutions, removal from the blacklist of the NGOs that defend human rights, easier diplomatic avenues for pressing one's interests in the global arena. Second, the major global players also have an interest in presenting to their internal publics the image of carrying out foreign policy in partnership not with dictators and authoritarian regimes, but with countries that strive to realize democracy 'within the limits of their context'. These two powerful forces converge in an attempt to establish a view of democracy as merely a set of procedures, exportable anywhere and universally preferable to outright conflict or explicit oppression – a view of democracy as a mere going through certain democratic motions (campaigning on the part of a plurality of parties, perhaps debating on TV, voting, tallying the vote in a fair way, forming majorities, governing). Such view is misguided from a normative point of view: democracy so conceived can easily lead to the self-destruction of the democratic regime, as the example of Hitler and the countless other authoritarian or totalitarian regimes brought into being by popular vote can attest. It is also descriptively inaccurate: Egypt and Tunisia were countries where elections were held – in fact Mubarak was re-elected for a fourth time with an overwhelming majority – and it would be an utter mystery why people would want to risk their lives in order to obtain what they already have, if democracy were equated with voting.[6]

For these reasons, democracy's success and its becoming a taken-for-granted horizon for thinking the legitimacy of government poses the challenge of offering an understanding of what fully-fledged democracy means. Paraphrasing a distinction that Weber eloquently drew between 'capitalism' and the 'spirit of capitalism' – respectively exemplified by the profit-seeking activity of usurers, military contractors, traders, and large merchants in Greece, Rome, and Florence, versus entrepreneurs in Manchester in the eighteenth and nineteenth century – we could say that true democracy is 'democracy with the spirit of democracy'. That is also where our difficulties begin: it is easier to export the formal procedures that supposedly define democracy than the culture that turns democracy into a distinctive form of political and social life where all can live at one with themselves.

In another paper (Ferrara 2010) I have tried to reconstruct a genealogy of the 'spirit of democracy' by tracing cultural presuppositions of democracy that in turn generate an affective infrastructure of basic democratic attitudes – a passion for the common good, a passion for equality which results today in a passion for equal recognition, a passion for individuality, and a passion for openness. In the light of the multiple modernities debate, the relevant question is: does the 'spirit of democracy' so conceived resonate with one and only one specific version of modernity?

Kateb has famously (and, unbeknownst to him, problematically) noted that democracy *qua* ethos and way of life, as understood for example by Emerson, Thoreau and Whitman, 'is the culmination of radical Protestantism' (Kateb 1992: 85).[7] To remain within parochial Christian boundaries, is democracy then doomed to remain imperfect in non-radical protestant contexts, not to mention Catholic contexts? What about non-Christian contexts? For those who are not 'among Jefferson's fortunate heirs' (Habermas 1996: 62–63), is democracy doomed to remain a mere procedural form forever disjoined from the true 'spirit of democracy'? This is where the idea of 'multiple democracies' can be of help.

In order to facilitate this process, what we political philosophers can do is to disentangle significant aspects of the 'spirit of democracy' from the original

---

6   So acute has become the awareness of the necessary but not sufficient conditionality of voting for democracy, that the catchphrase 'elections without democracy' has become popular: see Sadiki (2008), see also Diamond (2002).

7   For a similar way of raising the problem of a non-protestant or 'post-post-protestant' democracy with its own spirit of democracy, see Rosati (2009: 112–15).

cultural seedbed related to the Puritan ethos, and then to work out versions of it that may be compatible with other cultural configurations.

The following considerations constitute some preliminary and tentative exploration in that direction. First, I will highlight moments of *convergence* that relate to at least three of the sub-components of the 'spirit of democracy' or democratic ethos: the orientation to the common good, to equality, and to the intrinsic value of individuality. I will look at diverse cultural sources that could sustain these orientations with a force comparable to that which has been the case with Protestantism. Second, I will highlight moments of persisting *dissonance* between the fundamentals of Western modern liberal democracy and the various religious cultures of the world. Unless we come to terms with these, we will not be in a position to grasp how the alternative modalities of the 'spirit of democracy' can still be variants of the same thing.

Consonances Across Diversity

Let me begin with the orientation to the common good, or the willingness to yield to the general interest in deliberation. Arguably, this is the first and most important distinctive trait attributed to democracy. Its origin can be traced back to Montesquieu. The democratic (no less than the aristocratic) version of what he called 'republic' famously rests and depends on the existence of the 'political sentiment' of 'virtue' among the citizens (Montesquieu 1989: Book III, n. 2). Here 'virtue' is a complex attitude which includes an orientation towards the common good and a readiness to stand back and yield to what the common good requires – a kind of attitude so fundamental for democracy that it becomes an indispensable ingredient of Rousseau's 'general will' (as distinct from the 'will of all') (Rousseau 1967: 30–31), and whose reflection can still be seen in the Rawlsian notion of reciprocity and in the priority of 'political values' over other kinds of values within 'political liberalism' (Rawls 2005: 50–51, 139).

The Common Good

An equivalent emphasis on the priority of the common good can be easily found in a plurality of religious cultures. We need only recall the Confucian idea of 'harmony' and of the good of the people as the object of rulership, the Buddhist view of community and of the 'brotherhood' of fellow believers as in the service of the advancement of the good of the larger society,[8] and the Moslem Ulamas's continuous emphasis on the promotion of the common good as a legally significant concept (Zaman 2006: 130–39). In the Hindu tradition as well, one can find authoritative reference to the overarching notion of the common good even in Kautilya's (c. III century BCE) *Arthashastra* and in King Ashoka's Sixth Rock

---

8   See The Teaching of Buddha, Mahaparinirvana-sutra, AN 3–118: 242.

Edict (where *dharma* is said to be the object of his policies because it leads to the common good),[9] not to mention Gandhi's teaching in modern times.

A more difficult task, but at the same time crucial, is to find equivalents of the connected and counterbalancing notions – crucial to democratic theorizing – of every individual's having an *equal say* in what the common good is and of the resulting acceptability of a plurality of legitimate visions of the common good, of the notion of every citizen's equal entitlement to try to advance their vision of the common good, and of consent as a standard of legitimacy. Consequently, the convergence of a plurality of religious sources will be discussed in the remainder of this section with respect to three further aspects of the spirit of democracy over and beyond an emphasis on the common good. These are convergence towards a) accommodating pluralism, b) consent as the *ground* as opposed to being a *sign* of legitimate rule and c) accepting the equality of all citizens.

Pluralism

Multiple sources for accommodating pluralism – sources other than mere equivalents of the tradition that runs from Voltaire's scepticism to Rawls's 'burdens of judgment' – are relatively unproblematic to find. Islam, for one, is argued by distinguished scholar Ali İhsan Yitik never to have included, let alone mandated, a motto like *extra ecclesiam nulla salus,* but to have always accepted the possibility of salvation outside its borders (Yitik 2004: 1).[10] In the Confucian tradition, a fundamental difference separates 'agreeing' and 'harmonizing', where harmonizing preserves a central place for respect of plurality.[11] Throughout Chinese

---

9 See Boesche (2002: 14).

10 Along the same lines, the late Nasr Abû Zayd wrote: 'The Qur'ân is the "speech of God"; there is no dispute about this doctrine, but the discourse structure of the Qurân reveals multiplicity of voices not only one. As a discourse the Qur'ân is polyphonic not monophonic; there are so many voices in which the "I" and/or "We" speaker is not always the Divine voice' (Abû Zayd 2004: 19). And furthermore: 'there is no one single verse in the Qur'ân stipulating world punishment, or legal penalty, for apostasy; freedom of religion in the form of "no coercion" is widely quoted even by the traditional "ulamâ"' (Abû Zayd 2004: 27). Under the heading of allowing for 'epistemic humility', the Islamic acceptance of pluralism is discussed in Rosati (2009: 124–6).

11 A famous passage from the traditional commentaries to Confucius's Analects illustrates the point. To the Marquis of Qi's question 'Is there a difference between agreeing and harmonizing?' Master Yan answered: 'There is a difference. Harmonizing is like cooking soup. You have water, fire, vinegar, pickle, salt, and plums with which to cook fish and meat. You heat it by means of firewood, and then the cook harmonizes the ingredients, balancing the various flavors, strengthening the taste of whatever is lacking, and moderating the taste of whatever is excessive'. The contrast with 'agreeing' could not be sharper and is illustrated by the character of Ran Qiu, whom we would call today a yes-man: 'What his lord declares acceptable, he also declares acceptable; what his lord declares wrong, he also declares wrong. This is like trying to season water with more water. Who would be willing

history, although *he* (harmony) has often resulted in mere *tong* (uniformity), the conceptual resources are there for always addressing this degeneration and restoring a unity which contains plurality.[12] Hindu religiosity also includes the acceptance of pluralism as one of its core notions, as eloquently stated in the famous Vedic verse according to which truth 'is One, though the sages know it variously' (*Ékam sat vipra bahudā vadanti*) (Rig Veda 1.164.46) and reasserted in the Bhagavad Gita where all paths are said to lead to God, leaving then room for the notion of other religions embedding specific aspects of the truth. Similarly, Buddhism embeds at its core a pluralistic combination of the 'unity of Ultimate Being with the freedom of different paths for realizing it' (Murti 1980: 341).[13] In the Hebrew tradition, the line of prophecy originating with Amos has been argued by Walzer to exclude that there is one and only one chosen people and path to salvation, and even the phrase 'evil in God's sight' should not be interpreted as identifying just one set of evil acts, but rather as suggesting that God 'blesses each nation differently' and that 'there is a set of evil acts for each nation, though the different sets certainly overlap' (Walzer 1990: 516).[14]

Consent as the Ground of Legitimacy

Moving on to the second element, consent as the ground of legitimacy is very evident in Sunni Islam, though less so in Shi'a Islam. More specifically, leaders (*imams*) of the Muslim community are supposed to be selected on the basis of communal consensus and on their individual merits; though certainly this has been only an episodic practice during history, the principle is certainly there (Hallaq 1986).[15] With reference to both adjudication and deliberation, furthermore, it has been argued that 'diversity and differences among human beings are claimed in the Qur'anic discourse as merciful divine gifts to humankind' (11:119) (Abou El Fadl 2006: 11). Also within Buddhism the notion can be found that kings derive their legitimacy from the general consent of the people they rule. Several of the Jakata stories in the *Pali Canon* implicitly suggest that the people had a right to

---

to eat it? It is like playing nothing but a single note on your zither. Who would want to listen?' (Confucius 2003: 150).

12 See Tu Weiming (2009: 55).

13 For a different view, see Hayes (1991: 72–7).

14 For a discussion of tradition and the space for pluralism, see also Seligman (2000: 139–40).

15 Abû Zayd, on the other hand, underlines the conservative moment in the Sunni doctrine of consensus (even though it was in turn certainly less autocracy-leaning than the Shi'a's emphasis on hereditary succession), and notes how the Muslim reformists had to 'break through the principle of consensus by re-invoking the principle of rational reasoning, ijtihâd (…). By undermining the principle of "consensus", they were able to navigate through the volumes of law, fiqh, without limiting themselves to following a specific school, which gave them more freedom to choose opinions and to build legal syllogisms' Abû Zayd (2004: 48).

overthrow a king who was cruel, unjust or incompetent (Jataka I, 326; III, 513–4; VI, 156).

Confucianism can be argued both to contain and intrinsic idea of consent as the ground of legitimacy and a *sui generis* idea of equality, which leads us into the third dimension of non-Western notion of the 'spirit of democracy'. By contrast to the received notion of a Confucian natural penchant for authoritarianism – active rulership being conceived as the prerogative of those who display moral exemplarity – it has been argued that underlying the Confucian idea of dedication to the common good on the part of the ruler is a notion of equality as the equal possession, on the part of all the members of the people, of a moral capacity to reach perfection. As Herr has suggested,

> If due respect for the people is not forthcoming and leaders neglect or vitiate the people's well-being, then the people are entitled to complain to, criticize, dissent from, and even actively depose the leaders, precisely because their equal moral potentiality entitles them to the most optimal social conditions for realizing such potentiality. Therefore, equality among Confucian persons is the fundamental idea undergirding and safeguarding Confucian politics. (Herr 2010: 280)

The Equality of Citizens

The idea of the equality of citizens constitutes perhaps the single most important dividing line between a fully fledged liberal-democratic polity and what counts for Rawls as a 'decent polity'.[16] What makes a political order into a decent polity is the presence of an overwhelmingly shared view of the common good, but also questioned at the margins, and the presence of a 'decent consultation hierarchy' when decisions are to be made, which allows pluralism to find expression. What distinguishes a decent from a liberal-democratic polity is the non-equal or equal

---

16   For the definition of what a 'decent', as opposed to liberal-democratic, polity is, see Rawls (1999: 59–60). On the side of democracy, the flourishing of democracy with the 'spirit of democracy' requires a passion for equality that Tocqueville associated with the success of democracy in the American society of the 1830s. As he wrote, equality in its most complete form includes freedom: 'all the citizens take part in the government and each of them has an equal right to do so' (Tocqueville 1969: 503). Anticipating the 'free and equal' phrase that so often recurs in contemporary liberalism, Tocqueville observes that in an ideal democratic order, 'men will be perfectly free because they are entirely equal, and they will be perfectly equal because they are entirely free' (Tocqueville 1969: 503). In contemporary views of democracy, Tocqueville's insight lives on not just in the liberal ideal notion of 'free and equal citizens', but also in a certain 'recognitional' twist that the passion for equality has received. Authors such as Honneth, Margalit and Taylor always connect their notion of recognition with an implicit 'equality' of recognition. A democratic and just society is one where everyone obtains recognition in the legal sphere (Honneth 1996), where no one is 'humiliated' or treated as less than fully human (Margalit 1996), and where recognition automatically means 'equal recognition' (Taylor 1992).

right of every citizen to express their views. Underlying the project of 'multiple democracies' is the question whether a diversity of paths of progression 'from decency to democracy' can be reconstructed on the basis of the different religious and civilizational bedrocks upon which decent polities rest.

In this respect, whereas the Lockean and later Jeffersonian idea that 'all men are equal because they were created equal' cannot be easily generalized beyond the boundaries of Christianity, the 'political-liberal' idea that the ground of equality resides in the equal possession of the 'two moral powers' on the part of all human beings and in their potential for constituting 'self-authenticating sources of valid claims' is much more versatile. Over and beyond the case for a Confucian egalitarian and democratic polity,[17] similar cases can be made for Hinduism, Islam and Buddhism. In the *Bhagavad Gita*, Krishna's message to his followers is 'I am equally disposed to all loving entities; there is neither friend nor foe to me' (9, 29). In the *Dhammapada* of the Buddhist canon, the idea can be found that to become a Brahmin is not a matter of birth or natural disposition: only one dedicated to searching for the truth, whatever his station in life, can be a Brahmin.[18] As far as Islam is concerned, in the wake of his Sudanese mentor Ustadh Mahmoud Mohamed Taha's interpretation of the Qur'ân as envisaging the equality of all human beings, An-Na'im has maintained that the parts of the Qur'ân connected with the Mecca period of Mohammed's prophecy, as opposed to the later Medina period (during which concerns about ruling over unruly tribes and unrestful polyethnic populations inspired a more conservative message) constitute its normative core and ground the idea of a *full equality* of all those included in the polity, to the point of granting them religious freedom and gender equality (An-Na'im 2008: 54–62 and 106–8).[19] An-Na'im goes further than a mere compatibility thesis and argues that *shura* – the practice of non-binding consultation in matters of public decision-making on the part of the rulers – could be made to evolve into a practice of resorting to 'institutionalized constitutional principles that include the

---

17 See Herr (2010: 269–80) and Tan's discussion of the unique equality-grounding passage of the Analects (17.2) where Confucius maintains that 'Men are close to one another by nature; they diverge as a result of repeated practice', in Tan (2004: 101–3). See also the interesting collection edited by Chang and Kalmanson (2010).

18 'By birth one is no Brahmin, by family, austerity. In whom are truth and Dhamma too pure is he, a Brahmin's he' (Dhammapada, 26, 393).

19 See also Taha 1987 and An-Na'im 1990. Khaled Abou El Fadl has argued that 'A fundamental Qur'anic idea is that God vested all of humanity with a kind of divinity by making all human beings the viceroys of God on this earth: "Remember, when your Lord said to the angels: 'I have to place a vicegerent on earth,' they said: 'Will you place one there who will create disorder and shed blood, while we intone Your litanies and sanctify Your name?' And God said: 'I know what you do not know'" (2:30). In particular, human beings are responsible, as God's vicegerents, for making the world more just. By assigning equal political rights to all adults, democracy expresses that special status of human beings in God's creation and enables them to discharge that responsibility' (Abou El Fadl 2006: 3–4).

population at large' (An-Na'im 2008: 108).[20] Having said this, however, the task remains to specify how the equality of citizens takes on a specific coloring when it comes to gender lines and to lines of religious multiconfessional diversity, and how the concepts of public reason and reasonability resonate in contexts where the background culture is significantly different.[21]

Individuality as a Value

Another area of convergence is that of *individuality*, the one which the 'democratic individualists' such as Thoreau, Emerson, Whitman and later Kateb identified as quintessential for defining the spirit of democracy and yet the most difficult to detach from the Puritan background.[22] Yet even on this most impervious terrain, equivalent cultural resources can be found. For example, in the idea of the individual members of an Islamic polity sharing in the quality of being 'vicegerents' of God, or 'vicegerents' of the Prophet in another version, lies the challenge of interpreting the Qur'ân along more inclusive lines and deriving from it a conjectural argument leading to a less suspicious attitude towards the Western notion of individual autonomy (El Fadl 2006).[23]

With reference to Confucianism, it has been argued that the Confucian self is a 'reflective, and ceaselessly transformative being' (Tu 1989: 45) and that the ability for self-reflection is the primary means through which the imperative of self-perfection is responded to (Cheng 2004: 124–35). Although such self-reflection cannot be equated in all respects with the Western notion of individual autonomy, it does provide for many of the results associated with moral autonomy, notably with the capacity for rethinking and reimagining the web of social relations within which the self emerges and develops (Kupperman 2004). One of the *loci* where a Confucian concept of personal autonomy can be found is provided by the eloquent passage of the *Analects* where the Master points out that 'the Gentleman agrees with others without being an echo. The small man echoes without being in agreement' (XIII, 23).

A more complicated task is to work out the locus of autonomy in the 'no-self view of the self' characteristic of Buddhism. In order to discover the moment

---

20   See also Abou El Fadl's interesting reconstruction of shura as potentially a 'symbol signifying participatory politics and legitimacy' (Abou El Fadl 2006: 8–9).

21   An-Na'im moves some steps in that direction with his concept of 'civic reason', as distinct from public reason (An-Na'im 2008: 97–101).

22   Democracy is nourished by a 'passion for individualism'. Democratic individuality, as opposed to 'individualism pure and simple' (Kateb 1992: 83) is the name given to this inspiration, which revolves around the idea of self-reliance, 'independent thinking, newly innocent perception, self-expressive activity, unexpected creativity' (Kateb 1992: 33) and around the suggestion that 'democracy's most elevated justification lies in its encouragement of individuality' (Kateb 1992: 78).

23   For a conjectural argument leading to acceptance of pluralism and equality within Islam, see also March (2009).

of contact between the apparently opposed Western and Buddhist conceptions, one has to direct attention to the more encompassing notion of the *person*. The enlightened person, who has understood the illusory quality of *ātman* or the unitary, volitional self, and has learned to attend the void or substanceless of any supposed core of identity, has done so certainly not in order to put herself at the mercy of external stimuli and unbridled inner urges. On the contrary, that person has attained a higher-level of self-control and self-awareness, and transcended the particularity of attachments, expanding her boundaries somehow from the limited ones of an insignificant self to the limitless ones of a 'great self'.[24] The *arahant*, namely the person who through the Noble Eightfold Path (*āryāṣṭāṅgamārga*) has carried the process of personal development to perfection and has developed all the good aspects of the personality, is described as 'one with a mind like a diamond': like a diamond, the mind of such a person can 'cut' anything but cannot itself be cut.

Persisting Dissonances: The 'Spirit of Democracy' in the Plural

After highlighting the convergence of a plurality of religious cultures onto a set of distinctive aspects of the spirit of democracy – orientation towards the common good, acceptance of pluralism, consent as the ground of legitimate rule, equality of citizens, the capacity of the person to rise above the received cultural inputs – we need to cast a glance also at the *dissonances,* namely on those points of friction between the fundamentals of Western modern liberal democracy and the various religious cultures of the world. By focusing on dissonances, it is possible to launch the critical imagination well beyond the existing forms and it is possible, for those who inhabit Western liberal-democratic polities, to enrich their critical self-understanding by way of, to use Chakrabarty's felicitous expression, 'provincializing' their own, up to now mainstream, ways (Chakrabarty 2007). Additionally, by focusing on dissonances, we can exert the political imagination in order to envision a plurality of paths of progression from a decent polity to a fully fledged but not necessarily Westernized liberal-democratic polity.

---

24   Interestingly, it has been argued that the Buddhist idea of the self as composed of an empty core and expendable layers of illusory self-images, as well as the underlying understanding of the Absolute as void, leads to a receptivity towards openness, to which a parallel can be found in the Hebrew rejection of all images of the absolute and of God as idolatry: 'the teaching of voidness does not really mean that everything is nothing … Emptiness has a sense that something has an open inside, a free inside. One can translate emptiness as freedom, so that everything is free of being pinned down by what one person or one group or one community thinks it is … in the ancient Hebrew tradition, the fact that they would not include vowels with the consonants in the name of God in order to make it humanly unpronounceable is in the same direction of what we would call voidness or freedom' (Thurman 1997: 394).

Among the points of dissonance which a comparative analysis of understandings of democracy can highlight, I find it promising to start from two which appear at first sight of crucial importance: a) the idea of rights and b) the role of political conflict within a democratic polity.

The Idea of Rights as Trumps and their Priority over Duties

Compared to the ideas of a required orientation to the common good, of a plurality of legitimate version thereof, of 'government by consent', of the equality of citizens, and of the person as a independent source of valid claims, much more unpalatable to non-Western cultures appears to be the very idea of *subjective rights*, *qua* prerogatives of the single individual against authority and potentially against the whole political community. In a way, a major distinctive feature of the Western modern form of political association is the priority of rights, *qua* subjective entitlements, over duties. This priority runs against the grain of all religiously framed approaches to communal life. As Soroush has very eloquently put it, in Western modern polities

> Rights are honored over duties. One of the markers of the modern – in contradistinction to the traditional – world is the emergence of 'rights carrier' as opposed to 'duty bound' human being. The language of religion (especially that of Islam as exemplified by the Qur'an and the Tradition) is the language of duties, not rights. In these texts, human beings are given commandments by a supremely sovereign authority. The language of *shari'ah* is that of commanding, as the picture of humanity in the mirror of religion is that of a duty-bound creature. Human beings are required to believe, pray, give alms, and conduct themselves in such matters as matrimony and inheritance in accordance with traditional guidelines . . . Of course, the religious texts do occasionally address the rights of humans, but such passages are very rare and exceptional. (Soroush 2002: 61–62)

This is true of the Muslim perception of the Western 'rights-discourse' but it applies to many other religious cultures.[25] In the Muslim context, rights are invoked only as a restorative concept after a harm has been inflicted or a tort perpetrated. Rights come into the picture as compensations for torts and damages. What remains difficult to metabolize is the idea of rights 'in general', as preordained to any legal action and as the 'property' of individuals before they become victims deserving compensation.[26] Within the Confucian tradition, again, the individual

---

25   See also Seligman (2000: 130).

26   One of the possible avenues for the transformation of this picture is pointed out by Abou El Fadl. One could consider 'prior', 'abstract' or 'immutable' those rights which 'are necessary to achieve a just society' according to the Islamic view and in order to apply the principles of Islam with the virtue of 'mercy'. They could coincide with the five values

is not a bearer of rights but the center of a network of social obligations which do give her the entitlement to a certain solidarity, help and recognition, but not to an unconditional set of 'abstract' rights vis-à-vis the collectivity. Justice is achieved through interpersonal mediation, rather than impersonal procedures, and through the requirement of *benevolence (ren)* which binds the rulers and whoever is a position of social dominance. The duty of benevolence has its roots directly in the *Analects*, where at VIII, 7 Confucius states that a Gentleman 'takes benevolence as his burden'. It is impossible to track here all the various epiphanies of this basic idea of social justice as a harmonious network of relations, as distinct from its resting on procedures that secure respect for individual rights, in the other religious cultures such as Buddhism or Hinduism.

The point is that such a view is well represented also within Western culture and forms the backbone of the indigenous Western resistance to Protestant-modernity. Max Weber wrote a memorable reconstruction of the clash between the traditional Catholic ethic of brotherliness, centered on the reciprocal care of the neighbors for one another, under the principle 'Your want of today may be mine of tomorrow', which obviously knew of no individual rights but only of required benevolence (Weber 1975b: 329). In the wake of the French Revolution, Burke on the one hand and De Maistre on the other reacted with repulsion to the 'abstractness' of the rights of man as such and to the priority of rights over duty. De Maistre, in fact, famously spoke of the 'rights of God'. Hegel too argued that modern ethical life was traversed by a tragic rift, between the 'abstract' morality of the Kantian-type individual subject, who sets himself as a judging tribunal for the whole of social practices in the name of a formal law-like principle, on one hand, and the thick values embedded in practices and customs which contribute to the cohesion of the social fabric and project a concrete, situated, 'rational' normativity of their own.

In the wake of this dual line of development, within Western political cultures the Catholic and the Hegelian and later Marxist traditions have been very wary of anchoring the just polity in the observance and enforcement of abstract individual rights, and this resistance can be observed in the mistrust that Christian-Democratic and Communist party-elites have displayed vis-à-vis the whole 'rights-discourse'. Finally, the emphasis on a nomocentric order, based on a comprehensive conception of the good of religious or secular derivation and the duties, not the rights, that it generates for its adherents, has continued to inspire a critique of liberalism from well within the ranks of Western philosophy. One need only recall here the communitarian critique of liberalism, and notably Taylor's articulation of a notion of 'duty to society' (Taylor 1985: 197–98),[27] of which the liberal 'rights-

---

mentioned by Abou El Fadl as those which spell out the necessities (daruriyyat) constitutive (along with needs or hajiyyat and luxuries or kamaliyyat) of the good for the citizens: religion, life, intellect, lineage or honor, and property. See (Abou El Fadl 2006: 13). For interesting comments on Abou El Fadl's understanding of rights, see Rasmussen (2008).

27   The central critique raised by Taylor contends that 'Primacy-of-rights theories in other words accept a principle ascribing rights to men as binding unconditionally, binding,

discourse' becomes entirely forgetful, the preoccupation with the anomic outcome and the parasitic relation between liberal institutions and pre-liberal reservoirs of meaning from Durkheim to Böckenförde, and the feminist opposition of an ethics of *care* versus one centered on rights.[28] Taylor has gone so far as to argue the case for a *Liberalism 2* (1992: 58–61), as distinct from the classical liberalism centered on rights. *Liberalism 2* allows for a normative public discourse on the good, which could resonate much more harmoniously with the Confucian, Islamic, Catholic, Orthodox, Buddhist and Hindu understanding of the democratic polity. An emphasis on duty has also gained wide acceptance over the past decade on the scene on international law, through the acclaimed doctrine of the 'Responsibility to Protect', elaborated on UN input by a Commission on Intervention and State Sovereignty, and later adopted by the UN at the initiative of Secretary General Ban Ki-moon. At the center of the Responsibility to Protect view is no longer a clash of rights – the single states' right to freedom from interference with their sovereignty versus the international community's right to stop, if needed through military force, all massive and perduring violations of human rights – but one and the same 'duty' or 'responsibility' to protect human life, which is entrusted primarily to nation states but can be legitimately fulfilled by the international community if for any reason, voluntary or involuntary, states fail to discharge it.[29]

The Positive Role of Intra-systemic Political Conflict

Finally, another point of friction between contemporary Western right-centered liberal democracy and the various nomocentric, comprehensive or 'duty'-oriented versions of it concerns the role of social and political conflict within democratic life. First, what is meant here by conflict? Rights-centered democracies expand and institutionalize an insight which dates back to Machiavelli's reflections on the positive role of the conflict or 'disunion' between nobility and common people in

---

that is, on men as such. But they do not accept as similarly unconditional a principle of belonging or obligation. Rather our obligation to belong to or sustain a society, or to obey its authorities, is seen as derivative, as laid on us conditionally, through our consent, or through its being to our advantage' (Taylor 1975: 188).

28   See Böckenförde's dictum, 'The liberal secular state lives on premises that it cannot itself guarantee. On the one hand, it can subsist only if the freedom it consents to its citizens is regulated from within, inside the moral substance of individuals and of a homogeneous society. On the other hand, it is not able to guarantee these forces of inner regulation by itself without renouncing its liberalism' (Böckenförde 1991: 112, quoted in Habermas 2008: 101). A true representative, within Western discourse, of the Confucian emphasis on a benevolence now renamed as care, is Gilligan's conception of an ethics of care as reflective of women's approach to the moral life (Li 2008: 176). On the other hand, Toni Woodiwiss has explored the Confucian equivalent of a right in labor protection, a right-equivalent realized as a legally enforceable benevolence, on the part of the employer for the benefit of the employee (Woodiwiss 2008).

29   See ICISS (2001).

the Roman republic (1998: Book I, Ch. 2). They see the vigorous confrontation of contending interests and values in the public arena as a sign of a healthy democratic life. Far from endangering social and political cohesion, contestation and political conflict, often rooted in social and cultural diversity, can lead to the better articulation of points of view, to a better public choice, to the selection of a more efficacious leadership, to an invigorating sense of a political community of equals who jointly determine the fundamentals of their shared life.[30] This insight then branches out in a plurality of institutional implications and assumptions about a viable democratic infrastructure, such as party pluralism, the idea of majority rule within a constitutionally secured framework, the notion of a vibrant public sphere nourished by an independent press, by a plurality of electronic media and more recently by an open access internet combined with social media, the idea of transparency in public administration and of the protection of privacy, the idea of transparency in the private funding of political parties and more recently also of a control over the maximum level of expenditure in electoral campaigns. Also the separation of powers, from Montesquieu to the reconsideration recently offered by Ackerman can be understood as a fundamental principle which responds to the factual ubiquity and the normative desirability of strong confrontations in the public arena of a democratic society.

When placed, transplanted or emerging from 'nomocentric', comprehensive or otherwise duty-centered political cultures, democracy rests on, and has to meet the challenge of, a democratic ethos which is much more wary of the 'disharmony' implicit in conflict, much more suspicious of the divisive potential unleashed by a plurality of organizations, parties, associations, newspapers, media, and by standards of transparency and of privacy to be imposed on respectively administrative activities and areas of private concern. Political cultures nurtured within Catholic, Islamic, Confucian, Buddhist, or Hindu religious backgrounds, and their secularized successors, when and where they do prize pluralism, majority rule and the separation of powers, nonetheless inject into the spirit of democracy underlying their institutions an instinctive aversion to conflict and confrontation, to voting and coalition forming, and constantly compare the costs and benefits of living with injustice versus the instability produced by exposing injustice. The fear of divisions and conflict often paralyzes the democratic institutions which are implanted in these cultures. To give just one example, while it is one thing for majority rule to operate in contexts where the political culture admits of and even invites fruitful confrontation in the public arena, it is quite another for the same procedural rule to operate in contexts where close majorities up to 60 per cent are perceived as indicative of a pernicious 'split' or 'rift' within the deliberative body

---

30 In a sense, the idea of conflict and agonistic confrontation implicit in liberal-democratic views incorporates Simmel's view of conflict not as the opposite of social cohesion but as one of the forms of social cohesion. See Simmel (1964: 13–20).

and not fully legitimated in pursuing their ends.[31] In some contexts unanimity is suspicious – it reeks of hidden oppression or bribery; in other contexts unanimity is the highly appreciated sign of a successful 'mediation'. Thus we can have a distinction between democratic cultures which are tendentially consociationalist and democratic cultures that tend towards a more agonistic view of the process.[32]

Conclusion

Throughout this discussion the plausibility of the thesis has been corroborated that adequate consonances can be found in all historical religions for the major components of the 'spirit of democracy', namely, for an orientation to the common good, for a positive notion of pluralism, for a notion of legitimate rule as resting on the consent of the governed, for the equality of the citizens, and for a positive appraisal of individuality. Finally I have also shown that the priority of rights over duties and the valuing of contestation and agonism within democratic life are the two components within the 'spirit of democracy' for which it is most problematic to find equivalents in non-Western and non-Protestant cultures.

Provisionally then, the analytic differentiation of the concept of democracy must start from here, from construing four versions of the spirit of democracy which represent alternative paths of transition from a Rawlsian 'decent polity' to a 'liberal-democratic one'. The classical path which reductive theories of modernization have taken as canonical and exclusive has combined an agonistic and rights-centered understanding of the democratic process, a combination most resonant with the Protestant and especially Puritan version of Christianity. Other possibilities exist, however. Agonism and the valuing of contestation could be combined with a duty-centered political culture, which emphasizes political mediation of conflict over juridified litigation. This is the combination that we observe in all forms of strong republicanism, endorsed by Machiavelli and Arendt, such as Athens and the Roman republic in ancient times, Harrington's Venice and Machiavelli's Florence before 1512, and the Puritan republic of Cromwell. In modern times it is difficult to find examples of this version of the democratic ethos except in transient stages of history: the Paris commune, the Kronstadt uprising, and the Spanish Republic at the time of the Civil War of 1936–39.

---

31   As Lijphart puts it, a consociationalist democratic culture accepts majority rule just as much as an agonistic culture does, but 'it accepts majority rule only as a minimum requirement: instead of being satisfied with narrow decision-making majorities, it seeks to maximize the size of these majorities' (Lijphart 1999: 2).

32   In the literature consociationalism is identified through the concurrence of features such as the presence of a 'Grand Coalition' ruling the country, of practice of mutually recognizing veto power among the major parties, strong proportionality in appointing people who belong to parties and factions to office and prominent positions, presence of locally autonomous governemnt institutions.

On the consociationalist (or confrontation-averting) side of the spectrum, democratic cultures built on an aversion to conflict and contestation may be combined with a propensity for the centrality of duties over rights, as might be the case with the Islamic retributive and restorative understanding of rights, with the Confucian emphasis on harmony, and with Buddhism. Examples could be here the Malaysian and Turkish forms of democracy for Islam, Thailand's Buddhist democracy, and Taiwan's Buddhist-Taoist culture as background for its democracy, and a possible avenue for a future Chinese Confucian democracy. On the other hand, democratic regimes exist that formally endorse and prize the priority of rights in so far as their constitutions are concerned, but do so with a consociationalist bent and a strong aversion to democratic contestation, one example among the major democracies being Italy's former Christian-Democratic dominated democratic polity (in a pluriconfessional Christian political culture, Belgium and Switzerland may also offer examples of consociationalism).[33]

Finally, it should be emphasized that these are just initial and tentative analytic distinctions, which should give way to a more detailed typology of democratic forms which function as developmental but culture-specific paths for the transition of decent polities towards full democratic forms that can still preserve the mark of their civilizational distinctiveness. As the twenty-first century begins to unfold, an age-old dictum can be inspirational when aptly reformulated: 'Cuius religio, eius res publica'.

References

Abou El Fadl, K. 2004. *Islam and the Challenge of Democracy*. Princeton: Princeton University Press.

Abou El Fadl, K. 2006. Islam and the Challenge of Democracy. *Boston Review*, http://www.bostonreview.net/BR28.2/abou.html.

Abû Zayd, N. 2004. *Rethinking the* Qur'ân: *Towards a Humanistic Hermeneutics*. Utrecht: Humanistics University Press.

An-Na'im, A.A. 1990. *Toward an Islamic Reformation. Civil Liberties, Human Rights, and International Law.* Syracuse: Syracuse University Press.

An-Na'im, A.A. 2008. *Islam and the Secular State. Negotiating the Future of Shari`a.* Cambridge, MA: Harvard University Press.

Arnason, J.P. 2005. The Axial Age and Its Interpreters, in *Axial Civilizations and World History*, edited by J.P. Arnason, S.N. Eisenstadt and B. Wittrock. Leiden-Boston: Brill, 19–48.

Bellah, R.N. 1957. *Tokugawa Religion. The Values of Pre-Industrial Japan*. Glencoe: Free Press.

Böckenförde, E.W. 1991. *Recht, Staat, Freiheit*. Frankfurt: Suhrkamp.

---

33   Other interesting examples are half-way or semi-consociationalist cases such as Canada and Israel. See Lijphart (1977: 119–33).

Boesche, R. 2002. *The First Great Political Realist: Kautilya and his* Arthashastra. Lanham: Rowman & Littlefield.

Chakrabarty, D. 2007. *Provincializing Europe. Postcolonial Thought and Historical Difference.* Princeton: Princeton University Press.

Chang, W. and Kalmanson, L. (eds) 2010. *Confucianism in Context. Classic Philosophy and Contemporary Issues, East Asia and Beyond.* Albany: State University of New York Press.

Cheng, C. 2004. A Theory of Confucian Selfhood: Self-Cultivation and Free Will in Confucian Philosophy, in *Confucian Ethics. A Comparative Study of Self, Autonomy and Community*, edited by K. Shun and D.B. Wong. Cambridge: Cambridge University Press, 124–47.

Confucius. 2003. *Confucius' Analects, with Selections from Traditional Commentaries*, translated by E. Slingerland. Indianapolis: Hackett.

Cortella, L. 2011. *L'etica della Democrazia. Attualità della* Filosofia del Diritto *di Hegel.* Genova: Marietti.

Diamond, L.J. 2002. Thinking About Hybrid Regimes. *Journal of Democracy*, 13 (2), 21–35.

Duso, G. (ed.) 1988. *Filosofia Politica e Pratica del Pensiero. Eric Voegelin, Leo Strauss, Hannah Arendt.* Milano: Angeli.

Eisenstadt, S. (ed.) 1968. *The Protestant Ethic and Modernization. A Comparative View.* New York: Basic Books.

Eisenstadt, S. 1986. *The Origin and Diversity of Axial Age Civilizations.* Albany: State University of New York Press.

Eisenstadt, S. 1996. *Japanese Civilization. A Comparative View.* Chicago: University of Chicago Press.

Ferrara, A. 2008. *The Force of the Example. Explorations in the Paradigm of Judgment.* New York: Columbia University Press.

Ferrara, A. 2009. Authenticity Without a True Self, in *Authenticity in Culture, Self, and Society*, edited by P. Vannini, J.P. Williams. Farnham: Ashgate, 21–36.

Ferrara, A. 2010. 'Democracy and the Passion for Openness'. Paper read to the Conference 'Democracy and Affects', University of Virginia, 2–3 April 2010.

Frankfurt, H. 2007. *The Importance of What We Care About. Philosophical Essays* (1988). Cambridge: Cambridge University Press.

Fukuyama, F. 1992. *The End of History and the Last Man.* New York: Free Press.

Habermas, J. 1984. *The Theory of Communicative Action* (1981). Vol. I and II. Boston: Beacon Press.

Habermas, J. 1990. *The Philosophical Discourse of Modernity* (1985). Cambridge, MA: MIT Press.

Habermas, J. 1995. Reconciliation through the Public Use of Reason: Remarks on John Rawls's Political Liberalism. *Journal of Philosophy*, XCII (3), 109–31.

Habermas, J. 1996. *Between Facts and Norms. Contributions to a Discourse Theory of Law and Democracy* (1992), translated by W. Rehg. Cambridge: Polity Press.

Habermas, J. 2008. *Between Naturalism and Religion.* Cambridge: Polity Press.

Hallaq, Wael. 1986. On the Authoritativeness of Sunni Consensus. *International Journal of Middle Eastern Studies,*18, 427–454.

Hayes, R.P. 1991. Gotama Buddha and Religious Pluralism. *Journal of Religious Pluralism* 1, 65–96.

Herr, R.S. 2010. Confucian Philosophy and Equality. *Asian Philosophy: An International Journal of the Philosophical Traditions of the East*, 20 (3), 261–82.

Honneth, A. 1996. *The Struggle for Recognition. The Moral Grammar of Social Conflicts* (1992). Cambridge, MA: MIT Press.

Honneth, A. 2000. *Suffering from Indeterminacy: An Attempt at a Reactualization of Hegel's Philosophy of Right.* Amsterdam: Van Gorcum.

Huntington, S. 1997. *The Clash of Civilization and the Remaking of World Order.* New York: Simon & Schuster.

ICISS. 2001. *The Responsibility to Protect: Report of the International Commission on Intervention and State Sovereignty*. Ottawa: International Development Research Centre.

Jaspers, K. 1953. *The Origin and Goal of History.* New Haven: Yale University Press.

Kateb, G. 1992. *The Inner Ocean. Individualism and Democratic Culture.* Ithaca: Cornell Univesity Press.

Korsgaard, C. 1996. *The Sources of Normativity.* Cambridge: Cambridge University Press.

Korsgaard, C. 2009. *Self-Constitution.* Oxford: Oxford University Press.

Kupperman, J. 2004. Tradition and Community in the Formation of Character, in *Confucian Ethics. A Comparative Study of Self, Autonomy and Community*, edited by K. Shun and D.B. Wong. Cambridge: Cambridge University Press, 103–23.

Larmore, C. 2004. *Les Pratiques du Moi.* Paris: PUF.

Li, C. 2008. The Confucian Concept of *Ren* and the Feminist Ethics of Care. A Comparative Study, in *Confucian Political Ethics*, edited by D. Bell. Princeton: Princeton University Press, 175–96.

Lijphart, A. 1977. *Democracy in Plural Societies. A Comparative Exploration.* New Haven: Yale University Press.

Lijphart, A. 1999. *Patterns of Democracy. Government Form and Performance in Thirty-Six Countries.* New Haven: Yale University Press.

Machiavelli, N. 1998. *The Discourses on the First Ten Books of Titus Livi* (1531), edited and with an introduction by B. Crick. Harmondsworth: Penguin.

March, A. 2009. *Islam and Liberal Citizenship: The Search for an Overlapping Consensus*. Oxford: Oxford University Press.

Margalit, A. 1996. *The Decent Society.* Cambridge, MA: Harvard University Press.

Menke, Ch. 1996. *Tragödie im Sittlichen: Gerechtigkeit und Freiheit nach Hegel.* Frankfurt: Suhrkamp.

Montesquieu. 1989. *The Spirit of the Laws* (1748). Edited by A.M. Cohler, B.C. Miller, H.S. Stone. Cambridge: Cambridge University Press.

Murti, T.R.V. 1980. *The Central Philosophy of Buddhism: A Study of the Madhyamika System* (1960). London: Unwin.

Rasmussen, D. 2008. Islam and Democracy, Paper to the Istanbul Seminars, 2–6 June 2008.

Rawls, J. 1997. The Idea of Public Reason Revisited, in J. Rawls, *The Law of Peoples* 1999. Cambridge, MA: Harvard University Press, 129–80.

Rawls, J. 1999. *A Theory of Justice* (1971). Revised edition. Cambridge, MA: Harvard University Press.

Rawls, J. 2005. *Political Liberalism* (1993). Expanded edition. New York: Columbia University Press.

Rosati, M. 2009. *Ritual and the Sacred. A Neo-Durkheimian Analysis of Politics, Religion and the Self.* Farnham: Ashgate.

Rousseau, J.J. 1967. *The Social Contract* (1762). In J.J. Rousseau, *The Social Contract and the Discourse on the Origin of Inequality*, edited by L.G. Crocker. New York: Simon and Schuster.

Sachsenmeier, D., Riedel, J., and Eisenstadt, S. (eds) 2002. *Reflections on Multiple Modernities. European, Chinese and other Interpretations*. Leiden-Boston: Brill.

Sadiki, L. 2008. *Rethinking Arab Democratization: Elections Without Democracy*. New York: Oxford University Press.

Salvatore, A. 1997. *Islam and the Political Discourse of Modernity*. Reading: Ithaca.

Salvatore, A. and Eickelman, D.F. (eds) 2006. *Public Islam and the Common Good.* Leiden-Boston: Brill.

Schluchter, W. 1981. *The Rise of Western Rationalism: Max Weber's Developmental History.* Berkeley: University of California Press.

Seligman, A. 2000. *Modernity's Wager. Authority, the Self and Transcendence.* Princeton: Princeton University Press.

Simmel, G. 1964. Conflict (1908), in G. Simmel, *Conflict and the Web of Group Affiliations*, translated by R. Bendix. Glencoe: Free Press, 13–123.

Soroush, A. 2002. *Reason, Freedom, and Democracy in Islam*. New York: Oxford University Press.

Storr, R. 1984. *A History of Modern Japan* (1960). Harmondsworth: Penguin.

Taha, M.M. 1987. *The Second Message of Islam.* Syracuse: Syracuse University Press.

Tan, S. 2004. *Confucian Democracy. A Deweyan Reconstruction.* Albany: State University of New York Press.

Taylor, C. 1985. Atomism. In C. Taylor, *Philosophy and the Human Sciences.* Vol I of *Philosophical Papers.* Cambridge: Cambridge University Press, 187–210.

Taylor, C. 1992. The Politics of Recognition, in *Multiculturalism and 'The Politics of Recognition'*, edited and introduced by A. Guttman. Princeton: Princeton University Press.

Taylor, C. 2007. *A Secular Age.* Cambridge, MA: Harvard University Press.

Thomassen, B. 2010. Anthropology, Multiple Modernities and the Axial Age Debate. *Anthropological Theory*, 10 (4), 321–42.

Thurman, R. 1997. Seeking the Roots of Pluralism: Buddhism. *Journal of Ecumenical Studies*, special issue of the Rabbi M.H. Tanenbaum Foundation on *Seeking the Roots of Pluralism*, 34 (3), 394–8.

Tocqueville, A. 1969. *Democracy in America.* Edited by J.P. Mayer, with a new translation by G. Lawrence. Garden City, NY: Doubleday & Co.

Tu, W. 1989. Pain and Suffering in Confucian Self-cultivation, in *Way, learning, and politics: Essays on the Confucian Intellectual*. Singapore: Institute of East Asian Philosophies.

Tu, W. 2009. Cultural Diversity, Intercivilizational Dialogue, and Harmony. A Confucian Perspective. *Proceedings of the IVR 24th World Congress: Global Harmony and the Rule of Law.* September 15–20, Beijing.

Voegelin, E. 1957. *The World of the Polis* (vol. 2 of *Order and History*). Baton Rouge: Lousiana State University.

Voegelin, E. 1974. *The Ecumenic Age* (vol. 4 of *Order and History*). Baton Rouge: Lousiana State University.

Walzer, M. 1990. Two Kinds of Universalism, in *Nation and Universe*. Tanner Lectures on Human Values. Salt Lake City: University of Utah Press.

Weber, M. 1964. *The Religion of China* (1915). Translated by H. Gerth and with an introduction by C.K. Yang. New York: Free Press.

Weber, M. 1975a. The Social Psychology of the World Religions (1915), in *From Max Weber*, edited by H.H. Gerth and C. Wright-Mills. New York: Oxford University Press, 267–301.

Weber, M. 1975b. Religious Rejections of the World and Their Directions (1915), in *From Max Weber*, edited by H.H. Gerth and C. Wright-Mills. New York: Oxford University Press, 323–59.

Wittrock, B. 2005. The Meaning of the Axial Age. In *Axial Civilizations and World History*, edited by J.P. Arnason, S.N. Eisenstadt and B. Wittrock. Leiden-Boston: Brill, 51–85.

Woodiwiss, A. 1998. *Globalisation, Human Rights and Labour Law in Pacific Asia*. Cambridge: Cambridge University Press.

Yitik, A.İ. 2004. Does Qur'an Approve Religious Pluralism? *Journal of Religious Culture/Journal für Religionskultur*, Johann Wolfgang Goethe-Universität Frankfurt am Main ISSN 1434–5935, 68, 1–5.

Zaman M.Q. 2006. The Ulama of Contemporary Islam and their Conception of the Common Good, in *Public Islam and the Common Good*, edited by A. Salvatore and D.F. Eickelman. Leiden-Boston: Brill, 1–55.

Chapter 2

Multifaceted or Fragmented Public Spheres in Turkey and Iran

Uğur Kömeçoğlu

Introduction

Modernity, like many allusive concepts, defies any definite explanation. The answers given to the question "what is modernity?" are highly diverse and it is difficult to grasp the meaning of all explanations with simple analytical tools. But there is one point of commonality shared by the many scholars who put forward the claim of a close connection between the idea of "modernity" and that of "secularity" (if not simply secularization).

Both terms, however, have been subject to reconsideration, as recent studies of religious movements and communities offer strong evidence that the concept of "secularism" does not provide an adequate analytical tool to understand the meanings and functions of new religious developments. This difficulty of dealing with the novel religious developments in secular societies has led academicians to use the concept of "postsecularity" as a new analytical lens.

Similarly, the social and cultural changes in the historical period starting from the second half of the twentieth century to the present phase of the new millennium have called into question the assumption of "modernity" as a singular social form constructed by core western countries and their historical experiences. This questioning and judgment created the multiple modernities perspective. It seems plausible that the idea of "multiple modernities" and the notion of "postsecularity" are closely connected, just like the earlier pairing in which a close connection between "secularity" and "modernity" was constructed.

Scholars need to contextualize this new level of conceptualization, however, otherwise many arguments become suspended in the air. One way of contextualizing the idea of postsecularity is to provide an analytical framework by focusing on contemporary Islamic movements. In its traditional locations, Islam triggers the emergence of quite hybrid and sometimes paradoxical social forms in the process of "westernization" in Muslim countries. In understanding this complicated process Turkey can be seen as one of the most significant and exemplary contexts to pursue the traces of "postsecular condition", because secularism is the main pillar of the Turkish modernization experience that began in the nineteenth century and reached its westernized institutional peak in the early Republican period. Turkey had a very long tradition of modernist ruling elites which have been engaged in secularizing and reforming Turkish society. Since the 1980s, however, new Islamic actors have challenged this essentially westernist model of change and today the Turkish form of the moderate Islamic movement has been incorporated into politics and legitimated by the democratic parliamentary system. This development suggests strongly that Turkey is an important anchorage of the postsecular condition.

Similarly, Turkey appears to offer insights that help us to understand the multiple modernities paradigm. As Göle points out, "the project of multiple modernities presents a challenge to the monocivilizational narratives of western modernity" (Göle 2000: 91). In Turkey, modernity is continuously reappropriated or reshaped by blending westernist and Islamic perspectives. The Turkish mélange of western modernity and Islamic historicity as well as temporality already introduces an example of "multiplicity into the model of modernity", which inevitably brings forth Turkish experience as a pluralistic form of the modern (2000: 91–2). The Turkish mode of development provides us with a creative tension between "the specificity of Islam and general principles of modernity, without one annihilating the other". As such, Turkish Islam can be thought of as "a critical introduction of Muslim agency into the modernity" (2000: 93). This situation suggests an intersection of the multiple modernities project and the postsecular condition. The Turkish Islamic idiom, voices and practices in everyday life, in urban spaces and in politics "throw new challenges at classical premises of modernity, especially of secularism and western-boundedness" (2000: 93).

In this essay, the public expressions of the Islamic movement under the secularizing conditions of Turkey will be elaborated. As a Turkish academician, first I will concentrate on the Turkish context, but to increase the comparative dimension of this chapter within a counter example, my interpretations will involve the public experiences of young "secularist" actors in Northern Tehran, who enter into conflict with the religious paradigm of the Iranian regime.[1]

> The Turkish and Iranian examples can be seen as cases of reverse mirroring …
> What is at stake in both countries is the decline of the hegemony of the state over
> the definitions of the secular and the religious … Both countries are Republican
> states but the secular-religious divide is reversed … Despite differing levels of
> pluralism and democracy, in both cases the political distinctions of the religious-
> secular divide are unsettled. (Göle 2010: 45–46)

There are striking similarities and differences in the histories of modernization of Turkey and Iran, and these have left their particular legacies on the public sphere.

---

1   I was part of a research project titled "Youth, Authority and Public Space in Iran" supported by SSRC. This chapter can be evaluated as a product of the SSRC project. I would also like to thank Prof. Nilüfer Göle for her valuable support. Her supervising role was an important part of the study and she accompanied my second visit to Tehran as the consultant of the project.

Before the Islamic revolution, the project of secularization in Iran was almost a replica of the Turkish mindset of secularism. However, by leaving past issues of temporality to historians, in present time, we can observe two contrasting types of authority in these countries, based on secularism and Islamism in Turkey and Iran respectively.

*   *   *

In Turkey the dominant conception of the public sphere was based on secularism and westernism. It is a country which has been transformed from a multi-ethnic, multi-religious empire to a nation state. Notwithstanding some counter-arguments, it could be claimed that the Turkish modernization project has been historically quite successful. The most privileged identity at the level of social habitus is still the secular and westernized identity. Of course this is already a debatable issue, especially after the coming to power of the conservative Islamic party. But in Turkey, by using the concept of habitus or semiotics, one can refer to dominant or sovereign signs and symbols of the cultural profile in the central parts of big cities like Istanbul to reinforce the argument about the success of the modernization project. These signs and symbols are related to the western forms of dress, leisure, fashion, life-style, entertainment, art, home decoration, youth cultures, music, movies and so on. Another exemplary indicator of this modern state of affairs is the value accorded to education in "English-medium schools" as a highly-desired cultural capital by all sections of society including Islamic sectors. The famous dictum of the Republic's founder, which formulates the aim of the nation as "reaching contemporary level of civilization" refers to a western consciousness or a civilizational shift. The public sphere or this consciousness was introduced from above by the modernizing elites. The Turkish modernization project, which was strongly influenced by the French model, was based on the purification of the public sphere from religious and regional particularisms. It dictated the removal of religious signs and practices from the official public sphere.[2]

At this point, today's Iranian public sphere with its anti-western character can be introduced as the opposite vision to the Turkish public sphere. These two public spheres present two monolithic pictures in retrospective terms. But in this chapter I will try to dissolve these monolithic pictures to show their multifaceted and fragmented reality under the present conditions.

---

2   The closure of dervish lodges and shrines, the replacement of the Islamic calendar with the Gregorian calendar, the replacement of Arabic script with the Latin alphabet, the adoption of metric system, the acceptance of Sunday instead of Friday as the official day of rest, compulsory civil marriage ceremony, prohibition of Islamic polygamy, the replacement of Sharia with various European codes of law, the ban on the fez (Ottoman headgear) and the adoption of the Panama hat for males, the prohibition of old religious seminaries; the temporary prohibition of Ottoman classical music on radio channels during the single-party period were the main measures taken in this direction.

If we move from historical to present time, or if we leave behind the surface images of the dominant urban public sphere and delve into the deeper social layers, we can see that the Turkish and Iranian public spheres are no longer monolithic.

In Turkey, this fragmentation occurs along the lines of rural-to-urban migrants vs. old urban population, Sunnis vs. Alevis, *laicist* vs. Islamist, Turks vs. Kurds, Muslims vs. non-Muslim minorities; and at the level of everyday life, neo-traditional coffeehouses vs. purely European style cafes, veiled women vs. unveiled women, middle class urban youth vs. youth in squatter areas or idiosyncratically defined categories of White Turks vs. Black Turks. For a micro level example, one can set *arabesk* music (a hybrid music genre that captured the passions of migrants) against western music and so on. All of them prove that the initial design of a homogenous and modern universalist public order is challenged by different social forces.

In Iran, fragmentation similarly occurs along the lines of the Islamic way of life vs. secular western life styles (though secular western life styles are mostly experienced in private or semi-public spaces); traditional vs. modern urban spaces; migrants vs. old urbanites, Kurds vs. Iranians; liberal and reformist elites vs. fundamentalist religious elites, feminists vs. male Islamists; the new urban generation vs. the old generation, and so on.

Of course, in a Derridean sense, all the above-mentioned categories look like "undecidables", or "ambivalent" orderings in Bauman's terms, or "fields" in a Bourdieuan sense. That is, they are not always mutually exclusive binary oppositions, though many of them have borrowed aspects from each other or hybridized each other, yet the degree of hybridization or pluralization is less apparent in Iran due to the dominance of the post-revolutionary Islamist regime. We need a subtler analysis to make it more perceivable or visible.

There are cross-cutting cleavages and allegiances too. For example, Alevis as religious minority in Turkey are also divided along ethnic lines. Although the majority of Alevis are ethnically Turks, Kurdish Alevis are also publicly active. When faced with Sunni Islamism, the Alevis (who share many symbols with Iranian Shiites) tend towards the political choice of secularism. When confronted with secular leftist Kurdish nationalism, Turkish Alevis in particular stress their religious identity (cf. Çamuroğlu 1998). To delineate micro-level, everyday mundane manifestations of hybridization or allegiances, I can offer the examples about the rural-to-urban migrants who prefer to drink whisky with the traditional food called *lahmacun*; you can see restaurant names like "Lahmacun & Café", McDonalds produce hamburgers with a Turkish taste. *Arabesk* music is becoming more like westernized pop music, while pop music becomes more *arabesk*. Famous secular Turkish models are "veiled" in Islamic fashion-shows. These fashion-shows, as well as Islamic holiday sites, Islamic hair dressers, wedding saloons and even Islamic beauty parlours are becoming popular among the new Islamic middle classes. So after the 1990s, the secularist civic public sphere is experienced more or less in a sort of "all that is solid melts into air" situation, and thus more flexible and postsecular identities have emerged. But it is possible to observe the social and cultural borders – sometimes insurmountable borders – within these different "publics" as I suggest below in terms of the notion of competing publics.

The Politics of Islamic Veiling

There are various reasons for comparing Turkey and Iran; a particularly good example is the practice of Islamic veiling.

In Turkey, veiled women are not allowed to work in official public spaces like government offices, work-spaces of civil servants, and parliament. Official institutions have no emancipatory character in terms of employment for veiled women in Turkey. On the other hand, in Iran women without their "hijab" cannot enter the public space.

When I first arrived at Tehran airport, even my first glimpse of the veiled women working at passport control made the differences between two countries more perceivable. Of course I was not surprised by the hijab, because in Istanbul since the 1990s you can see veiled women all over the city. Yet the image of veiled women working behind desks in such official jobs was something that my social gaze is not used to experience, since veiling in official institutions is forbidden in Turkey. In Iran, official public spaces have an inclusive capacity for those veiled women. Especially for females coming from the lower classes and strongly patriarchal uneducated families, the spaces of employment and education have a quite emancipatory role. However, one should bear in mind that in Iran there is no category of "unveiled woman in public" because of the compulsory use of the hijab.

In Turkey, although veiled women are excluded from official public spaces, they find new types of public existence in civil spaces like cultural centres, spaces of art courses, "cafes in the historic courtyards of old Ottoman *medreses* (religious seminaries)" and even in cyber space. Many veiled students, because of the official ban on the headscarf (which was valid until 2011) applied to American universities to get a diploma; some of them preferred distance education. Whereas in Turkey the preference for education in the West on the part of veiled female students is a way of being in the educational public with their headscarves, for the young Iranian females, the West may represent the opportunity to be unveiled in public. For these female actors both in Turkey and in Iran, the geographical destination is the same but the reasons behind escape movements are totally contrasting. Yet they are both consequences of authoritarianism. One is secularist authoritarianism, the other religious authoritarianism.

From this perspective it is also possible to create a translation of politics through comprehending the debates over the proper dress-codes of female deputies of parliament, both in Turkey and Iran. This translation of politics can be related to a case of discrimination against a veiled female deputy in Turkish parliament and a contrasting conflict in Iran.

Tohidi (2002: 865–866) has written about the international negative reaction to the "black chador" which is the traditional religious female dress in Shiite Islam. This negativity was so obvious that it created a public debate in Iran, especially among male Islamist diplomats, Islamist women activists and associates of the Foreign Ministry. Some male diplomats argued against female delegates who wear the black chador in foreign offices while attending international events, because of the black chador's "counter-productive impact". Instead of the chador, they recommended wearing "manto-rusari" (a long loose overcoat with a head scarf). But some female Islamists argued against this recommendation on the grounds that they should not compromise on such a "critical Islamic symbol" because of international prejudices. Yet it took over many years according to Tohidi, to revive the debate around the question of "chador" versus "manto-rusari". The debate was initiated by three elected female deputies who were determined to wear "manto-rusari" instead of the "black chador" in parliament (Tohidi 2002: 865–866).

While in Iran some female deputies were trying to enter parliament without a black chador, in Turkey in May 1999, a first-time elected female deputy Merve Kavakçı was barred from taking her seat in the Turkish parliament because she was wearing a head-scarf (Tohidi 2002: 866; cf. Göle 2002). (There is still no head-scarved female deputy in Turkish parliament.) When she entered parliament, hard-core secularist deputies shouted "Merve out, Mullahs to Iran". According to Tohidi's research, in reaction to this exclusion in Turkish Parliament, about 200 chador-clad women in Iran, led by a conservative female deputy, took the streets of Tehran to protest against the secularist Turkish deputies "for violating the basic rights of a Muslim woman". However, Merve Kavakçı, who had been contested by the secularists in the Turkish parliament with the slogan "Mullahs to Iran", voiced her anger against the chadored women's demonstration by saying, "I do not need the support of those who do not believe in democracy and the right to choose one's style of life and dress code, be it the Iranian Islamists or Turkish secularists". Just after the general elections, some Islamist female politicians in Iran threatened to bar elected female deputies from parliament because they chose not to wear a black chador but *manto rusari* (Tohidi 2002: 866).

Iran is like a mirror or a distorted mirror of Turkey because it reflects the implementation of a purified official public sphere, but it is a counter-reflection because Turkish secularist elites see the authoritarianism of their "Other" in the mirror of Iran, and Turkish Sunni Islamic politicians see their sectarian Other, namely Shia fundamentalism, in Iranian Islamism. We can argue that the mainstream Turkish political understanding of the difference between "the veiled" and "the unveiled" can be translated to the political understanding of the difference between "the chadored" and "the *unchadored*" in Iran. The empty category of "the unveiled" in Iran is filled by the category of "the *unchadored*". However when we leave aside the official and political side of the story and enter into the complex texture of daily life, one can encounter competing forms of authority both in Turkey and Iran.

Turkey: Subverting the Secular Texture of Public Space

There is a built-in paradox in the political systems of many Muslim countries. On the one hand, attempts at secularization were realized through authoritarian regimes, on the other hand transitions to democracy or multi-party regimes were often accompanied by a revival of Islamic value-systems, practices and oppositional movements (Göle 2002). The secularization model in Turkey has preferred the removal of religious symbols, identities and similar forms of particularisms from the official public sphere, as mentioned above. Yet the claims of Islamic actors to the public sphere (since the 1980s) were characterized by their group particularity in challenging the neutrality/universality/cultural sterility of the secular Republican public sphere or citizenship. Islamic actors ideologically contested the secularist public space through their collective identity.

From Islamic Politics to Postsecular Identifications

In the last two decades, less and less politicized but more postsecular Muslim identities have weakened or blurred the perceived social boundaries between secularist and Islamic publics in Turkey. The more Islam becomes self-limited, independent from ideological politics, contextualized and aestheticized, the more it loses its radical fervency, and moves into the postsecular cultural domain. One of the best indicators of such a transformation can be observed in the new consumption patterns of Islamic actors. Consumption as one of the most visible public activities can also be viewed as an active process involving the symbolic construction of Islamic identity. It is possible to evaluate this process through some significant examples at the level of public space and consumption simultaneously.[3]

The transformation of Islamism in Turkey from radical and political struggles to postsecular representations in everyday life can be linked to a new ethics of consumption among Islamic groups. Some of the major changes in Islamism are related to its accommodation to the market economy and consumer society. Islamic actors who appropriate new forms of urban life in economic or cultural fields reshape Islamism in a postsecular style. As they pursue their economic interests, these Islamic actors interact with secular sectors at large. Especially in the inclusionary contexts where upward social mobility prevails, new Islamic actors, both as entrepreneurs and consumers, participate and become visible within the given secular public sphere on the one hand, and try to mould new public spaces of their own in conformity with the requirements of Islamic faith in a postsecular manner on the other.

By using the advantages of engaging in business in an open market economic system, Islamic groups are now able to develop their own middle and upper middle classes. This upward social mobility has also helped them to form their

---

3   For a more detailed discussion of the consumption analysis below, see Kömeçoğlu 2007: 57–69.

own educated elite. Through secular and modern education, Islamic actors have also succeeded in transforming their newly-acquired economic capital into cultural capital. As a result of this process of embourgeoisement, consumption has gained a prominent place amongst Islamic groups. They have become as much a part of consumerism as secular sections of society.

Affluent Islamic social groups have used their purchasing power to claim social status through the visible display of commodities signalling high social standing. Patterns of consumption among Islamic sectors have radically changed. Cultural patterns and life styles associated with secular middle-class consumption as markers of status have been attractive to the Islamic circles. Modern home decorations, western style furniture, luxurious head scarves, attractive outfits, jeans, perfumes, summer holidays, new swimsuits for Muslims, and other secular significations have been emulated by the emerging Islamic groups.

Although urbanization has altered the patterns of consumption among rural-to-urban migrants, the use of identical products and the meaning attributed to them can vary across groups and categories within society. The Islamic movement simultaneously both adapts to and resists lifestyles associated with secularity. This proves the mutual interaction between the Islamic and secular sectors, and shows the characteristics of postsecular positioning among Muslim actors.

The reality of living in the secular city of Istanbul has increased the awareness of style and the need to consume within a repertory or code among Islamic actors, which is both distinctive to Islamic social groups and expressive of individual preferences. The urban Islamic individual is no longer the old austere type who would not spend on relatively trivial items of clothing or adornment. Rather he/she consumes in order to articulate a sense of postsecular identity. Islamic status groups use patterns of purchasing not only as a means of demarcating themselves from secularists, but also as a means of winning social acceptance by appropriating the well-recognized social signs of their secular others. The status markers Muslims use to differentiate themselves are neither identical to nor completely different from those used by secular groups, and signify group values as well as individual esteem.

Islamic status is linked with a specific style of life, which involves the kinds of clothing, foods, drinks, holiday sites, even the types of music enjoyed, that are thought to be appropriate to Muslim status groups. These publicly visible practices of new Islamic actors are embedded in broader cultural relations through which goods acquire meanings.

The embeddedness of the Islamic way of life in a secular domain is realized within systems of signification, of making and maintaining distinctions, establishing boundaries, for example, within both Muslim women's intra-group relations and their inter-group relations with secularist women. Headscarf consumption among middle or upper middle class urban Islamic women has different symbolic dimensions. First, luxurious fabrics, colours and styles of the headscarves stand in direct contrast to the casual appearance of the traditional way of head covering generally practiced by rural women or rural-to-urban migrant women. The traditional way of covering one's head that leaves a part of the hair visible contrasts with the present use of the headscarf in urban middle class Islamic circles. Second, the usage of codes and signs of high status secular groups in the advertisements of headscarves – such as "noble", "first class", "creation" and "collection" – reveals the desire to be accorded the same status, but still to be differentiated from them by the very practice of Islamic veiling (Okur 1997). Third, this type of veiling, by its variation from the traditional head covering that lacks any political dimension, accentuates the meaning of veiling on the one hand, but with its emphasis on luxury and stylishness strengthens postsecular dimension of their identity and weakens the radical Islamic dimension characterized by pure modesty on the other.

Similarly, in the domain of cultural consumption, Islamic youth's concern with the new coffeehouses in Istanbul that have a religious character shows the postsecular character of their identities.[4] The districts where the Islamic coffeehouses are situated have a common pattern. All those districts have historic and architectural Muslim texture in spatial terms, such as *Üsküdar, Fatih, Sultanahmet* or *Çemberlitaş*. These coffeehouses correspond to the cultural aspirations of Islam in Istanbul because they are so far from the oppositional claims of radical Islam. Two of the sixteenth century *medrese*s (religious seminaries) in Çemberlitaş have been converted into coffeehouses by educated urban Islamic actors. They show consideration for some Islamic norms, in that alcoholic drinks are not served in these coffeehouses, and one of them is named the *Medrese Café*. It has an authentic atmosphere with its classical architectural style and artistic columns. These restored *medrese*s are representational spaces associated with a kind of Islamic value. The *Medrese Café* is an attempt to resuscitate the cultural memory of the old Muslim coffeehouse tradition where literary activities took place, of course in an altered form for modern times. And no doubt these places are the result of the postsecular cultural revitalization pioneered by Islamic and intellectual university students since the nineties.

The spatial separations representing the gender-based segregation in Islam are removed in these postsecular neo-traditional coffeehouses. The non-existence of religious gender-based spatial segregation leads to the intermixture of veiled women and Islamic men. This presents opportunities for strange encounters through religious and highly intellectual discussion groups as well as mere flirtation between males and females. The Islamic actors, especially university students, cannot remain outside the modern gender sociabilities emerging from the intermingling of the sexes in public spaces.

Young veiled actors and Islamic males do not feel comfortable in European-style cafes, for instance in the cafes at the westernized district of Taksim in Istanbul. However they did not name their spaces *kahvehane* (coffeehouse in Turkish with its Muslim connotations) but rather cafe, because the traditional Muslim term

---

4   For a detailed discussion on Islamic coffeehouses in Istanbul see Kömeçoğlu, 2006: 163–189.

kahvehane connotes degeneration in today's urban environment of Istanbul. *Kahvehane*s are seen as shabby places filled by the unemployed, uneducated, rural or elderly retired people. The *kahvehane* is also a male space. It does not create a cultural capital or urban educated feeling for new Islamic actors. But these actors do not like the European café tradition either. So they transformed the courtyard of an old *medrese* and named it *Medrese Café* instead of *Medrese Kahvehane*, neither *kahvehane* nor cafe, neither Islamic nor secular, but more postsecular designation. These young actors are not indifferent to the values of secular youth but they are also concerned with their own religio-cultural sensitivities. They communicate with and talk to their secular others both on discursive and spatial levels through such and similar practices.

Another example of the spatial performance of new Islamic actors, namely Islamic holiday sites, can be understood as spaces that both resemble and differ from secular worldly lifestyles. The simultaneity of the acts of resemblance and difference strengthens the postsecular dimension of their identities. Actually, holiday sites in the south of Turkey offer a comfortable exoticism, prioritizing pleasure for all. Although words like tranquil and peaceful are not frequently used in the advertisements for secular holiday sites in Turkey, Islamic hotels in the same region frequently promote the slogan of *huzurlu tatil* (peaceful, tranquil, untroubled vacation) to emphasize that Islamic morality is protected, especially with respect to gender relations. The hotels offer summer vacations in conformity with Islamic rules: prayer times are respected and only non-alcoholic beverages are served. With its Islamic connotation, *huzurlu tatil* also refers to maintaining the Islamic border between licit and illicit. This is provided by the architectural design of the hotels, which offer separate beaches and swimming pools for Muslim women.

There are several Islamic holiday sites on the western and southern coast of Turkey. A cursory survey of these sites shows that most of them carry foreign brand names. A postsecular paradox is seen in the TV advertisement for Sunset Beach Hotel, which begins with the image of a "whirling dervish", symbolically representing the asceticism inherent in Sufi Islam that encourages the annihilation of the self and withdrawal from worldly pleasures. In the advertisement, entertainment within the limits of Islamic morality is visualized side by side with an otherworldly appeal; worldly pleasures are juxtaposed with ecstatic meta-worldly pleasures. Thus, secular lifestyles of consumer society are mixed with the religious symbols of Islam, and the resulting hybridization increases the postsecular dimension of their identities.

From the spatial perspective, sports centres for veiled women, non-alcoholic restaurants, Islamic holiday places, Islamic hairdressers and beauty parlours, and the coffeehouses illustrate the formation of new pious but postsecular middle-class identities, attempting to carve their own alternative spaces. These are the sites where the boundaries between the secular and religious, moral and immoral, licit and illicit, private and public are problematized. The illustrations of Islamic experiences of public space which I have described are not only adaptations to secular mass society or market rationality but also self-reflexive postsecular experiences. In this regard, we can speak of a postsecular framework in which Islamism is waiving its "religious" claims but increasingly permeating "secular" life practices.

Iran: Subverting the Islamic Texture of Public Space

In the Iranian context, in contrast to Turkey, uniformity has been imposed on social semiotics by Islamism after the revolution in 1979, yet the public sphere is *multi-layered* or fragmented too, as I will show below using visual information gathered via participant observation. The ideal of a homogenous public order legitimated by communitarian conscience as designed by Islamic revolution is contested in a myriad of ways.

It is possible to observe the fragmentation of the public sphere in Tehran especially in civic public spaces like central streets, squares, shrines, cafes, restaurants, shopping centres, parks, bazaars, and food courts. On the longest street of Northern Tehran, the Veli-Asr Street, especially in the Park-ı Millet area (Public Park of Nation), I observed men and women sharing together open and closed civic public spaces. At the late afternoon and especially in the evening, youngsters (and also families with their children) go out to enjoy being in public, to eat and drink, to take a walk while eating corn and fancy ice-creams. Nocturnal public life is quite lively in this area. Public parks are important in Tehran, because they signify places where people who do not know each other can meet and enjoy each other's company, with various attempts at challenging the religious fundamentalist imaginary. Parks in Tehran provide unusual contexts for improvised secular performativities. The secular Iranian youth is especially quite aware of this spatial opportunity. Islamic morality is written upon the bodies of chadored females through the compulsory practice of veiling. However veiled bodies are not only written upon, but they also have the capability to write their own secular meanings and feelings upon space. This became manifestly clear when I observed young veiled girls rollerblading or playing badminton in Park-ı Millet. In fact, rollerblades as well as skateboards are vehicles that western youth use to contest various forms of spatial restriction that they encounter in their lives. Veiled Iranian young females, who are expected to be modest, diffident, calm and virtuous, subvert the Islamic texture of public space by engaging in this performance. The speed and sound of the rollerblades on the solid concrete competes with the sound of Islamic messages coming from the loudspeakers which are situated in the park by the official authorities. The rapid motion of the veiled bodies on the rollers was creating a kind of dance, maneuvering with their waving long dresses against the pre-supposed corporeal female passivity of Islamist moral imagery. Rollerblading offers a peculiar form of sociability to youngsters creating a specific emancipatory feeling of secularity. On a visual level, an idealized veiled figure is often identified by the religious regime with the representation of Islamic modesty. Her body is the bearer of acts which should fit to religious moral norms of female docility. She is seen therefore as literally embodying religious norms. However, I suggest here that the above-mentioned performative practices transgress the urban Islamic form of modesty. This also shows that women's bodies cannot be reduced to religious political vehicles.

At the other side of the Veli-Asr street, opposite to the Park-ı Millet, I had the opportunity to participate in the public environment of the shopping centres, restaurants and cafes, "the big food court and super market" called *Jam e Jam*, where one can find Mexican, French, Lebanese and Mediterranean fast food corners side by side. At the Safevih Bazaar where shops sell clothes, customers were mainly women. Women in this area do not wear long dark overcoats or black chadors. In summer they are wearing tunics in various pastel colors and trousers or jeans under these tunics, a dress-style which is completely in contrast with fundamentalist Shia veiling. Tunics are not very long, mostly not reaching to their knees, shaped at the waist, and they are not loose fitting but tight garments which highlight the feminine shape of their bodies. Thus they turned the compulsory religious veiling into a secular statement of fashion practice. Many young women wear open shoes which show their feet and it can be seen that they paint their toe and finger nails in very attractive colours like pink or red. They also use quite seductive make-up especially on their eyes. In this middle-class publicness, with a variety of pastel colours, tunics and trousers, high heeled shoes and make-up, women are expressing their secular femininity in the religious public sphere within the limits of Islamic dress-code. The style of covering their heads also contributes to this impression. They push their headscarves back to reveal more hair. In Turkey, young Islamic women cover their head in such a style that social audiences cannot see any part of their hair. Here in Iran, almost half of women's hair at the front side as well as their necks are exposed. Young women use this front side of their well-prepared hair to express secular femininity against compulsory veiling, and it was clear that they had spent a lot of time at the hairdresser's having their hair tinted blonde or other colours.

Near to the Safevih Bazaar, at a bigger shopping centre there are four cafes side by side all facing the street, and a "Sandwich and Snacks House" as it is named by the owner in English. The interiors and decor of these cafes are completely Western in style: they are like small American cafes. Western-style furniture, advertisements in French and English, all cold and hot western drinks, foreign cigarettes and the latest technology and mobile phones on the tables, the latest fashionable handbags, imported equipment to prepare cappuccinos, espressos, sundaes and milk-shakes, and western music and menus dominate these small spaces of northern Tehran. Although the Islamic revolution rejects the "pollution" of secularist culture and values, in this sense at least, it is losing its legitimacy.

By exchanging phone numbers, sitting together, getting spatial proximity, looking eye-to-eye, forming intimacy, creating friendship and sociability, these youngsters establish new secular meanings through renegotiated gender relations in Tehran. These secular children of the revolution challenge the Islamic norms of public relations. They develop worldly gender socialization while drinking their "non-alcoholic beer" (due to the ban on the use of alcohol) or "choco glassé"; or while they are eating their "pizza" or smoking "western cigarettes". One of the cafes is named "Star Café" and in the menu, written in English, there were more than 70 types of cold and hot foreign drinks, representing the western consciousness and taste. (Men are also adapting western-style clothes in these particular spaces. It was interesting to observe a young man with a big cowboy hat and some others with sunglasses over their baseball hats. Their sport-shoes and jeans were all western-branded.)

These cafes and open-air spaces around them serve the purpose of providing a peculiar secular place in which western life-styles are appropriated by effective forms of secular gender sociability whereby religious structures of rules and norms are challenged. We need to see this process of new life style formation among the youth of Northern Tehran as a performative process of secularity that has specific spatialities. Youth identity, as well as being about secular corporeality and fashion is also about spatiality. In fact, these western style cafes, fast food courts, Fereshteh street, Gandhi shopping centre (with brands such as Levi's and Esprit) act as sites for the performance of a new secular identity in opposition to the dominance of Islamist imagery. For the young habitués, these places provide a focus for a new sense of belonging, that is, they are succeeding in making a particular place, a new sense of belonging which acts against the religious indoctrination represented by vast murals of revolutionary martyrs and black chadors. Thus these secular Iranian youngsters may begin to contest religious adult authority more directly.

The actors attending these places exhibit similar characteristics with respect to their bodies. It should be remembered that the body is the site for constructing the modern secular subject. Just as the body decoration of young male actors in these spaces does not fit the traditional construct of the Islamic body, the hyperfeminine appearance of the fashion-conscious veiled girls with their exaggerated make up refers to a change in the expression of the self in a Shiite society. Empowered with such socio-spatial practices, these young secular actors recast their needs of gender socialization, thereby increasing the extent of their secular presence in the Islamic public space. Thus gender relations in northern Tehran are becoming more and more informal and less governed by religious rules and conventions.

The presence of women in open and closed public spaces of Northern Tehran, with their demands to socialize with males, and to have spatial closeness with them, reverses the classical Islamic formula pertaining to their visibility in public. As young veiled women occupy new urban spaces, they initiate a disruptive or subversive process. Uncontrollable encounters and physical proximity between men and women change the religious texture of the ideal Islamic space. They support the quest for new forms of secular intimacy. And as they start to grasp the internal dynamics of secular publicness, they also start to question the traditional norms and conceptions of marriage, as well as sexuality. Affective or emotional individualism, the establishment of secular marriage on the basis of personal selection guided by "romantic love" (instead of the conservative "ethico-legal love" in Hegelian terms) emerge among these urban actors. So entry into the unsegregated gendered public space and the quest for new forms of secular sociability would change their life-practices. Thus the strongest element of Islamic public realm, that is, gender politics, is increasingly becoming subject to the questioning of the fundamentalist imaginary of women's visibility, and opens up a new context of secularity in Northern Tehran.

In Tehran, like many other big cities in Muslim countries, these young secular actors transform and subvert Islamism as they blend into modern urban spaces and consumption patterns. The main reason for these young actors to be in these particular spaces is that they want to try different public behaviour, manners and actions, everything from appearance, dress codes, styles and flirtation to new forms of sociabilities. It is a matter of readapting, testing and sometimes reacting to the taken-for-granted Islamic limits. These new forms of public visibility transform the composition of the fundamentalist imaginary of the public sphere as Iranian youth familiarize themselves with norms of secularity and reflect upon their new spatial practices. As they enter into or contribute to the formation of middle class urban spaces, what emerges is a secular subjectivity as a function of public space.

Of course, other impressions in the old part of Northern Tehran (Tecrish) and in Southern Tehran remind me that there are opposite social realities of publicness in the city. I visited the Tecrish area during the commemoration of death of the Prophet Muhammed's daughter, Fatimatuz-Zehra. On the day of commemoration, it was possible to observe that pious people, mostly adults, turned the courtyard of the Shrine of Imamzade Salih into a public gathering place. Men and women from different parts of the city were arriving by bus to pray at the shrine with the aim of commemoration. Adult women in black chadors were lighting candles for their prayers. Families were sitting at the courtyard of the shrine having their home-prepared meals and teas. The space of the courtyard was very crowded; women were dressed in black and men were mostly bearded. I noticed that the public spirit or landscape had turned completely into a religious space dominated by pious actors exhibiting more Islamic and traditional bodily images.

Thus two contrasting and competing social habitus or corporealities can be observed in two close locations – Tecrish is just at the end of Veli-Asr Street. Interestingly, on ordinary days (when there is no commemoration), youngsters use the courtyard of another shrine, Imamzade Ismail Shrine, as a meeting place since it is a less controlled space. This shows how both secular and religious meanings are attributed to the religious space by different social actors having different social backgrounds.

One can see women in black chadors lighting candles in the courtyard of the shrine (a practice that may even be dismissed by clerics as a superstitious belief), and within five or ten minutes drive, one can observe in a modern shopping mall women in completely contrasting secular images, as well as big Mickey Mouse toys, numerous computer games, DVDs of western movies, high-tech computers, the newest programs, and many Sony products. One can also interpret similarly the Persian translations of "Harry Potter" in book stores named "Book City" or huge restaurant advertisements for "Country Fried Chicken". The broadcasting of football matches between European teams or censored foreign movies in Persian after religiously- and politically-oriented TV programs can be perceived from the same perspective.

During flights on Iran Airlines, and also in Tehran, one can taste "Zam Zam Cola". "Zam Zam" is the name of the sacred water that Muslim pilgrims drink in Mecca. Cola may be conceptualized as a western consciousness of consumption or dietary taste (or may be conceptualized as the symbolic representation of western capitalism). But "Zam Zam Cola" and other examples represent a neither purely secular nor purely Muslim way of understanding the world. In fact, in Tehran's social context, secular middle-class youth practices are struggles focused on areas of cultural reproduction and on issues like individual self-realization and participation rather than simply marking their class and status differences. Similar practices can also be observed among the youth coming from lower classes, who make use of every legal opportunity for collective public gathering to create temporal but secular dispositions. Soccer matches create opportunities for demonstration, shouting, making noise, entertainment, blocking the flow of traffic, playing drums and dancing. Similarly, even the Sacred Ashura nights may also turn into less religious and more secular occasions by linking the consecrated to the profane. In principle, these nights are composed of heavy religious mourning rituals with pious theatrical acts, yet since the collective effervescence of youth is not inhibited in these nights, they use the performative opportunity to transform a solemn religious ritual into secular ways of having good time in public. In short, young people from various class backgrounds try to reverse the religious normative structure of space into a more secular temperament.

It is also possible to focus on opposing visual signs and images which exist side by side representing multifaceted reality of public life in Tehran. For instance, pictures of revolutionary Muslim leaders, Ayatollahs Khomeini and Hamaney can be seen on the walls of the most westernized spaces, like *Jam e Jam* shopping mall. Western menus and large, framed pictures of fast food dishes are displayed on the walls adjacent to those posters of religious leaders who are the political images of the revolution. The co-existence of these religious symbols with the highly stylish appearance of young secular women prove that the "revolutionary ideal" of rejecting the *gharbzede* (toxicated by the west or westoxicated) is no longer overwhelming in the organization of Northern Tehran's public spaces.

Similarly, Valentine's Day takes a unique form in Tehran. According to the editors of Frontline World:

> The holiday is not approved by Iran's Islamic government, but unofficially Valentine's Day has caught on, especially among the young. In her short video, Iranian-American filmmaker Shaghayegh Azimi captures the giddy atmosphere of the day, as she speaks to people on the streets, in the malls and gift shops, and in cafes where couples are out on dates. Of course, Iranians have their own ancient traditions of romance and poetry that transcend any commercial

import. But Iran's own cultural history seems to inspire some to take part in the Valentine's Day festivities, including one man who says he is searching for 'his metaphysical calling', his soul mate. (Frontline World 2006)

For Shaghayegh Azimi "a new culture now exists that fuses Iranian and western lifestyles and values, Valentine's Day is part of this" (Azimi 2006).

We can also put forward the notion of a more emancipatory hidden society, the assertion of a secular "private life-world" encountering the public restrictions of the Islamic regime which appear as the main development in the post-revolutionary Iran. In one of my conversations with secular Iranians, they talked about the acts of praying and dancing, which metonymically connoted the relative nature of the private-public distinction. It is said by way of a joke that "people used to pray at home and dance in public before Islamic revolution, now they dance at home and pray in public". Of course I am not taking "prayer" and "dance" simply in their empirical manifestations. But if "prayer" and "dance" can be taken as performative metonymies of the "religious" and the "secular" respectively, the private or semi-private sphere in Iran becomes a metonymy of the freedom of speech by people talking to each other, perhaps more importantly, reacting to fundamentalism. So a characteristic of the public turns into a characteristic of the private. The distinction between the public sphere (which is conventionally associated with secularity) and the private sphere (which is conventionally associated with religiosity) has little reflexivity in the Iranian context. On the contrary, one can observe the existence of the transformative influence of "secular private sphere" over the "religious public sphere". In some ways, the most apparent feature of the private or semi-private sphere in Iran has been a vision of power so that the "transformation of private sphere" is itself a major strategy of the secularists against compulsory or pseudo religiosity in public domain. It is an awareness of how the "secular" private sphere competes with the dominant representations of the "religious" public sphere. Thus the private sphere protects its residents from the mainstream styles of religious publicness and provides an environment of secular inner sociation that can be interpreted as an alternative life strategy, which in turn may shape the secular public performances of participants. The private sometimes transforms or shapes the public. Even Habermas (1989) in his classical study conceives the early bourgeois public sphere as the sphere of private people coming together as a "public". This unified private sphere functions like a secret public sphere, or like a public behind closed doors. As Fraser points out, after all, to interact discursively as a member of a counterpublic [semi-public sphere in Iran] is "to aspire to disseminate one's own discourse to ever widening arenas" (Fraser 1992: 124). For Fraser, Habermas captures well this aspect of the meaning of publicness when he notes that: "however limited a public may be in its empirical manifestation at any given time, its members understand themselves as part of a potentially wider public, that indeterminate, empirically counterfactual body we call 'the public at large'" (in Fraser 1992: 124). The point is that the private sphere in Iran has a dual character: on the one hand, the private sphere in Northern Tehran functions as a space of withdrawal and secular regroupment; on the other hand it also functions as a secular basis and training ground directed toward a wider religious public (1992: 124).

While travelling on the highway, one can observe the image of a street fighter on a huge billboard which says both in Persian and English "The Islamic world is against all the enemies of Palestine" – a political Islamic message. After a while you see another billboard which says in English "Sports Not Drugs" with a picture of a cycling sportsman. In the inner city, one can encounter graffiti which reads "Pink Floyd the Wall". These sensorial significations represent the contrasting social imaginaries at the visual level, including both religious and secular messages. It is no coincidence that the slogan "Sports not Drugs" is written in English. It points to the increasing drug use among urban youth and the inability of the authorities to cope with it. According to a newspaper article by Judah:

> more and more young Iranians are turning to metaphorical means of escape. In the wealthier northern suburbs of Tehran, kids pop Ecstasy tabs and smoke dope at secret parties. In the poorer south, it is heroin and opium. Addiction has grown, too; and like anywhere else, drug addiction is sometimes intertwined with another growing phenomenon: prostitution. (Judah 2002)

At this point maybe Judah makes a debatable interpretation concerning modernity. In his opinion, in Iran the cultural products of western modernity – music, video-games and films, internet chat, satellite television – are spreading among youth, and as is the case in other societies "modernization has also brought along all the familiar evils: a widespread sense of alienation, drug addiction and prostitution". These facts could be taken as the evil sides of modernity but are we sure that in Iran "a widespread sense of alienation, drug addiction and so on" are simply products of modernization? It is not an easy question. Durkheimian anomic facts can be related to social and economic variables in the West, but the reasons behind anomic facts in Iran should be traced back to the domain of a restrictive or non-emancipatory experience of the religious public sphere, which creates alienation or a reified understanding of society.

In the context of postsecularity paradigm, how can we interpret the various "secular" youth practices in the "religious" texture of Tehran presented by departing from the spatial context of a public park? Are they ordinary assimilations to modern western cultures, consumption and lifestyles or are they an expression of political opposition?

It is not feasible to explain such an appropriation of secular western youth practices in Tehran merely as an assimilation to the global youth culture that has spread all over the world. It is possible to conceive these practices of appropriation within the framework of secular socio-cultural movements in Iran, in which active political opposition of secular youth movements is mostly suppressed, be it leftist or liberal. When the notion of "profane culture" and its agency enter the "religious scene", the new cultural practices of the secular Iranian youth can be read as attempts at appropriating certain elements of cultural secularity and absorbing them into the oppressive Islamic culture, thus showing their transformative potential. In Tehran, the acquisition and appropriation of secular cultural practices – through active and subjective motives – create interaction and communication between young actors who see and observe each other, thus establishing a transformative relationship with the religious public sphere. As Sadria points out, in the model of socio-cultural movements, interaction and communication primarily leads to the recognition (not simply seeing) of these actors by others resembling themselves. In Tehran, this recognition brings about their "becoming" through the construction of a new way of living and exploration of secular cultural meanings. Through the continual process of interaction and communication, secular elements incessantly enter into circulation and are shared by the participants, and perhaps becoming transferred into the existing religious culture (Sadria 2003: 5–7). These interactions and appropriations can create different forms of action particular to the peculiarities of different societies; that is, a different social context would give the same secular cultural elements completely different functions. In fact, under the Islamicizing circumstances of Iran, western youth cultures could turn into means of realizing these actors' secular counter-life objectives. Hence, to consider the adoption of western styles and values by middle-class secular youth in Tehran only in terms of cultural assimilation would be an explanation devoid of any analytical value. Via such practices, secular youth in Iran are challenging the political discourses of religious oppression, and these life projects then enter into circulation, thus turning into common secular practices that leave their own distinctive traces on the religious space.

There is no intention here to attribute a high ideological consciousness to the young secular actors in Tehran but rather a strong awareness in face of the religious restraints they encounter. In Tehran even the quest for joy, music, fashion and fun turn into components of a secularist movement. Therefore the acceptance of western cultural practices does not imply an identical process for all societies. In Tehran all these cultural practices connote the "symbolic and secular power" of resisting monologizing Shiite religion.

Anti-regime secularist political action is not possible in Iran. But the sociology of socio-cultural movements cannot be separated from a representation of society as a system of social forces competing over a cultural field. Touraine defines this kind of secular movement as a socially conflictual but also culturally oriented form of behaviour. The secular action should not necessarily be oriented towards the state, and cannot simply be identified with hard-core political engagement for the control of power. For Touraine, such social action transcends the political level and functions at the level of historicity i.e. the capacity of a society to produce itself. It is a competition over cultural orientations by which relationships are normatively organized (Touraine 1985).

In this context, even friendship, joy, emotions and love can be politicized relations in Iran, in the sense that the "profane becomes political". The memory of the pre-revolutionary secular composition of life in Northern Tehran has not disappeared among permissive parents, and is reflected in the life-world of their children. Secular forms of emotions and intimacy are meaningful not only in the private sphere. Emotions and the ways that individuals negotiate their relations may comprise characteristics of publicization as it can be observed in the youth spaces of Tehran within the limits of regulatory Islamic codes. Despite the fact that they are liminal secular practices, they show that emancipation in the religious public is not wholly exiled to the semi-private sphere. Especially for youth, a disposition towards secular leisure and entertainment weakens the validity of Islamism, and the processes of social change are articulated in everyday life. Secular youth also tends to reinvent the pre-revolutionary worldly traditions of Iranian culture. It is a secularist disposition which comprises all that is considered immoral by the religious ideologues of the regime.

Conclusion

Multiple modernities can be seen to be a prominent feature of the two contexts that I have analysed here: Turkey and Iran. In both cases, a religious and a secular reality co-exist, often in striking contrast yet in close proximity. In Turkey, urban middle-class circles creatively subvert and adapt elements of western consumerism with Islamic codes and norms, as the examples of headscarf usage, *medrese* cafes and Islamic holiday sites effectively reveal. Middle-class Islamic actors are able to create their own distinct modernity which is neither Western consumerist nor traditional Islamist.

In marked contrast, where modern Turkish women adopt a head covering that simultaneously symbolizes style and fashion yet hides the hair completely, the comparable urban middle-class woman in Tehran is at pains to subvert the state-prescribed veiling, revealing her hair and tinting or styling it to feminize her appearance as much as possible. The example of Iran, as mentioned by Göle (2010: 45–46) at the outset, provides a striking mirror to the practices in Turkey: where in Istanbul, Islam reshapes imposed secularity and creates an alternative, less secular identity, in Tehran, western elements are used to subvert an imposed Islamism and to construct an alternative, less religious identity.

Yet both examples reveal critical issues for Islam's significant encounter with modernity. Both in Tehran and Istanbul, distancing from primordial traditions, participation in secular conditions, weakening of ideological Islamism within market structures, and novel interpretations of religious morality and processes of cohabitation all force us to reflect on multiple modernities paradigm. The complex social semiotics of both Turkish and Iranian urbanity can be perceived as varying indicators of an exchange between western and Islamic conceptions of modernity, religious austerity and consumerism. They can be seen as postsecular criticisms of modernity that prove that Muslim societies are not predestined to choose between assimilation to globalism and dependence on local religious indigeneity. The creative transformation of Islamic locality opens the way for a reflexive nexus between religiosity and secularity with multiple, unexpected effects. As I have discussed, treating this undermining of the classic Islamic formula as nothing more than an example of the all-pervasive impact of globalization is to fail to understand the underlying processes that forge co-existing multiple modernities in a postsecular environment. In both cities and both countries, actors, more or less secular or religious, create their own modernity as a form of discreet challenge to the authority of the state.

References

Azimi, S. 2006. Notes from the Filmmaker. [Online]. Available at: http://www.pbs.org/frontlineworld/blog/2006/02/valentines_day_2.html [accessed 14 February 2006]

Çamuroglu, R. 1998. Alevi revivalism in Turkey, in *Alevi Identity*, edited by T. Olsson et al. Istanbul: Swedish Research Institute, 79–85.

Fraser, N. 1992. Rethinking the public sphere: A contribution to the critique of actually existing democracy, in *Habermas and the Public Sphere*, edited by C. Calhoun. Cambridge: MIT Press, 109–142.

Frontline World 2006. *Valentine's Day in Iran*. [Online]. Available at: http://www.pbs.org/frontlineworld/blog/2006/02/valentines_day_2.html [accessed 14 February 2006].

Göle, N. 2000. Snapshots of Islamic modernities. *Daedalus* (winter), 91–117.

Göle, N. 2002. Islam in public: New visibilities and new imaginaries. *Public Culture*, 14 (1), 173–190.

Göle, N. 2010. Manifestations of the religious-secular divide: Self, state and the public sphere, in *Comparative Secularisms in a Global Age*, edited by L.E. Cady and E.S. Hurd. New York: Palgrave Macmillan, 41–53.

Habermas, J. 1989. *The Structural Transformation of the Public Sphere*. New York: Polity Press.

Judah, T. 2002. The sullen majority. *The New York Times*, 1 September.

Kömeçoğlu, U. 2006. "New Sociabilities: Islamic Cafes in Istanbul", *Islam in Public: Turkey, Iran and Europe*, edited by N. Göle and L. Amman. Istanbul: Bilgi University Press, 163–189.

Kömeçoğlu, U. 2007 "Islamic Patterns of Consumption", *Cultural Changes in the Turkic World*, edited by F. Kıral et al. Würzburg: Ergon Verlag.

Okur, Ö. 1997. Alternative advertisements on Turkish television channels. Unpublished M.A. thesis. Boğaziçi University, Istanbul.

Sadria, M. 2003. Cultural social movements, unpublished paper.

Tohidi, N. 2002. The global-local intersection of feminism in Muslim societies: The cases of Iran and Azerbaijan. *Social Research*, 69 (3), 851–887.

Touraine, A. 1985. An introduction to the study of social movements. *Social Research*, 52 (4), 749–788.

Chapter 3
The Turkish Laboratory: Local Modernity and the Postsecular in Turkey

Massimo Rosati

It is well known that Turkey is a country in a state of flux. The ongoing debated and contested transition from a Kemalist ideology to a post-Kemalist one has a deep impact on many different levels and domains of Turkish national life (see Gülalp 2004; Dagi 2011). The Western-like profile of the Kemalist project of modernization is beginning to give way to alternative forms and understandings of modernity. Though the liberalization process started in the eighties, under Turgut Özal's government, it was only in the nineties that the liberalization of the public sphere and of political life started to challenge with more conviction the centralist doctrines of the Kemalist ideology, with its homogeneous understanding of public space, and to make visible alternative interpretations of nationalism and secularism (see Dressler 2010). Intellectuals and columnists daily openly debate the Kemalist legacy, how to vernacularize Western modernity, how to recover parts of the Ottoman heritage, and how to reshape both secularism and nationalism to accommodate those hundreds of differences – religious, cultural, and ethnic – that characterize the Turkish landscape. This debate is becoming more and more intense, following the general election of June 2011, on the eve of the promised writing of a new Constitution. Needless to say, the transition from a Kemalist Turkey to a post-Kemalist one is highly controversial, perceived as threatening to Kemalist sensibilities. From international relations – the Minister of Foreign Policy, Ahmet Davutoglu, is a fine intellectual and theoretician of civilizations (Davutoglu 1993 and 1997) – to TV soap operas and fictions, Turkey seems in search for itself. What is interesting is how this process deeply affects the balance of power between civil and military power, the State and civil society, the centre and peripheries (cultural, ethnic, religious, sometimes geographical) of the country. Although it is very difficult to predict the outcome of the ongoing processes, one can easily imagine that they will continue to question the profile of the Kemalist Turkey, and they will shape an alternative form of modernity, a form of *local* modernity, to use Nilüfer Göle's expression (Göle 2010).

Given the abundant literature on Turkey in political, constitutional, and philosophical terms, I want to try to throw a different light on the above-mentioned processes by choosing a different route, characterized by a cultural analysis of the changes in the symbolic value system of contemporary Turkey. At the level of the dynamic of the Turkish central value system, one can witness a process of pluralization of the image of modernity, of transformation of the notion and practice of secularism, and above all the making of a postsecular society. The transition from a Kemalist Turkey to a post-Kemalist one is not only *reflected*, but also *produced* at the level of struggles over symbols. I will mention three symbols expressing different views of modernity and secularism: an *old symbol in transformation,* an *emergent new symbol*, and an *ancient symbol in between past and future*. Each of them is as controversial as it is shared, as is frequently the case with symbols. Struggles over these symbols are the ground on which nowadays the reconfiguration of an alternative modernity to the Kemalist one – ideologically though not always in fact Western-like – is taking place. After briefly showing the relevance of the three selected symbols, I will try to draw from the Turkish case some broader conclusions on the meaning and the making of a postsecular society.

Contested Symbols

Mustafa Kemal Atatürk: An Old Symbol in Transformation

No other symbol is more at the centre of the Turkish value system (Shils 1975; Mardin 2006) than the image of the founder of the modern Republic himself. As Esra Özyürek correctly notes (Özyürek 2006: 93), visitors and newcomers are immediately greeted in Turkey with images of Atatürk, as much in Istanbul as elsewhere in the country, from airports to streets, in public buildings as well as in private shops, on coins and banknotes. Images of Atatürk, above all statues (whose construction must follow codified and detailed rules), are an integral part of Kemalism as a state doctrine that has a canon of sacred texts, rituals and pilgrimages, sanctuaries and feasts (Jenkins 2008: 81; Meeker 1997). What matters, however, in the present context, is the progressive transformation of the iconography referred to Atatürk, and of the meaning of this powerful, shared, virtually incontestable symbol, protected by law as well as by the morally coercive force of the public opinion.

There are basically three different types of representation of Atatürk's body: as a soldier, as a statesman, and as a man of the people (Özyurek 2006: 96). However, if the first and the second are part of the traditional iconography of the Republic, and symbolize the ideal of the independent nation, unified under the banner with the six arrows (nationalism, republicanism, populism, laicism, transformationism, statism; the nucleus of the rightist corporatist view of society proper to the charismatic leader, see Parla and Davison 2004), the third one is the outcome of a process of transformation that started in the nineties. More than representing Atatürk as a triumphant hero (see Giesen 2004), now the new commercialized Atatürk paraphernalia (stickers, pictures, t-shirts, ashtray, lighters and hundreds of other commodities), miniaturize the image of Atatürk, and frequently depict him as an ordinary human "with a social life and desires" (Özyurek 2006: 105), representing the same western style and tastes (his hats, clothes) but penetrating in a different space. In fact, if the monumental images of the soldier and the statesman occupy basically the public space of streets, squares, public buildings, now the new miniaturized and "humanized" images of Atatürk, "are displayed in private businesses, homes, and, more important, on the bodies of private citizens, all outside the direct authority of the state. In such miniature forms, Atatürk's representations, although still icons of the state, become a part of the bourgeois subject's domestic sphere" (Özyurek 2006: 105). Atatürk's image is added to those of family weddings within the domestic space, and is displayed in small barbershops or drug-stores. It is a process of miniaturization, and in a sense of privatization, of the leader's image that is not only part of a broader commodification of lifestyles and identity symbols (Navaro-Yashin 2002), but expresses, according to some interpreters, a privatization of secularism, the retreat of secularism into the private space under the onslaughts of an Islam that is increasingly present in the public sphere. "My Atatürk" is displayed at home, at work, on one's car, or on one's own body, as a symbol of the nostalgia for the modern, against "your veils" (Özyurek 2006: 99).

However, there is yet another transformation of this powerful symbol. It does not express only the triumphant Kemalist ideology, secularism included; or in its miniaturized and privatized form, the present, alleged weakness of the secular, "white" Turkey in comparison with Muslim and "black" Turkey.[1] Atatürk's image is a symbol so sacred, intangible, shared, that in recent decades even Islamic movements are trying to re-interpret it and to appropriate it. So, for example, during the celebrations for the seventy-fifth anniversary of the Republic, in 1998, the then ruling Islamist Welfare Party showed pictures of Atatürk in public prayer, praying with chest-level palms turned upward, or with his then-wife Latife Hanim veiled. More recently, in October 2010, after months of controversies, President Gül commemorated the establishment of the Republic of Turkey by merging receptions that in the previous years were kept separated. In fact, since his election in 2007, Gül had always held two separate receptions, one for the military and senior government officials, and another in the evening for the media, NGOs, artists and others. The latter hosted the spouses of the invitees, covered or not. However, in 2010 he merged the two receptions, and a few days later, his wife, who wears a headscarf, officially welcomed Germany's representatives, walking down the red carpet and greeting Turkish soldiers. By introducing the headscarf in public spaces, Gül was trying to make places related to the memory of Atatürk (such as the Dolmabahçe Palace, where Atatürk died in 1938, and where official receptions take place) open to religious markers; he was trying to separate the memory of Atatürk from Kemalism and from a Kemalist understanding of secularism. In a

---

1 "Black Turk is used to designate those Anatolians and Rumelian (the Balkans) who were excluded from the political and economical system, whereas the White Turks are those who have been dominating the system", Yavuz 2009: 309, n. 31

recent interview, a member of the Saadet Partisi (The Felicity Party, the heir of the Islamist Movement of Nemcmettin Erbakan) told me (implicitly quoting Erbakan himself) that if Atatürk was alive, he today would be a member of the Saadet Partisi! These examples show how respected and untouchable his memory is, even in a time of appropriation by non-Kemalist groups, and in a time of incipient de-mythologization of his figure, quite evident in recent biographies and debates on them (see Hanioğlu 2011).

Hrant Dink: The Emergent Symbol

Hrant Dink was a Turkish-Armenian journalist, the founder and director of Agos, a weekly Turkish-Armenian magazine committed to bridging Turkish divided memories on the Armenian uprooting. He was shot on January 19, 2007, in Istanbul, in broad daylight, outside Agos' premises. The killer was a young Turkish nationalist, soon arrested. However, after more than four years, Dink's family and friends, and the public opinion, are still waiting for justice: in fact, nobody yet knows who armed the young Turkish nationalist, although there have emerged clear responsibilities of the Turkish police and other sectors of the institutions, which though informed of the plans to kill Dink, failed at least to protect him. The murder of Dink is part of a more complex picture of a deep-state power aimed at destabilizing the country and fostering a new military intervention to restore the principles of Kemalism, by a secret organization called Ergenekon. Dink's funeral turned into a huge demonstration of anti-Kemalist Turkey in favour of freedom, justice, and equality. Every year, on January 19, thousands of people gather together outside Agos' premises to commemorate his memory and sacrifice, and to ask for justice.

Around the figure of Dink there is now developing a set of symbols (the white dove above all, now for example reproduced in a public park dedicated to Dink's memory in Mersin) and a ritual that binds together broad sectors of civil society: ethnic, cultural and religious minorities (Armenians and Kurds in first place); sectors of mainstream Sunni Islam that share a common anti-Kemalist feeling; leftist political parties and movements, trade unions and civil rights activists. Dink is becoming the symbol of a pluralistic, democratic Turkey, strongly centred on human rights and cosmopolitan values, but also concerned with the value of cultural and religious differences and particularities. "Friends of Dink" are quite frequently secular leftists; however, though not particularly enamoured of religious rituals, Dink himself was well aware of the meaning of religions for individual and collective life, and he considered them part of a pluralist public space. Dink's figure is becoming the symbol of a Turkey in search of democratization, where secularism is interpreted not as an assertive and aggressive form of repression, control and privatization of religions, but as a condition for equal access for every culture and faith to the public space. Dink's memory challenges above all secular nationalism. Sociologically, Dink represents not a triumphant hero, such as Atatürk, but rather an example of a process of social construction of victimhood that deeply alters the relationship between centre and periphery, bringing categories relegated in the past to the margins of society towards the centre, altering and changing the sacred centre itself (see Giesen 2004). From a sociological point of view, it is extremely interesting that Dink's memory is taking shape in a highly ritualistic way: the annual commemoration outside Agos' premises reproduces the spatial form of the temporary, "unofficial sanctuary" (Kong 2010; Della Dora 2011) that was spontaneously shaped soon after he was killed. As his friends at Agos told me during interviews, through the ritualistic event of the commemorations, the space in front of Agos, the premises of the magazine and now the foundation itself are becoming a sacred space. Though space does not permit me here to develop the idea fully, there is a sort of "grammar" of sacred spaces, that has to do with the working of ritual and the sacred, and with the functions they perform. Roughly speaking, sacred spaces (unofficial postsecular sanctuaries included) have four features: an orienting function, the capacity of mirroring a transcendent and more perfect order, being a meeting point between man and the sacred, and finally containing and representing (always in a partial and limited way) the sacred. A detailed analysis, that is beyond the scope of this chapter, would show that the temporary sanctuary built on the occasion of Dink's commemoration exactly meets the properties of this grammar, and that through ritualistic actions a new sacred symbol related to Dink's memory is taking shape.

Ayasofya: Glimpses of a Postsecular Sanctuary

Recently, since the so-called spatial turn, a methodology of urban sanctuary research aimed at studying the relevance of sacred spaces for the development of virtues of appreciation of religious pluralism is under development (see Knott 2005; Beaumont, Jedan, Molendijk 2010; Greve 2011). Postsecular sanctuaries are set urban spaces where religious rituals foster social solidarity in cosmopolitan socioscapes. In Turkey, one historical sanctuary is of particular interest as a possible candidate for the role of postsecular sanctuary. Its history is not unique in Turkey; other sanctuaries share the same story,[2] but no other has the same artistic and symbolic magnitude. I am talking about Ayasofya, or Hagia Sophia, or St Sophia, in Istanbul. Built by the Byzantine Emperor Justinian I, the Great, between the years of 532 and 537, the Church was dedicated to Sophia, referring to Christ as the Word or as the Wisdom made flesh. After having served as the Cathedral of Constantinople for 1123 years, it was to become the mosque of Ayasofya for another 481 years, and has been a museum since 1934. It was turned into a museum by Atatürk himself. Ayasofya is not only an astonishing architectural heritage of humanity, but also a multilayer religious symbol, the frozen memory of religious groups.

One of Maurice Halbwachs' lessons is that memories are always particularistic, given that memory is always the memory of a group, and groups are plural in

---

2   Another example is St. Savior in Chora (Kariye Camii or Kariye Kilisesi) in Istanbul.

modern societies (Halbwachs 1950 and 1992). Hagia Sophia, the Byzantine cathedral, is a sacred place at the centre of the memory of Orthodox Christians; Ayasofya, the mosque, is a sacred place at the centre of the memory of Muslims. Nowadays, it is the perfect spatial manifestation of the Kemalist understanding of secularism: by turning it into a museum, religious differences and conflicts were neutralized, banning them from the public space and turning them into aesthetic differences good for tourists and art lovers. At the same time, Ayasofya is still today a contested symbol. While Kemalists want to keep it as a national museum, Orthodox Christians want it reopened to the religious cult for Christians, whereas Muslims want the same but for Muslims. However, there is also a fourth group, not large in number but which included Hrant Dink in its ranks, composed of people who would like to see it transformed into a multi-faith sanctuary, the symbol of a multi-religious country. Solutions proposed by columnists, scholars and individual political personalities suggest the building be open to Christian worship on Sunday, Muslim on Friday, and the rest of the week to visitors. Leaving technicalities aside, what matters is the different understanding of secularism that these positions reflect. The present state of the museum of Ayasofya reflects a secularism understood both as the privatization of religion and the control of the state over religious symbols, that is the form of secularism proper to the Turkish state-tradition. Those among Orthodox and Muslims that lobby in favour of the reopening for single-faith worship dream of the prevailing of a single memory, while those – among them Orthodox, Muslims, and secularists – who think of a multi-faith and multi-purpose sanctuary see it as the symbol of a different understanding of secularism. Once again, in this context space does not permit me to enter into details, but the state and future of Ayasofya has a particularly relevant symbolic meaning, for Turkey of course, but also for a multicultural and multi-religious Europe.[3]

Alternative Modernities and the Postsecular in Turkey

Transformations of Atatürk's iconography and of official political liturgies framed by Atatürk's memory (such as receptions at the Dolmabahçe Palace, or at the Anitkabir, the Atatürk Memorial in Ankara), the emergence of a new symbol, such as the figure of Hrant Dink, and controversies about the status of Ayasofya, are the expression of a deep revision, among other things, of the Kemalist understanding of secularism. However, consistently with a causalist understanding of ritual, according to which ritual is not only the expression of beliefs, but also a means to generate beliefs (see Rosati 2009), my view is that the kind of liturgies that take place on occasions such as the commemorations of the Independence, the establishment of the Republic, or Atatürk' death, and the kind of liturgy that characterizes the annual commemoration of Dink's death, are also

---

3   It was also Dink's opinion, see Dink 2006.

responsible for changes both in the central value system of the Turkish collective identity, and in the understanding of secularism. Ayasofya is the symbol of a divided memory, and just in principle, considering positions in the debate about its status, a possible symbol of a different understanding of secularism.[4] Shifts in the representations of Atatürk's body and in the use of public spaces related to his memory are the evidence of a new balance between the Kemalist memory and above all Sunni Muslim culture. Hrant Dink, a still contested symbol because of the Kemalist hostility towards minorities, is becoming the symbol of a different view of the national identity, open to the rights of minorities and to cultural and religious differences. Both a new memory of Atatürk and the memory of Dink are shaped ritualistically, by means of rituals that have all the ingredients of liturgical rituals,[5] in that they take place in sacred – even if not religious – spaces, that are real sanctuaries; they occur regularly; they follow a precise protocol, observing a structure fixed over the years, but capable of balancing canonical and self-referential meanings; and they have performative effects.

The overall effect of these ritualistic performances is a progressive challenge to the Kemalist central symbolic system. As I said before, the process started in the eighties, it has its roots in the fifties, after the end of the single-party system, and it gained momentum first in the nineties, and again in the years of the AK Party government. The AK Party (Justice and Development Party) is a crucial actor in understanding contemporary changes in Turkey, and current disputes over the idea of secularism (see Cizre 2008; Tepe 2008; Hale and Ezbudun, 2009; Yavuz 2009). It can be considered the last (provisional) outcome of the process of liberalization started by Özal, and the (provisional) outcome of a process of transformation of the National Outlook Movement. Under structural factors (political participation, neo-liberal economic policies and the expansion of the market) and agency (reinterpretation of the religious tradition), the AK Party is undergoing a transformation from a Islamist movement to a party which is conservative in terms of social morals (and religiously inspired in its visions of gender roles, family life and so on), close to the Reagan-Thatcher ideology of neo-liberalism in terms of de-regulation of the economy, and fully committed to the language of human rights (Cizre 2008: Yavuz 2009). Even if it looks more often than not like a *modus vivendi*, the AK Party seems to be committed to bridging not only Turkey and Europe, but also different sectors of Turkish society: Kemalist and Islamists, Kurds and Turks, Turks and Armenians, Sunnis and Alevis, Muslims and other religious minorities. It is hard to say whether the AK Party is moved by pragmatic instances but lacks visions of the future of Turkey, as social scientists sometimes say. However, it seems to me hard to embark on a very risky political process such as the so-called "democratic opening" (concerning the solution of the Kurdish question but also the accommodation of other minorities, cultural

---

4   The status of Ayasofya is not, currently, in the agenda. However, it is an issue that every now and then enters debates.

5   For the distinction between liturgical and mystical rituals, see Rosati 2009.

and religious differences) without vision and prospects. In recent years it seems that the AK Party's ability to democratize the country, rather apparent in its early years in government, is waning, and many lament the weakening of its initial reformist stance. Limits and contradictions have emerged in its government, as well as expressions of authoritarianism towards the media and uncertainties in the "democratic opening". However, it seems apparent that the main obstacle to a further democratization of the country is still the Kemalist opposition.

Speaking of secularism, the AK Party's position, and that of intellectuals close to the ruling party (see Karasipahi 2009), is quite unequivocal: secularism is an integral part of Atatürk's legacy, an integral part of Turkish identity, a crucial constitutional principle, and above all a necessary condition in order to live together. However, it is necessary to live together differently. In other words, the AK Party's position is also unequivocal in contesting the Kemalist interpretation of secularism.

A useful distinction is that between laicism as it evolved in France, on the one hand, and religious freedom as it evolved in the Anglo-American context (Yavuz 2000; Diotallevi 2008; Yavuz 2009). In the first case, the separation between religion and politics, usually in a situation of religious monopoly, is meant to control religion and eradicate it from the public sphere: it is a form of anti-religious secularism, tolerant out of duty, to say the least sceptical towards the value of religions. In the second case, religious freedom aims at protecting religions, usually in a situation of religious pluralism, from state intervention, and encourages religions to unfold their capability of generating social capital within the public sphere. Depending on several other variables, such as religious pluralism, doctrinal beliefs and so on, this kind of separation can be judged convenient from the point of view of religions themselves, whose integrity can be protected against the corrupting effects of a more direct involvement in mundane and political affairs. In principle, the above argument can be a powerful reason to embrace secularism from a religious perspective (see Taylor 1998).

The Turkish case is particularly interesting and complex. The kind of secularism proper to Kemalist elites in different phases of the Republican history – during the mono-party system (1924–1950), in the years of the multi-party period (1950–1983), in those of the neo-liberal revolution (1984–1999), and finally in the recent period of the AK Party's rule, is a quite clear example of an assertive, militant, comprehensive or metaphysical (in Rawls' vocabulary) kind of secularism. In Turkey, state secularism can actually be understood as a form of colonization of the life-world by the political system (Habermas 1984), aimed at repressing religious and cultural differences at large – conceived of as threatening the integrity of the state and the republic – in the name of a homogeneous public space (Meeker 1997; Yavuz and Esposito 2003; Parla and Davison 2004). Secularism took (and still takes nowadays in significant sectors of the political and cultural systems) the form of a Jacobin laicism deeply embedded in the top-down process of nation-building, for a long time interpreted by the international literature as the only and almost "natural" way of modernizing and democratizing the country (Lerner 1958; Berkes 1998; Lewis 2002). In the light of old theories of modernization, frequently linked to orthodox theories of secularization, even the authoritarian aspects of Kemalism were justified in terms of theories of tutelary democracy (Parla and Davison 2004, 4).

The Habermasian concept of colonization of the life-world is particularly useful in reading this process of secularization as a means to prevent religious influences in the spheres of education, economics, family, dress codes, language expressions, everyday practices concerning almost every aspect of life. As a process of colonization, secularism in Turkey did not mean simply separation of politics and religion, and neutrality of the State, but the structuring of the means of control of religion (Islam) through a twofold process: the construction of an Oriental "other" on the one hand, and the shaping of a national Islam by means of the Directorate of Religious Affairs on the other (Yavuz 2009). *Lailik* in Turkey implied both separation and control (Davison 1998). In my view, the general but at the same time most characterizing feature of Kemalism's effort of creating a secular nation-state was the "scepticism, or fear of society" (Yavuz and Esposito 2003: xxiii), understood as intrinsically anomic. However, there are also other views of secularism in contemporary Turkey. According to Yavuz, there are at the moment at least three positions within the secularist camp: a) a rigid Kemalist version of militant secularism (assertive, metaphysical); b) "the conservative Turkish-Muslim understanding of secularism as the control of religion; and, c) the liberal conception of secularism stressing the separation of politics from religion (freedom of religion)" (Yavuz 2009: 153). The first version leaves no room for any kind and form of religious tradition, the second makes space for Sunni Islam but leaves out of the map the popular Islam of the Tarikats (see Özdalga 1998; Özdemir and Frank 2000), the Alevis (see Clarke 1999; Shankland 2003) and other religious minorities (see Kieser 2006), while the third one "is defended by Istanbul-based big business elites, some politicians and the Alevi community" (Yavuz 2009, 153).

As I will stress later on, I am sceptical about this picture. According to mainstream opinions, Turkey would be shifting, or would have to shift, from the Kemalist assertive view of secularism to a passive form of secularism, the difference paralleling that between secularism as a comprehensive doctrine and secularism as form of neutrality between world-views. I am not fully convinced by this opinion. If this is the case, Turkey is "simply", so to speak, shifting from one Western-like model of modernity to another one, from France (although the Kemalist model of secularism was not French-like at all, officially France was the model and source of inspiration), to England. Despite my admiration for the latter, I don't think this is the case. In my view, Turkey is interesting (theoretically, sociologically and perhaps from a normative point of view too) exactly because it is experiencing something like a "local modernity", an alternative way to arrange politics and religion, religion and society, drawing on its own resources and its Ottoman past. My feeling is that Turkey, through its political and cultural post-Kemalist but also post-Islamist elites (see Karasipahi 2009), is trying to transform *hüzün* (the feeling of a "deep spiritual loss", according to Orhan Pamuk, Istanbul's true soul, see Isin 2010) in a positive resource to shape a new modernity and a new way to deal with religions (in the plural) in a postsecular age.

The beginning of the processes of change crucial for the transition from a secular Turkey to a postsecular one has occurred, in waves, since the 1980s. It was Turgut Özal's reform policy that initiated Turkey's economic, social and political liberalization. Actually, already in the 1960s a new emerging bourgeoisie started to challenge the civilian-military bureaucracy over the definition of the process of modernization. However, it was during the Özal years that the rigid Kemalist iron cage started to weaken and "the new Anatolian business class, along with Istanbul-based industrialists, increased its power" (Yavuz 2009: 16; see also Tuğal 2009). This process, here outlined in almost "Marxist" terms, opened – in Mardin's felicitous expression – new spaces of opportunities, most obviously in the economic sector but also in the social and political spheres. Particularly relevant, from a sociological point of view, it is the role played by media networks (Yavuz 2003: chapter 5), the Said Nursi movement (Mardin 1989) earlier and the Fetullah Gülen movement later, (Yavuz and Esposito 1998) in reopening the public spheres (in the plural, see Çinar 2008; Grigoriadis 2009) to religious influences, and in vernacularizing modernity.

Contrary to early-modern theories of modernization, here the process of modernization (liberalization for example in the economic sphere) implied neither a secularist trend, nor a reactive revolt against modernity, but the creation of hybrid forms of life, practices and beliefs. Filling the gap opened by these new opportunity spaces, *conscious Muslims* (Yavuz 2009) started to negotiate (Çinar 2008) within the public spheres new understandings of justice and modernity. Sociologists, and here one must mention particularly the pioneering and authoritative work of Nilufer Göle, are nowadays capable of offering us detailed, illuminating and fascinating accounts of the socio-cultural practices that, while putting a strain on the Turkish society, transform it in a molecular way. Religious education and the headscarf issue are perhaps just the most visible and well-known of these phenomena (Göle 1996; Özdalga 1998; Göle 2006; Çinar 2008). From the sociological point of view, the postsecular in Turkey has to do, in my view, with the re-opening of Muslim cafés, where men and women negotiate gender roles; it has to do with literature, where new models of women and men are depicted; it has to do with architecture and music, where rationalist and *à la franca* ideal-types are compromised with Islamic revivals, and so on (Çayir 1996; Kömečoglu 1996; Yavuz 1998).

Turkey and Multiple Modernities:
Towards a General Definition of the Postsecular

Over the decades of its Republican history, Turkey experienced different ways of arranging relationships between religion(s), politics and society. Though I am more interested, in this context, in focusing on current changes in the Turkish landscape, it is my conviction that from Turkey one can derive more general considerations about the relationship between modernity(s) and religion(s). In the past, Turkey was thought of in the light of old theories of modernization and secularization, but now that the crisis of old theories of modernization goes hand in hand with the crisis of orthodox theories of secularization (Beckford 2003: chapter 2; Davie 2007: chapter 3), we can learn something from Turkey about possible new ways of interpreting the relationship between modern societies and religions. Trying to synthesise previous reconstructions, one could say that since 1923, Turkey has experienced at least three different forms of relationship between religion(s) and secular politics: a) mutual mis-recognition of religious and secular forms of life, b) an authoritarian secular politics vs. religion(s), and c) a paternalistic domestication by politics of religion(s). Though history is obviously much more complex than this, I would say that mutual mis-recognition was the main form of relationships between secular politics and religion(s) in the period 1923–1950, authoritarianism the form it took in the period 1950–1980, when faced with authoritarian Kemalist elites religion(s) started to play a democratizing role, and paternalism its form in the period 1980–2000, the period of Islamic-Turkish synthesis. The period from 2000 up to the present is that of a still ambiguous and open construction of a postsecular modernity.

At the end of our journey in Turkey, for sure too short for the enormous complexity of this fascinating country, my theoretical suggestion is that maybe one could try to derive from the Turkish case a sort of four-quadrant model to analyse the relationships between religion(s) and secular politics, the analytical utility of which could be tested in other contexts. Empirically, it is derived by generalizing the Turkish case. Theoretically, it is derived by focusing on the place and role of the idea of reflectivity both in religious and secular world-views. Space does not permit here a full account of the way I came to get the two dimensions of religious reflectivity and secular modernity's reflectivity, namely reconstructing the reading of Western modernity proposed by two very different (but in my view complementary) authors, namely Habermas and Seligman (Rosati 2011). From the theoretical point of view, suffice it to say that the four-quadrant model is the outcome of the intersection of these two dimensions: the reflective capacity of Western modernity, and the reflective capacity of religious traditions. Modernity's reflectivity means the ability to discuss rationally validity claims, taken as the sole source of legitimacy of social and political order, a skill that modernity must also apply to the claims of reason itself to satisfy completely needs of meaning and functional needs of modern societies. Towards religion, this reflective capacity of modernity results in abandoning imperial pretensions by reason, and abandoning a self-destructive secularism. The mutual recognition by reason and faith of each other's limitations leads Habermas to define the postsecular as a *process of complementary* learning between faith and reason, religious and secular world-views (Habermas 2006). On the other hand, religious traditions' reflectivity, a notion elaborated by working on Seligman's categories, means the religious traditions' capability of coping with modernity understood as a civilization, without giving up their particularities, without assimilating, but finding inner resources, specifically religious resources, to articulate a vocabulary of principled tolerance and pluralism. Religions' reflectivity means recognizing religious differences as visible and deeply practised by individuals and groups, and developing a 'principled tolerance' capable of recognizing the internal and the external 'other' on the basis not of liberal but of religiously coloured sources.

What I am suggesting is that the reflectivity of modernity on the one hand, and that of religions on the other, are two defining dimensions of the idea of postsecular society, at least from the socio-political point of view. However, this is only part of the story. In fact, they are not only two defining dimensions of the *idea* of postsecular societies, but also two constitutive dimensions and even conditions of postsecular embedded social practices. Roughly speaking, one might assume that high levels of modernity's reflectivity and of religious reflectivity will trigger a process of complementary learning between secular and religious forms of life that in turn will creatively give life to hybrid social practices, reshape the borders between the two, negotiate identities, roles and spaces, and so on. Postsecular forms of life are contingent upon postsecular social practices, that in turn depend on the levels of reflectivity of modernity and religions. On the basis of these two variables, we have four possible kinds of relationships between modernity and religions.

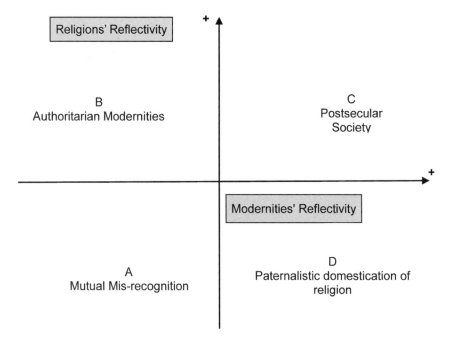

Figure 3.1   Relationships between modernity and religions

The first one (quadrant A) indicates a condition that I call of "mutual mis-recognition", reminiscent of the first phase of theories of secularization, when traditional religions were expected to disappear from the modern horizon and science was supposed to replace them as the new faith, and when religions felt at war with modernity's main cultural and socio-political features. It is the condition proper to post-revolutionary France, but also of contemporary disputes between neo-Atheists and religious integralists, which share the same Cartesian anxiety. In Turkey, it is the phase of the "golden" age of the Kemalist Republic, the time of the mono-party system, between 1923 and 1950. In a condition like this, no complementary learning process can be triggered.

The second condition (quadrant B) presents a different picture. Here we have low levels of secular modernity's reflectivity, and comparatively higher levels of religious reflectivity. I call a situation like this "authoritarian modernity", because here religious movements tend to have a democratising orientation towards the larger society. Solidarnosc in Poland might be a classical example, as well as Said Nursi in Turkey (Markham and Pirim 2011). Making claims for religious freedom, social movements may pave the way for larger categories of rights. Frequently, in claiming religious rights they consciously adopt the language of human rights reinterpreted from within their vocabulary – defending not only the rights of Catholicism, Islam or other specific traditions – against authoritarian but fully modernized regimes. The adoption of the human rights discourse shows that religious movements are capable of entering the public sphere, and defending their right to become actors within it, without either giving up their symbols and marks, or yet segregating themselves into "liberated zones" (Roy 1994: 80) separated from the modern society outside. In this quadrant, religions are peripheries in search of a way to penetrate into a hostile centre, while in quadrant A they are not necessarily at the periphery of the social system. In Turkey, quadrant B is the phase between 1950 and 1980, when religion (meaning here Sunni Islam) found political representation in the democratic party, and started to move towards the centre of the Turkish symbolic system.

The third possibility (quadrant D) is characterized by the opposite situation. Here we have a comparatively high reflectivity of modernity, but low levels of religious reflectivity. I would call this a state of paternalistic domestication of religion. This is typical of contexts characterized by a strong religious monopoly that forces secular actors to deal strategically at least with the mainstream religious tradition. In fact, instead of choosing a confrontational approach, here secular forces choose the way of instrumentalizing the religious mainstream tradition, to exploit it for functional reasons. It is neither an aprioristic refusal of religion, nor a sincere recognition of it, but an instrumental exploitation of its resources (integrational, identitarian and so on). Religion is not considered *qua* religion, or not sincerely, but as a functional resource. On the other hand, religious reflectivity is very low, because religious actors move between a radical refusal to have any contact with the secular world, on the one hand, and the willingness to be exploited in exchange for a public recognition, on the other. In Turkey, it is the phase between 1981 and 2000, when secular politics exploited above all Sunni Islam for nationalist purposes, under the Turkish-Islamic synthesis, and when the Refah party chose a confrontational approach with the secular state.

Let's consider now the fourth possibility (quadrant C), the one that indicates the postsecular condition. It is in a sense the opposite of quadrant A, and it indicates how, in order to have a postsecular society, two overarching demanding conditions need to be met. A society must present highly reflective modern social, cultural and political subsystems on the one hand, and a highly reflective religious social and political landscape on the other. This offers the only possibility to trigger a fruitful complementary learning process. A society must be, in Davie's words, "fully modern and fully religious" (Davie 2007: ix). Needless to say, this is a condition that runs against "orthodox" theories of secularization. At the same time, the co-presence of highly reflective modern structures, and of highly reflective religious actors within the public sphere, means that the idea of postsecular society has little to do with the idea of a de-secularized society (Berger 1999). If this were not the case, the notion of postsecular society would be useless as an analytical tool for societies that have never been fully secularized, or where religions have always been public religions in Casanova's sense (such as Italy, for example, and Spain, see Thiebaut 2010). We have to get rid of the idea that the postsecular age is equal to an obscurantist return to the Middle Ages.

More analytically, the postsecular condition requires

a. Reflexivity, historicity and agentiality, namely the three features proper to each Axial civilization;
b. The co-presence of secular and religious world-views;
c. De-privatized religious movements claiming public recognition *qua* communities of faith who share particularistic sets of beliefs and practices;
d. A condition of vibrant religious pluralism (including traditional religions, and not only the so-called new religious movements), that forces religious movements to increase their self-reflexivity and impedes strong positions of monopoly;
e. Secular citizens and groups that, to quote Habermas, "neither deny out of hand the potential for truth in religious conceptions of the world nor dispute the right of believing fellow citizens to make contributions to public discussions that are phrased in religious language" (2006, 260);
f. The reintroduction of genuine Axial visions as expression of the sacred. The sacred cannot be expressed only by civic symbols (the flag, the constitution, political religions and so on), and it cannot take only immanent forms.

If these conditions are sufficiently present, then in principle new postsecular social practices could generate hybrid forms of life, both on the social and on the political level. On the sociological level, postsecular practices can negotiate new relationships between genders and roles, new understandings of public and private, codes of decency and so on. On the political and constitutional level, they can generate new institutional arrangements, more or less different from the liberal ones. By definition, this in an open process, highly context-dependent, so that it is impossible to describe or anticipate it in detail. What is sure is that it will work as a potent multiplier of the forms that modernity can assume. The outcome of postsecular social practices would be not only multiple modernities, but alternative forms of modernity, or, "local modernities" (Taylor 2001; Eisenstadt 2003; Göle 2005). Furthermore, the shaping of a postsecular society implies a deep re-configuration of the relationship between centre and periphery, and a pluralization of centres in complex relation to one another and to multiple peripheries. My view is that Turkey can be considered a laboratory in the making of a postsecular society, and of a local form of modernity.[6]

References

Beaumont, J., Jedan, C. and Molendijk, A.L. 2010. *Exploring the Postsecular. The Religious, the Political, and the Urban.* Leiden-Boston: Brill.

Beckford, J.A. 2003. *Social Theory and Religion.* Cambridge: Cambridge University Press.

Berkes, N. 1998. *The Development of Secularism in Turkey.* New York: Routledge.

Berger, P. 1999. *The Desecularization of the World. Resurgent Religion and World Politics.* Washington: Eerdmans Publishing.

Çayir, K. 1996. Islamic Novels: A Path to New Muslim Subjectivities, in *Islam in Public. Turkey, Iran, and Europe*, edited by N. Göle and L. Ammann. Istanbul: Bilgi University Press.

Çinar, A. 2008. *Modernity, Islam, and Secularism in Turkey. Bodies, Places, and Time.* Minneapolis: University of Minnesota Press.

Cizre, U. 2008. *Secular and Islamic Politics in Turkey. The Making of the Justice and Development Party.* London: Routledge.

Clarke, G.L. 1999. *The World of the Alevi.* New York: AVC Publications.

Dagi, I. 2011. Why do we need a post-Kemalist Republic? *Today's Zaman*, 21/2.

Davie, G. 2007. *The Sociology of Religion.* London: Sage.

---

6   The same view seems to be shared by E. Fuet Keyman, who writes that "Turkey can be described as a *postsecular society*. Of course, postsecular society refers not to a ontological totality, but to an 'emerging reality' in the process of being made. This means that both empirically and normatively, Turkey remains a secularized social order but one in which religious worldviews and convictions continue to increase their power and influence in shaping and reshaping religious identity claims and recognition", (Keyman 2010, 155). Needless to say, such a process of making of a postsecular society is not an irenic one; on the contrary, it is often confrontational. Above all, considering that the postsecular has to do with reflectivity, disruptiveness and conflict are always ingredients of the increasing of the awareness. On this point, see above all Göle (2011).

Davison, A. 1998. *Secularism and Revivalism in Turkey*. New Haven: Yale.

Davutoglu, A. 1993. *Alternative Paradigms*. Lanham: University Press of America.

Davutoglu, A. 1997. Civilizational Self-Perception, *Divan*, Vol. 1, 144–62

Della Dora, V. 2011. Engaging Sacred Space: Experiments in the Field, *Journal of Geography in Higher Education*, May, 163–84.

Dink, H. 2006. Article in *Agos*, 7 July.

Diotallevi L. 2008. Church-State relations in Europe and the crisis of the 'European model', in *Religion and Democracy in Contemporary Europe*, edited by G. Motzkin and Y. Fisher. London: Alliance Publishing Trust, 125–39.

Dressler, M. 2010. Public-Private Distinctions, the Alevi Question, and the Headscarf: Turkish Secularism Revisited, in *Comparative Secularism in a Global World*, edited by L.E. Candy and E.S. Hurd. New York: Palgrave Macmillan, 121–41.

Eisenstadt, S.N. 2003. *Comparative Civilizations and Multiple Modernities,* 2 Vol. Leiden: Brill.

Giesen, B. 2004. *Triumph and Trauma*. Boulder and London: Paradigm Publishers.

Göle, N. 1996. *The Forbidden Modern*. Ann Arbor: University of Michigan Press.

Göle, N. 2005. *Interpénétrations. L'Islam et l'Europe*. Paris: Galaade Éditions.

Göle, N. and Amman, L. 2006. *Islam in Public. Turkey, Iran, and Europe*. Istanbul: Istanbul Bilgi University Press.

Göle, N. 2010. Manifestations of the Religious-Secular Divide: Self, State, and the Public Sphere, in *Comparative Secularism in a Global Age*, edited by L.E. Cady and E.S. Hurd. New York: Palgrave Macmillan, 41–53.

Göle, N. 2011. The Disruptive Visibility of Islam in the European Public Space: Political Issues, Theoretical Questions, paper delivered at the 'Centre for the Study and Documentation of *Religions and Political Institutions in Post-secular Society*', University of Rome Tor Vergata, 28 April.

Greve, A. 2011. *Sanctuaries of the City: Lessons from Tokyo*. Farnham: Ashgate.

Grigoriadis, I.N. 2009. *Trials of Europeanization. Turkish Political Culture and the European Union*. New York: Palgrave Macmillan.

Gülalp, H. 2004. AKP's Conservative Democracy: A Post-Kemalist Liberalism? Paper presented at the annual meeting of the American Sociological Association, Hilton San Francisco & Renaissance Parc 55 Hotel, San Francisco, CA (accessed online: http://www.allacademic.com/meta/p109912_index.html).

Habermas, J. 1984. *The Theory of Communicative Action*. Cambridge: Polity.

Habermas, J. 2006. On the Relations between the Secular Liberal State and Religion, in *Political Theologies. Public Religions in a Post-secular World*, edited by H. de Vries, L.E. Sullivan. New York: Fordham University Press, 251–60.

Halbwachs, M. 1950. *The Collective Memory*. New York: Colophon Book.

Halbwachs, M. 1992. *On Collective Memory*. Chicago: University of Chicago Press.

Hale, W.M. and Ezbudun, E. 2009. *Islam, Democracy and Liberalism in Turkey. The Rise of the AKP*. London: Routledge.

Hanioglu, M.S. 2011. *Ataturk: An Intellectual Biography.* Princeton: Princeton University Press.

Isin, E.F. 2010. The Soul of a City: Hüzün, Keyf, Longing, in *Orienting Istanbul*, edited by D. Göktürk, L. Soysal and I. Türeli. London: Routledg, 35–50.

Jenkins, G. 2008. *Political Islam in Turkey.* New York: Palgrave Macmillan.

Karasipahi, S. 2009. *Muslims in Modern Turkey. Kemalism, Modernism and the Revolt of the Islamic Intellectuals.* London: I.B. Tauris.

Keyman, E.F. 2010. Assertive Secularism in Crisis: Modernity, Democracy, and Islam in Turkey, in *Comparative Secularism in a Global Age*, edited by L.E. Cady and E.S. Hurd. New York: Palgrave Macmillan, 143–58.

Kieser, H.L. (ed.) 2006. *Turkey Beyond Nationalism. Towards Post-Nationalists Identities.* London: I. B. Tauris.

Knott, K. 2005. *The Location of Religion. A Spatial Analysis.* London: Equinox Publishing Ltd.

Kömeçoğlu, U. 1996. New Sociabilities: Islamic Cafés in Istanbul, in *Islam in Public. Turkey, Iran, and Europe*, edited by N. Göle and L. Ammann. Istanbul: Bilgi University Press.

Kong, L. 2010. Global shifts, theoretical shifts: Changing geographies of religions, *Progress in Human Geography*, March, 1–22.

Lerner, D. 1958. *The Passing of Traditional Society.* Free Press: Glencoe.

Lewis, B. 2002. *The Emergence of Modern Turkey.* Oxford: Oxford University Press.

Mardin, Ş. 1989. *Religion and Social Change in Modern Turkey. The Case of Bediüzzaman Said Nursi.* New York: State University of New York Press.

Mardin, Ş. 2006. Center-Periphery as a Concept for the Study of Social Transformation, in *Religion, Society, and Modernity in Turkey.* New York: Syracuse University Press.

Markham, I.S. and Pirim, S.B. 2011. *An Introduction to Said Nursi.* Farnham: Ashgate.

Meeker, M.E. 1997. Once There Was, Once There Wasn't. National Monuments and Interpersonal Exchange, in *Rethinking Modernity and National Identity in Turkey*, edited by S. Bozdoğan and R. Kasaba. Seattle and London: University of Washington Press, 157–91.

Navaro-Yashin, Y. 2002. *Faces of the State: Secularism and Public Life in Turkey.* Princeton: Princeton University Press.

Özdalga, E. 1998. *The Veiling Issue, Official Secularism and Popular Islam in Modern Turkey.* Surrey: Curzon.

Özdemir, A. and Frank, K. 2000. *Visible Islam in Modern Turkey.* New York: Palgrave Macmillan.

Özyürek, E. 2006. *Nostalgia for the Modern. State Secularism and Everyday Politics in Turkey.* Durham and London: Duke University Press.

Parla, T. and Davison, A. 2004. *Corporatist Ideology in Kemalist Turkey. Progress or Order?* New York: Syracuse University Press.

Rosati, M. 2009. *Ritual and the Sacred. A Neo-Durkheimian Analysis of Politics, Religion and the Self.* Farnham: Ashgate.

Rosati, M. 2011. Postsecular Modernities: A Sociological Reading, paper delivered at the annual BSA Conference, Birmingham (unpublished).

Roy, O. 1994. *The Failure of Political Islam.* Cambridge, MA: Harvard University Press.

Shankland, D. 2003. *The Alevis in Turkey. The Emergence of a Secular Islamic Tradition.* London: Routledge.

Shils, E. 1975. *Center and Periphery. Essays in Macrosociology.* Chicago: Chicago University Press.

Taylor, C. 1998. Modes of Secularism, in *Secularism and its Critics*, edited by R. Bhargava. Oxford: Oxford University Press.

Taylor, C. 2001. Two Theories of Modernity, in *Alternative Modernity*, edited by D.P. Gaonkar. Durham and London: Duke University Press.

Tepe, S. 2008. *Beyond Sacred and Secular. Politics of Religion in Israel and Turkey.* Stanford: Stanford University Press.

Thiebaut, C. 2010. Secularizing traditional Catholicism: Laicism and laïcité, *Philosophy & Social Criticism,* March, 36, 365–80, special issue on *Postsecularism and Multicultural Jurisdictions. Reset-Dialogues Istanbul Seminars 2008–2009.*

Tuğal, C. 2009. *Passive Revolution. Absorbing the Islamic Challenge to Capitalism.* Stanford: Stanford University Press.

Turam B. 2007. *Between Islam and the State. The Politics of the Engagement.* Stanford: Stanford University Press.

Yavuz, M.H. 1998. *Islam Political Identity in Turkey.* Oxford: Oxford University Press.

Yavuz, M.H. 2000. Cleansing Islam from the Public Sphere and the February 28 Process. *Journal of International Affairs*, 54, 21–42.

Yavuz, M.H. 2009. *Secularism and Muslim Democracy in Turkey.* Cambridge: Cambridge University Press.

Yavuz, M.H. and Esposito, L. (eds) 2003. *Turkish Islam and the Secular State. The Gülen Movement.* Syracuse: Syracuse University Press.

Chapter 4

Russia's 'Cursed Issues', Post-Soviet Religion, and the Endurance of Secular Modernity

Alexander Agadjanian

The Russian case is of twofold relevance for the overall problematique addressed in this volume. On one hand, located at the European periphery (and often referred to as both geographical and cultural 'Eurasia'), Russia is one of the world's proverbial cases of a perennial complex of backwardness and desperate thrusts to modernity. Moreover, with its communist experiment, it offered, in the twentieth century, an outstandingly novel, unique, and globally influential road of modernization. In this sense, the Russian case cannot be avoided in any discussion of 'multiple modernities'.

At the same time, with its almost overwhelming historical adherence to an Eastern Orthodox branch of Christianity, Russia provides exceptionally rich material on the degree and forms of confessional determination of a nation's history (especially in view of tacit or open comparison with the 'Latin west') and on religious/secular divide of the modern times, which reached its apex in merciless secularization under the Soviet regime, and a new revival after this regime fell. In this sense, the Russian case is equally and directly relevant to the second facet of this book – postsecularism.

The 'cursed issues' of Russian history, since at least the ninetieth century, have been how to catch up with modernity without losing the Orthodox Christian 'soul' or identity, or whether this 'soul' could be sacrificed for the sake of modernity, and what kind of 'soul' would be substituted?

In this chapter I first present a brief overview of the Russian encounters with modernity and then test applicability of the 'multiple modernities' and 'postsecular' theoretical frameworks to the Russian material. My initial presumption is that these two frameworks are not necessarily linked to each other: a specific religious tradition does not necessarily offer a conceptual key to explain a different kind of modernity. In other words, the modern 'multiplicity' can not be explained by the multiplicity of faiths, as might be deduced from the postsecular perspective. Additionally, in my opinion, the Russian case proves a stronger link between modernity and secularity than is usually held by the currently prominent critiques of the classical theories of modernization and secularization. Consequently, my understanding of the 'postsecular', with which I finish this chapter, may be somewhat different from that shared by the editors.

Russia's Encounters with Modernity

A brief overview of Russian history reveals unmistakably a number of attempts of reforms and then counter-reforms, creating a sequence of push-and-pull impulses. The most obvious (if we make a certain simplification) were Peter the Great's reforms in the early eighteenth century; then some by Catherine the Great; then partial reforms under Alexander I in the early nineteenth century; then crucial reforms under Alexander II in the mid nineteenth; then Revolutionary reforms in early twentieth century and Bolshevik modernization in their aftermath; and finally, the post-Soviet reforms in the late twentieth century. Each of these reform periods was followed by certain backlashes, which can be seen as manifestation of an inner duality of the Russian culture, possibly related to attractive-repulsive contacts with the west (see Lotman and Uspensky 1994, Akhiezer 1997).

The reform impulses were generated and stimulated by encounters with the European experience; all were reactions to perceived backwardness vis-à-vis European processes, that is, all of them were conceived *within* the paradigm of western modernity. This was the case even when the reformers were making a selection of what to follow and what to reject in the cultural program of modernity. We know that this was not a selection from a systematic, integral program, because such a program did not exist in the eighteenth or nineteenth century. However, every piece of reform was a reaction to a certain western impulse, and the overall vector of reforms was westward.

Because of this selectivity, each attempt at massive reform was ambiguous in its content and consequences, and therefore certain counter-reforms were inevitable (see for example Il'in et al. 1996). Peter the Great promoted modern European technologies (starting with the military), some organizational patterns, some forms of state bureaucracy, some values of a work ethic for a part of society, while at the same time dramatically reinforcing selfdom and autocratic kingship. He introduced religious tolerance for some groups and unprecedented religious intolerance for others, etc. We can speak of the same ambiguity in Catherine's model of the 'Enlightened monarchy' or Alexander II's 'great reforms', and we can provide a similar analysis of both Bolshevik modernization and post-Soviet reforms (for the Soviet period, see, i.a., Christian 1997, Suny 1998, Poe 2006).

However, the selection of priorities was made within the scope of the cultural program of modernity, understood as a dynamic, unstable repertory of ideas and practices. European modernity was certainly the beacon for state bureaucracies and for the dynamic ruling elites of Romanov Russia, and this is what can be called *the* model of reforms, whose proponents were identified as 'westernizers'. The idea of imitation generated the dominant discourse of backwardness, belatedness and unoriginality. These 'westernizers' were of two kinds: some of them, with a more radical stance, formed an opposition to the ruling regime; others, who were more moderate, were incorporated into the ruling regime.

These 'cursed questions' (as coined by Dostoyevsky) produced a counter-reaction, a romantic traditionalist response, which was in most cases based on religious arguments, and a discourse of an alternative path, often mixed with messianism, whose message was profoundly anti-modern. The most striking example is the Slavophil intellectual movement of the mid nineteenth century, which expressed a strong Romantic refutation of modernity and which was partly absorbed by the ruling elites (Walitsky 1975).

At the same time, however, the advance of modernity in Europe was itself a complex phenomenon that evolved over time and gradually incorporated new elements (see Wagner 1994). The Romantic reaction against modernity in Russia was similar to what we can find within the west itself; the Slavophiles, who were in search of an Eastern Orthodox 'soul' for the Russian civilization, were heavily influenced and inspired by German Romanticism and French Catholic reaction in post-Napoleonic Europe. The discourse of backwardness and belatedness was also strong among nationalist intellectuals in Germany and Italy; and anti-modern trends were found in Europe (the west). In this sense Russia was a part of the European cultural and political space.

What made the Russian case distinct was its meta-European, 'Oriental' imperial background, which made the conflicts of identity and respective societal clashes sharper and of a different nature than within the west (in this sense, Russian developments were closer in content to Turkey, Mexico or China).[1] The line of the Slavophiles promoted the alternative of a distinct Russian civilization – one of the strongest and most pervasive discourses in Russian culture, found on both the level of intellectual debate and the grass-roots level of everyday cultural practices. Interestingly, the Slavophil vision turned finally (the 'late Slavophiles' such as Nikolai Danilevsky and Konstantin Leontiev) into what Eisenstadt has classified as a form of 'modern totalism', based upon ontologization of a collectivity (nationality-and-civilization) (Eisenstadt 2000: 9). Therefore, paradoxically, the Slavophiles were both antimodern and, implicitly, modern; they represented a stage in the dialectic of modernity.

The communist revolution launched a new alternative: accelerated techno-centric, super-rational modernization combined with a radical communitarian, egalitarian, and universalistic ethos. This was another model of modernity. To use Eisenstadt's classification, the Bolsheviks represented another – Jacobin – form of 'modern totalism', with its belief in primacy of society's voluntaristic restructuring through mobilization (Eisenstadt 2000). This new model was seen as a radical break with both European modernity and with the idea of a Russian

---

1   We can find striking similarities in national literatures where the dilemmas of westernization are fully reflected; Turgenev's or Dostoyevsky' characters show the same torn sensitivities as, for example, Octavio Paz's or Orhan Pamuk's and other colonial and postcolonial authors.

civilization, although, as a matter of fact, it was an involuntary (and unexpected) combination of elements from both of them. There was a deep consonance between Marxist *post*-capitalism (*post*-democracy) and traditional *non*-capitalism (*non*-democracy). Within the Soviet Union, especially by the end of it, the tension between these two cultural/political agendas – advanced rationalistic modernity vs. anti-western traditional culturalism – revealed itself quite vividly, although under the shadow of an officially dominant, presumably distinct communist model. The still unsurpassed analysis was made by Berdiaev (1955). Overall, as Arnason writes, communism 'might – for all its disastrous flaws and irrationalities – have been a distinctive but ultimately self-destructive version of modernity, rather than a sustained deviation from the modernizing mainstream' (Arnason 2000: 61).

In the aftermath of the Soviet Union, both old agendas – rationalistic westernizing and organic anti-western – came back to light reflected in public debates and in structural transformations. Both seemed to have taken somewhat obsolete, 'scholastic', i.e. speculative forms. On the one hand, there was the pursuit of classic modernity which was supposed to have been missed (because of the 'communist interregnum'). On the other hand, there was the pursuit of a specific national tradition, mostly in civilizational or cultural terms, based on some essentialist and religiously-bound assumptions – the tradition that was supposed to have been lost (because of the same 'communist interregnum', a sort of unfortunate accident). There was also the phenomenon of 'Soviet nostalgia', a nostalgia for an unusual blend of modernity and tradition that the Soviet Union actually was.

In the twenty-first century, however, these two historical trends (following the west or promoting a specific model) seem to have lost their persuasiveness for current realities and dominant discourses both in Russia and worldwide. Both the idea of catching up with modernity (classic secular and liberal universalism) and the idea of reviving an idiosyncratic cultural tradition, based on religious values (classic civilizational, anti-Enlightenment relativism, going back to Slavophil historicism) can sound simplistic in a world where the very metanarratives of modernity and tradition are under question; in a world of 'global condition', transnational communities, permeable boundaries, and multicultural patchworks. We will see how all these recent mutations complicate the situation.

Modernities – How Multiple? A Critique

Now let me deviate for a while from the Russian case. Building upon what I have said in the above overview, I will plunge into the theoretical optic of multiple modernities. I will then consider, also theoretically, one particular aspect of multiple modernities theory, that of the secular/religious divide. Then I will move back to Russia to explore this aspect of secularity and the role of religion in modernization.

Assessing the multiple modernities theoretical perspective, my main thesis, contrary to now widely spread interpretations, is that modernity is a single project, a historically and culturally distinct phenomenon, related to certain *temporal and spatial* coordinates. The semantic ambiguity of the term modernity comes from the temporal meaning of the word 'modern', thus pretending to cover all spaces within a certain time, which is not true. Modernity, by its origins and formation, belongs not only to a particular time, but to a particular space – Europe. As Russian history shows, the cultural program of modernity (not of one piece, but as a dynamic repertory of impulses) worked as the only known form of modernity, and what we witnessed worldwide were certain combinations/playing with elements of this program. I argue that modernity is *one*, and it is originally a European product (even though Europe's encounters with the rest of the world affected the evolution of European modernity).

What then do we mean when we speak of 'multiplicity'? In fact, it is, as in the Russian case, selective responses, national adjustments, attempts at traditionalist legitimation of western modernity: various *forms* – but the forms of a single, dominant *content*.

It should be said that Eisenstadt himself did not deny the core content of all 'multiple modernitites'; he rather emphasized the multiplicity of *responses* to similar challenges of Modernity. What I am arguing against here is rather some widespread simplifications of Eisenstadt's theory. Eisenstadt's idea of multiple modernities may lead to some false interpretations. First, he is constantly asserting the multiplicity of ideological and institutional patterns, while at the same time he provides clear, fundamental, dominant traits and characteristics that form the cultural program of modernity as definitely one and definitely European/ western. These fundamental principles or shifts (as compared with the previous Axial civilizations) are: 'the new conception of human agency – autonomous self', 'intensive reflexivity'[2]; multiplicity of roles beyond narrow, fixed, familiar communities (translocal communities); blurring distinction between center and periphery; incorporating into the central cultural core of themes and symbols of protest, 'equality and freedom, justice and autonomy, solidarity and identity'; the idea of progress and the perception of history as a 'project' (of domination over nature) (Eisenstadt 2000: 3). We can add more modern characteristics from Arnason's similar list: the capitalist economy; the nation-state; democracy; the pursuit of scientific rationality (Arnason 2000: 63). All these traits taken together make up the cultural program of modernity as an ideal type. A multiplicity of responses, a multiplicity of appropriations of modernity, 'playing' with this program give us modernity as an 'interpretative space' (Wagner 2008); but there are no multiple 'specific modernities' as distinct authentic cultural programs.

Second, Eisenstadt refers to Marx, Durkheim and Weber as proponents of classical assumptions of linear, homogenizing, irreversible global modernization; and he repeats many times that the post-WWII development did not prove these classical assumptions. On the contrary, I would argue that the globalizing world and continuing spread of basic elements/values of modernity through the dense communication networks and migrations *did* prove the growing outreach of western

---

2   This was best treated by Anthony Giddens (1991).

modernity. Trends of juridification and commodization became ubiquitous. What we can indeed refute as not supported by evidence is the complete homogeneity of the 'flat world'. However, western modernity is still dominant, though the patterns of dominance have changed from colonial to postcolonial.

Third, Eisenstadt refers to many anti-modern themes and movements that reject the hegemonic patterns of western modernity, and he uses this as a proof of the fact that modernities are multiple. This thought evokes serious objections or requires clarifications. Eisenstadt himself speaks much about the internal conflicts inherent to western Modernity as such. These conflicts include the following oppositions: pluralism vs. totalism; creativity vs. bureaucratization; freedom vs. control (Eisenstadt 2000:7–8). Arnason, with a reference to Castoriadis, adds the 'problematic relationship between capitalism and democracy' and the conflict 'between two equally basic cultural premises: on the one hand, the vision of infinitely expanding rational mastery; on the other hand, the individual and collective aspiration to autonomy and creativity' (Arnason 2000: 65). Western modernity is indeed a complex tangle of deep inherent tensions. These tensions are even deeper than the contradictions Eisenstadt so pertinently observed. If we take the oppositions of pluralism vs. totalism, freedom vs. control etc., it seems that these pairs of opposed traits are not only opposed along the cleavages between particular groups of people, particular social forces and/or discourses; these oppositions are entangled, meshed with each other and spill into each other like *yin* and *yang*. For example, the notion of plurality may potentially become a totalistic dogma; the value of freedom potentially tends to be imposed as a disciplined rule, and so on. In this sense, for example, the extreme, blatant rationalization in Soviet (and Nazi) experiments should not conceal the terrifying, 'mystical' rationalism present also in European democracies. This line of thought, critical to liberal democracies, goes from Nietzsche and Marx to Foucault and Agamben (for the latter, see Foucault 1977, Agamben 1998). The visible ideological discipline in the totalitarian systems should not hide from us a less visible 'structural violence' behind the rigid disciplines of liberal regimes (Eisenstadt in fact refers to 'political correctness' as one such example). The perception of rationalistic alienation and oppressive control in liberal democracies should not mean, however, a relativization of differences between them and the extreme totalitarian version of modern rationalism.

In any event, this deep complexity inside the cultural program of modernity made it possible for active groups from other societies to use contradictory impulses within it to legitimize the selection process, to explore for their own purposes relevant themes and variations from this program. Other societies' reactions were a range of attempts to accept modernity to a certain degree and in various combinations with certain local elements (only very exceptional are cases of complete rejection of modernity through complete self-isolation and refuge). What seem to be anti-modern movements in nonwestern societies are in most cases in fact certain ways, conscious or unconscious, of responding to the advancement of western modernity, playing on its inherent contradictions. Therefore, multiplicity can mean not the growth of authentic different modernities but rather a variety of ways to accommodate western modernity and to be accommodated to the global climate of western cultural hegemony.

It seems that Eisenstadt does not fully acknowledge the degree and the consequences of this cultural hegemony: it seems that the message of his whole theoretical endeavor was to dismiss this hegemony as a delusion. He does point out the trends to over-rationalization and totalistic control inherent to western modernity, but he seems to believe that these trends are counterbalanced by the premise of pluralism and autonomy, which is also part of the cultural program of modernity. He speaks of an internal opposition within modernity, which, so to speak, tends to pluralize itself, to realize itself in multiple forms. For Eisenstadt, hegemonic universalism is counterbalanced by 'authentic traditional localism' which modernity allows and encourages. Yet, in my opinion, modern universalism only 'pretends' to be inclusive, all-embracing, and accommodating differences, while in fact it is exclusive in the sense that, in the long run, it excludes anything which is not 'modern', not 'dynamic', or not 'marketable'. Local traditions, however anti-global they may seem, are in fact searching to be included into the global regime and thus accepting its basic rules. Eisenstadt writes about these local reactions as markedly confrontational towards the west, wishing to 'appropriate the new international global scene and the modernity for themselves, celebrating their traditions and "civilizations"' (Eisenstadt 2000: 22). However, the global scene is by default *coded* in western modern terms, and while appropriating modernity for themselves, these anti-modern forces can *not* avoid modern western semantics, and do accept them, playing the same game and thus becoming *implicitly modern*. These forces accept the very *language* of modernity, and we know that, in Bourdieu's terms, those who control the language control its users (Bourdieu 1991).

Eisenstadt's idea of multiplicity might be reflecting, as Arnason writes in the same seminal issue of *Daedalus*, an epistemic shift of recent decades, namely:

> Changing views of the relationship between unity and diversity in the modern world opened up new perspectives at a more basic analytical level; a better grasp of multiple configurations (the different national, regional, and potentially global patterns of modernity) reflects – and is reflected in – a clearer understanding of the multiple levels and components involved in the formation of modern societies. (Arnason 2000: 64)

I can agree with the idea of multiplicity in this sense of the theoretical opening up and rejecting of simplistic schemes. It is certainly an antidote against westocentric simplifications. However, this same idea of multiplicity, interpreted radically, may lead to another sort of mistake: an illusion of the complete originality of various cultural programs of modernity. This illusion (sometimes deliberately maintained or operating as a self-deception) of originality ignores the fact of the hegemonic structure of the global world, with a certain cultural program – the cultural program of western secular modernity – being dominant and supported by the 'legitimate violence' of leading nation-states and supra-national agencies. It is true, that this cultural program of modernity is also an evolving and complex phenomenon, reflecting substantial variations in forms and degrees within the west; but overall, modernity seems to be *one* ideal-type with a few determinant characteristics.

Therefore, as a bottom line, I am not convinced by the attempts of Eisenstadt's radical followers to reject the evidence of western modernity's being a) historically *sui generis* and b) a globally dominant phenomenon – since approximately the eighteenth century and still now, in the twenty-first. I have tried to show this in the above overview of Russian history.

Religion and the Secular

At this point let me try to link the above discussion on multiple modernities to the issue of religion and secularity. Religious traditions of Axial civilizations have been mentioned as a crucial variable defining multiplicity. The continuous influence of religious meanings seems to be referred to as the main watershed that distinguishes the non-western versions of modernity from the western one. Indeed, it is assumed that secularity is one of the basic characteristics of western modernity. Most scholars of modernity refer to this close link between modernity and secularity, either directly or through the analysis of the advance of rationalism, of reason, based on immanent, anthropocentric epistemology instead of the system of transcendental references, essential in the religious (i.e. Christian) worldview.

This link between secularity and western modernity is sometimes contested. This trend has been especially obvious in recent scholarship, partly developed under the auspices of postmodern studies and in connection with the notion of the 'postsecular' (Connolly 1999). What are the grounds of such a contestation? It is argued that religion and religious (primarily Christian) worldviews have always been an integral part, rather than a rejected ballast, of modernity, and continued to evolve along with modernity, either adapting to it or even actively enhancing it. This thesis is illustrated by several examples: Max Weber's thesis of the Protestant ethic remains a *locus classicus* of similar reflections; religion's vibrant role in the American history of the seventeenth to twentieth century is another strong argument (see discussion in Warner 1993, Calhoun 2011). In a similar way, there have been studies showing the important role played by the evangelical revivals and evangelical networks in the English modernization throughout the eighteenth and nineteenth century; and the role of German Pietism may be mentioned as well in this respect. Yet another example is the argument about 'religious Enlightenment' as opposed to a usual view of Enlightenment as a thoroughly secular phenomenon (Sorkin 2008). There are also studies that try to find the very *roots* of modern secular rationalism in the theological developments of the late medieval Christianity (Gillespie 2009).

Most recently, in sociology, the secularization theory became an object of a frontal criticism: it is admitted that this theory has come to an impasse and that the earlier uncontested link between modernity and secularity is increasingly being questioned. What hugely contributed to this reinterpretation were, of course, the current developments of the growing public role of religions worldwide and especially the abounding evidence from post-colonial non-western societies (see Casanova 1994, 2006; Berger 1999; Martin 2005). In my opinion, the religious effervescence in these societies pushes historians to look in a different way at the role of Christianity in the path of western modernization, somehow projecting (maybe unconsciously) the blatant global developments upon historical epistemologies (see Sorkin 2008).

All these considerations questioning the link between secularity and western modernity should be taken seriously. However, I am convinced that overall secularity has been and continues to be an important part of the cultural program of modernity. This logical link can also be illustrated historically from the western experience. Even if we take into account all the phenomena I mentioned in the previous paragraph, and with all push-and-pull movements that we can admit, we can still say that secularity is a *magisterial trend* in the course of western modernization. The Protestant ethic and the evangelical revivals might have worked as sacral mediation and even intensification of new modern values and behavioral habits, but then these values and habits were deeply secularized. The pockets of *religious* Enlightenment might have been an important phenomenon of religious legitimation and mediation for modern forms of thought, but it was the *secular* Enlightenment that was a magisterial trend. Bases of rationalism might have been founded in Christian theological arguments from the nominalist revolution until the Reformation, but the secularization of reason has finally become the magisterial trend. There might have been serious differences between the ways how religion/secular divide operated in Latin-Catholic and Anglo-Protestant cultural realms (Casanova 2006 calls the first *collision* and the second *collusion* between religious and the secular forces). Yet in both cases religion was displaced and, so to speak, localized with the modern process of societal differentiation.

One very important fact was that, with the advance of modernity, the very notion of 'religion' as such has changed: it came to be perceived in a different way or, we can say, it was invented as a phenomenon with a distinctly *modern* meaning (Asad 1993). Casanova agrees with Asad and develops Asad's insistence that *the secular* as such emerged within Judeo-Christianity (Casanova 2006: 10), a view that was advanced earlier by some theologians, from Johann Metz to John Milbank (Metz 1962, Levingston and Fiorenza 2000: 278, Milbank 2008). This approach corroborates well the phenomena I have just discussed, such as the theological roots of modernity or the religious Enlightenment: they are parts of the magisterial trend. Here is what this trend was, in the final analysis: the secular as a newly emerged episteme has meshed with other European developments to produce the cultural program of modernity. Religion was rationalized and disenchanted; religion was objectified (becoming an object that people can accept or reject, use and manipulate, etc.). For example, speaking of Islam and then expanding this to other religions, Hefner refers to Bourdieu's expression 'objectification of religious knowledge' to describe how the Muslims 'have come to think of their religious as something complete, self-contained, and objective – a system (*minhaj*) that can be distinguished clearly from other ideologies and belief systems' (1998: 84–104).

This magisterial trend of secularization has been brilliantly discussed in Taylor's *Secular Age*. While he shows all obvious and hidden, complex and intricate links between modern developments and the Christian meanings in the course of the western history since 1500, he also insists that the dominant process consisted in a continuous emancipation from an enchanted cosmos (started in Axial Age) and the emergence to dominance of an 'exclusive humanism': one that relies entirely upon human agencies and capacities, and excludes any reasoning that refers to transcendental arguments and goes beyond the goals of the human flourishing here and now (Taylor 2007).

Thus, as I have tried to argue, secularity is indeed an undeniable condition of western modernity. Let us now turn back to the issue of multiple modernities. I argued in the previous section that, in spite of multiple local forms and combinations, modernity is *one* ideal model developed in the west. Therefore, secularity (as a magisterial trend) is definitely a part of all modern projects both within the west and outside the west. Secularity comes to Japan, China, India, Turkey, Russia or Mexico within the single package with modern technologies, modern work ethics, modern arts, modern bureaucracies, modern democratic politics, modern discipline, modern style of clothing, modern standards of hygiene, and so on. This repertoire of elements may vary and not come at one time, but it goes as one ideal package. The reactions to these elements may also vary in different non-western societies, and the combinations with local cultural elements were and are complex and idiosyncratic, and this is where, through a complex entanglement, multiplicity of forms comes into being (on 'entangled modernities' see Therborn 2003 and Stoeckl 2011). However, the basic package of modernity is largely the same, and secularity is always included. In the course of world history of the last three hundred years – the period when the western modernity package was offered beyond the west – secularity may not have become the mainstream in non-western societies, but it has initiated strong intellectual challenges, strong structural hotbeds and pockets, and some specific social agents/groups that were bearers of secular ideas. Let us go back to the Russian case to illustrate these trends.

Religion and Modernization in Russia:
The Heights and Paradoxes of Secularism

Eastern Orthodox Christianity has rarely been said to provide a symbolic or institutional legitimation to modernity. Indeed, assessments to the contrary have been common; or, at least, religion was seen as neutral to modern developments, a separate, semi-isolated culture distanced from the social forces which stood behind modernization. The real picture, however, was more complex.

It is true that the aristocratic and bureaucratic elites, the intellectuals (*intelligentsia*), and the elite of entrepreneurs, who were oriented towards the European modern forms of culture and social behavior, were largely de-linked from the traditional forms of Orthodoxy. However, this break was not as simple as it might seem. The Russian religious tradition was not an unchanging, closed subculture, a ghetto or a traditional enclave within a society undergoing an impulsive but inescapable movement toward modernity. The Russian religion underwent several stages of change that can be seen as a parallel process of modernization, in step with society as a whole. There were strong influences of western churches, Catholic and Protestant, starting as early as the middle of the seventeenth century. The *Raskol*, the Great Schism of the seventeenth century, was, in the final analysis, a traumatic experience of modernization. It is well known that, paradoxically, it was "reactionary" Old-Believers, who during the *Raskol* opposed modernization, that later developed a work ethic that was unquestionably linked to successful entrepreneurial activities (Zhuk 2004, Robson 2007).

The trend of religious modernization continued in the early eighteenth century, when a new system of church-state relations was introduced that followed the European model of confessionalization. 'Religion' started to be redefined according to a modern paradigm, as a 'confession', a particular cultural sub-system (the schismatic Old-Believers were one such sub-system, as distinguished from the mainstream Church). In the nineteenth century, the Orthodoxy of the Slavophiles was indeed a newly constructed modern 'religion' as a system or civilization. The same was true of the famous Russian religious philosophy of the late nineteenth to early twentieth century: it was a modern, newly constructed phenomenon, an intellectual response to modernity. In the early twentieth century the modernizing impulses in the Church followed the rapid changes in society. The seminal Land Council of the Russian Church in 1917–1918 sought to reject both submission to the state (gaining autonomy) and the secular model of neutrality.

In spite of modernity trends *within* Russian Orthodoxy, this newly invented religion was constructed and interpreted *from outside*, by emerging modern social forces, overall, in negative terms and as *opposed* to modernity (the deeply religious capitalist Old-Believers were a striking exception). In the great majority of cases, the Russian Orthodox narratives themselves were openly anti-modern and thus coincided with the public image of religion as a symbol of stagnation and regress. In the course of the nineteenth century, Russian Orthodoxy (as well as other rooted religions of the Empire) ceased to be seen as neutral and were definitely stigmatized as regressive and linked with the anti-modern regime. This conflict was acutely perceived from the very beginning of the Petrine reforms, but it was exacerbated by the total societal radicalization during the fifteen revolutionary years (1905–1920).

The forced secularization in the Soviet Union was the logical outcome of the old conflict. The Soviet modernity was decisively secular; as we have seen above, secularity was an inevitable element of any modernity program. The Soviet case in this sense, too, was within the mainstream of global modern developments: secularization in the Soviet Union coincided with similar, if not so fiercely radical, processes in many societies from Europe to various colonies where ruling and intellectual elites – harbingers of modernity – were definitely secular. In this regard, the Soviet experience was deeply unusual in the sense that it produced, due to its totalitarian claims, an alternative system of sacralized ideals and practices, a sort of "atheist religion" with its dogmas, mythologies, hagiographies, and practices, a religion, partly dwelling upon the legacy of the traditional religions (Berdiaev 1955, Besançon 1977, Lane 1981).

The Postsecular in Russia and Beyond

Let me now briefly follow the course of the most recent Russian developments and then to move back to a more general, theoretical discussion centered on a new paradigm – the postsecular.

Since 1988–91, the years of the breakup of the Soviet Union, there have been two trends in the Russian society: further secularization and religious revival; such was a paradox of simultaneous secularization/de-secularization. Both trends had particular causes.

The idea of building a civil society and a European democracy, quite popular during the early post-Soviet decade among the elites and the wider society, required religious neutrality, new multicultural approaches, and a sort of technocratic naiveté that made it possible to abstain from any kind of ideological programming (after of a sort of "ideological fatigue" in the Soviet Union). In fact, the post-Soviet regimes tried to introduce a new, European type of moderate secularism; it was the first real experience of *laïcité* in Russian history. Additionally, insofar as the Russian society was heading for a new stage of modernization, secularity was supposed to follow accordingly. (This was reflected in the first law on religious freedom adopted in 1990.)

At the very same time, a totally opposite process was under way. The cultural status of religion was raised, in the 'pendulum logic' – a glorification of what was formerly oppressed or forbidden. For many, religion was also perceived as a fresh spiritual and emotional compensation for the shocking and traumatic break-up of the social system. Finally, religion was viewed as a repository of cultural arguments, collective memories, and symbolic strength needed to build new national, group, and individual identities. Religious arguments, among others, were used to create a brand of new Russian nationalism. In sum, religion was objectified either as (a) a 'genre of identity' (Robertson 1991: 282), one in many others, to be included into a patchwork of an identitarian bricolage, or (b) as an ideology (a system of thought and behavior) that can be instrumentalized in the public sphere (see Agadjanian and Rousselet 2005).

The main paradox of this situation, as I said, was indeed the *simultaneity* of the two opposite trends: the first real experience of secularism and the rise of the public relevance of religion. What can we say about this combination? This paradox needs to be somehow explained, and it is exactly at this point where we can introduce a new theoretical frame – the 'postsecular'. It what sense this frame can be used?

In purely historical terms, the new period of Russian history was *literally post*-secular, *after* secularity. In this, straightforward sense, Russia shared the new condition of post-secularism with other post-Soviet states, Turkey, India, Indonesia, Israel, and a few other societies. At a deeper level, we can talk about postsecular (rather than post-secular) in a more structural, rather than merely temporal sense: the very configuration of religious and secular in society have changed. On the one hand, we see how secular forces, while reiterating their adherence to secularity, become much more tolerant to religions and are sometimes inclined to incorporate religions into their social projects. On the other hand, when we witness a partial 'return to religion', this is a return to a *different* kind religion, which is thematized in new ways. For example, we find new religious forms that we can call religious modernity; we find that religious fundamentalism, in spite of its anti-modern rhetoric, is, by its structure, a modern phenomenon; and we find an *implicit* modernity (in spite of explicit conservatism) in the discourse of the Church intellectuals who are active in the public sphere.

Let me put aside the issue of religious modernity and religious fundamentalism and dwell more upon the last point of religious implicit modernity, for I believe it is crucial. The examples of such implicit modernity in the Russian Orthodox context can be found in the official documents issued by the Church leadership, such as the documents on the Church social program (Osnovy sotsial'noi kontsepzii 2000) and on human rights (Osnovy uchenia 2008). There is there an attempt to negotiate with secular modernity, accepting the *translation proviso* proposed by Rawls (1987) and developed by Habermas (2001, 2005). As we remember, these two scholars acknowledge the right of any 'comprehensive doctrine' or *Weltanschauungen* (including religions) to be present and voice their opinion in the public sphere; however, the condition of such presence and role must be the translation of such comprehensive doctrines from the esoteric idiosyncratic languages into the common, neutral, secular language accessible to all citizens. The Church documents I just mentioned showed exactly this translation project (Agadjanian 2003, 2010). And here we face the paradox of acceptance-through-refusal I mentioned earlier: while the *discourse* and the *position* of the Church towards modernity might be definitely critical and reactionary, the very process of translation from religious language to the common (secular) language means the acceptance of this latter as *the* universal language. Even though the program of modernity (for example, the idea of individual human rights, the topic of the second Church document) is explicitly rejected, the rules of the modern semantic universe, I argue, are nevertheless accepted. And this acceptance is crucial indeed, for we know that language, after all, is the tool of domination (Bourdieu 1991).

This complex, controversial situation is exactly what we can call the postsecular: neither complete, public secularity, nor the return to old forms of religiosity. To help untangle this complexity, I would like to mention one interesting fact. Some Russian Orthodox intellectuals find useful and truthful the postmodern critique of secularity. They believe that secularity must be refuted as one of the hegemonic grand narratives of modernity (Kyrlezhev 2008). The 'secular monoculture' has also been systematically criticized by the current Russian Patriarch and his core associates. However, the very same people might be promoting the idea of Eastern Orthodox supremacy in Russian cultural life. They reject the grand narrative of secularity but support the grand narrative of 'traditional religion'. This ambiguity is quite significant: Russian Orthodoxy may claim hegemony, but this hegemony is only relevant locally, within a certain particular territory, and not *universally* – for it is western secular modernity that is seen as claiming universality, and this universality of the 'secular' is rejected, because postmodernism celebrates a relativistic plurality of many choices. And though any allusion to the local hegemony of particular religious traditions is a denial of such plurality, it is also a part of a paradoxical and dynamic postsecular setting.

Concluding Discussion

In what way, then, can we apply the postsecular approach to the Russian case? All major thrusts towards modernity in Russian history have been initiated and carried out by secular forces. Moreover, as we have seen, Eastern Orthodoxy produced some examples of reactive implicit modernization, even though the results were not as far-reaching as in western Christianities. The driving force behind the post-Soviet stage of modernization is certainly also secular. Secularity is a premise by default, and in this sense Russia is no different from most European societies. The *immanent frame* seems to be unquestionably dominant. At the same time, similar to Europe, religion is back in the public sphere; but, also similar to Europe, it is a recognized minority rather than the main rival in the struggle of truth-claims. Religion is not the main rival any more, and the prevailing secularity changes to a more flexible accommodation of this minority. In this sense, I would prefer to speak of a certain phase in an evolution of secular modernity, rather than a completely new era. The transformed, modernized phenomenon of religion tends in a way to be incorporated into the late modern regime of secularity instead of being rejected as the main rival force (as was the case of the communist period and earlier in Europe at least in continental 'culture wars').

There is, however, an important difference between the Russian case and the western situation. In a recent debate, Habermas and Taylor discussed the new place of religion and mutations of secularity (Mendiata and Van Antwerpen 2011). They disagree in a few points, but what is common for both is their perception of liberal democratic modernity as a natural and neutral environment rather than a 'program'. This view seems plausible in the west, where modernity is a mainstream, more or less systemic set of characteristics. For Russia, as for many other non-western societies, 'modernity' is still considered as a 'program' to be realized, and secularity is seen as a part of this program. In Russia or India or China, a 'pluralist democracy' or 'market economy' are certainly not the natural environment; they possess something more, namely a particular content, a set of ideals and values, etc. They may be pursued or rejected, and they are not seen as 'natural or neutral', but subject to interpretation. The fact is that modernity is certainly the dominant, hegemonic global program that continues to define, as a major reference point, local discourses, practices, social differentiation and movements. The multiplicity of responses should not divert us from recognizing this dominant – admitted, rejected or admitted-through-rejection – ideal type of modernity. Modernity mutates but endures.

Substantial secularity, in my view, continues to be a part of this program. While registering changes, we still witness that secularity as such has not vanished; it has abandoned its hegemonic claims but has not ceased to be the 'default-condition' of western type of modernity (or even late modernity). In the Russian case, at least, religion, in any mutated or evolved form it may take, can *not* operate as an underpinning of some specifically Russian, hypothetical type of modernity. Indeed, religion is no longer rejected, as it used to be in the classic modern project, and indeed religion is no longer relegated exclusively into the private sphere. But this does not mean that the project of modernity, as a definitely secular phenomenon, is abandoned, for the impulses of modernization are generated by secular classes and forces; they are inspired by secular goals; and they are orchestrated by secular legal and ethical norms. Religious meanings can be admitted, and even incorporated into the secularity-dominated public sphere, but they are not, structurally, included in the core of still dominant program of modernity. In *this* sense, the term postsecular opens up a new space of discussion and a fascinating new research agenda, but it does not usher a new era of non-secular modernities.

References

Agadjanian, A. 2003. Breakthrough to Modernity, Apologia for Traditionalism: The Russian Orthodox View of Society and Culture in Comparative Perspective. *Religion, State and Society* 31 (4), 327–46.

Agadjanian, A. 2010. Liberal Individual and Christian Culture: Russian Orthodox Teaching on Human Rights in Social Theory Perspective. *Religion, State and Society* 38 (2), 97–113.

Agadjanian, A. and Rousselet, K. 2005. Globalization and Identity Discourse in Russian Orthodoxy, in *Eastern Orthodoxy in a Global Age*, edited by V. Roudometof, A. Agadjanian and J. Pankhurst. Walnut Creek, CA: Altamira Press, 29–57.

Agamben, G. 1998. *Homo Sacer: Sovereign Power and Bare Life*. Stanford: Stanford University Press.

Akhiezer, A. 1997. *Rossiia. Kritika istoricheskogo opyta*. Novosibirsk: Sibirskii khronograf.

Arnason, J. 2000. Communism and Modernity. *Daedalus* 129 (4), 61–90.

Asad,T. 1993. *Genealogies of Religion. Disciplines and Reasons of Power in Christianity in Islam*. Baltimore: Johns Hopkins University Press.

Berdiaev, N. A. 1955. *Istoki i smysl russkogo kommuniszma*. Paris: YMCA Press (*The Origins of Russian Communism*. First published in 1938).

Berger, P. (ed.) 1999. *The Desecularization of the World: Resurgent Religion and World Politics*. New York: Wm. B. Erdmans Publishing Company.

Besançon, A. 1977. *Les Origines Intellectuelles du Léninisme*. Paris: Gallimard.

Bourdieu, P. 1991. *Language and Symbolic Power*. Cambridge, MA: Harvard University Press.

Calhoun, G. 2011. Afterword: Religion's many powers, in *The Power of Religion in the Public Sphere*, edited by E. Mendieta and J. Van Antwerpen. New York: Columbia University Press, 118–134.

Casanova, J. 1994. *Public Religion in the Modern World*. Chicago: University of Chicago Press.

Casanova, J. 2006. Rethinking secularization: A global comparative perspective. *Hedgehog Review* 8 (1–2), 7–22.

Christian, D. 1997. *Imperial and Soviet Russia: Power, Privilege and the Challenge of Modernity*. Basingstoke: Palgrave Macmillan.

Connolly, W. 1999. *Why I Am Not a Secularist*. Minneapolis: University of Minnesota Press.

Eisenstadt, S.N. 2000. Multiple modernities. *Daedalus* 129 (1), 1–29.

Foucault, M. 1977. *Discipline and Punish. The Birth of the Prison*. New York: Pantheon Books.

Giddens, A. 1991. *Modernity and Self-identity: Self and Society in the Late Modern Age*. Stanford: Stanford University Press.

Gillespie, G. 2009. *The Theological Origins of Modernity*. Chicago: University of Chicago Press.

Habermas, J. 2001. *Glauben und Wissen: Friedenspreis des Deutschen Buchhandels 2001*. Frankfurt a. Main: Suhrkamp.

Habermas, J. 2006. Religion in the Public Sphere. *European Journal of Philosophy* 14 (1), 1–25.

Hefner, R. 1998. Christianity, Islam, and Hinduism in a Globalizing Age. *Annual Review of Anthropology* 27, 84–104.

Il'in, V., Panarin, A. and Akhiezer A. 1996. *Reformy i Kontrreformy v Rossii*. Moscow: MGU Publishers.

Kyrlezhev, A. 2008. The Postsecular Age: Religion and Culture Today. *Religion, State, and Society* 36 (1), 21–31.

Lane, C. 1981. *The Rites of Rulers: Ritual in Industrial Society – The Soviet Case*. Cambridge: Cambridge University Press.

Levingston, J. and Fiorenza, F. 2000. *Modern Christian Thought, Vol. II, Twentieth Century*. Upper Saddle River: Prentice Hall.

Lotman, Yu. and Uspensky, B. 1994. *Rol' dual'nykh modelei v dinamike russkoi kul'tury (do kontsa XVIII veka). Izbrannye Trudy, tom 1.* Moscow: Gnozis, 117–152.

Martin, D. 2005. *On Secularization: Toward a Revised General Theory.* London: Ashgate.

Mendieta, E. and Van Antwerpen, J. (eds) 2011. *The Power of Religion in the Public Sphere.* New York: Columbia University Press.

Metz J. 1962. *Christliche Anthropozentrik: über die Denkform des Thomas von Aquin.* Munich: Közel Verlag.

Milbank, J. 2008. Politicheskaia teologia i novaia nauka. *Logos* 4 (67). (Russian translation of Political Theology and New Science of Politics, chapter 1 of Theology and Social Theory. Beyond Secular Reason, 2006).

Osnovy sotsial'noi kontsepzii. 2001. *Osnovy Sotsialnoi Kontseptsii Russkoi Pravoslavnoi tserkvi.* Available at: http://www.mospat.ru/en/documents/social-concepts/ [accessed 10 November 2011].

Osnovy uchenia. 2008. *Osnovy Ucheniya Russkoi Pravoslavnoi Tserkvi o Dostoinstve, Svobode i Pravakh Cheloveka.* Available at: http://www.mospat.ru/index.php?page=41597 [accessed 10 November 2011].

Poe, M. 2006. *The Russian Moment in World History.* Princeton: Princeton University Press.

Rawls, J. 1987. The idea of an overlapping consensus. *Oxford Journal of Legal Studies* 7 (1), 1–25.

Robertson, R. 1991. Globalization, Modernization, and Postmodernization. The Ambiguous Position of Religion, in *Religion and Global Order*, edited by R. Robertson and W. Garrett. New York: Paragon House Publishers, 281–291.

Robson, R. 2007. *Old Believers in Modern Russia.* DeKalb: Northern Illinois University Press.

Sorkin, D. 2008. *The Religious Enlightenment.* Princeton: Princeton University Press.

Stoeckl, K. 2011. Europe's Entangled Modernities, in *Borders Constructed and Deconstructed – Orthodox Christianity in Europe*, edited by Alfons Brüning. Leuven: Peeters.

Suny, R. 1998. *The Soviet Experiment: Russia, the USSR, and the Successor States.* London and New York: Oxford University Press.

Taylor, C. 2007. *A Secular Age.* Cambridge, MA and London: The Belknap Press of Harvard University Press.

Therborn, G. 2003. Entangled Modernities. *European Journal of Social Theory* 6 (3), 293–305.

Wagner, P. 1994. *A Sociology of Modernity: Liberty and Discipline.* London and New York: Routledge.

Wagner, P. 2008. *Modernity as Experience and Interpretation. A New Sociology of Modernity.* Oxford: Polity Press.

Walitsky, A. 1975. *The Slavophile Controversy: History of a Conservative Utopia in Nineteenth-Century Russian Thought.* Oxford: Clarendon Press.

Warner, S. 1993. Work in Progress toward a New Paradigm for the Sociological
    Study of Religion in the United States. *American Journal of Sociology* 98 (5),
    1044–1093.
Zhuk, S. 2004. *Russia's Lost Reformation. Peasants, Millennialism, and Radical
    Sects in Southern Russia and Ukraine*, 1830–1917. Washington, DC: Woodrow
    Wilson Center Press.

Chapter 5
European Integration and Russian Orthodoxy: Two Multiple Modernities Perspectives

Kristina Stoeckl

Accompanying the return of religion as a vibrant research-topic in the social and political sciences over the last couple of decades, there has been a diffusion of the theoretical paradigm of multiple modernities.[1] Multiple modernities offer a historical and sociological analysis of cultural differences that avoids the strong implications of *clash-of-civilization* type of approaches, highlighting instead the persistence of religious, cultural and traditional patterns in modernizing societies. In particular with regard to Europe, the view that variations in patterns of secularization and socio-political development may be explained through the study of religious-cultural trajectories seems to have gained acceptance (Foret and Itçaina 2011). European integration – defined as a cultural and political process which, in its most general sense, implies the overcoming of ideological divisions since the breakdown of the communist regimes in Eastern Europe, and in its more concrete forms refers to the creation of common institutions such as the European Court of Human Rights and the European Union (see also Katzenstein 2006) – becomes, from this angle, a matter of defining or achieving common ground between Europe's multiple modernities.

Two recent applications of the multiple modernities approach to the religious situation in Europe – Wilfried Spohn's article 'Europeanization, Religion and Collective Identities in an Enlarging Europe: A Multiple Modernities Perspective' (Spohn 2009) and Timothy Byrnes and Peter Katzenstein's edited volume *Religion in an Expanding Europe* (Byrnes and Katzenstein 2006) – demonstrate, however, that the paradigm can be used in two different ways, leading to different conclusions and results. In a comparative-civilizational key, European integration becomes a matter of encounter between a thoroughly secularized western Christian civilization and the Eastern and South-western Orthodox Christian and Muslim civilizations. For Spohn, these different civilizational spheres and their varying religious-secular trajectories constitute the main obstacle to European integration (Spohn 2009).

---

1 The original version of this paper has been published in *The European Journal of Social Theory*, 14/2 (2011) by Sage Publications Ltd, All rights reserved. © SAGE Publications Ltd, 2011.

From a perspective focused more narrowly on actors and institutions, it is rather religious actors and transnational religious alliances that appear as a hindrance to further integration (Katzenstein 2006). In this chapter, I would like to clarify the different starting points and implications of these two variants of the multiple modernities paradigm, which I call 'comparative-civilizational' and 'postsecular' respectively. Looking more closely at present religious-secular debates and using Russian Orthodoxy as an example, I want to show that fault-lines of religious-secular conflict oscillate between civilizational borders and ideological secularist-religious conflict-lines. The paradigm of multiple modernities can help to explain both of these phenomena, and for this reason it is in need of further specification.

Russian Orthodoxy Confronting Secularism and Religious Pluralism

Orthodox Christianity in Europe today could be seen as a religion on the rise, re-emerging after decades of suppression under communist regimes and intrinsically bound up with the nationalist revival in many Eastern European countries. In all Orthodox countries in former communist Europe, the Churches have benefited from an increase in the religious attachment of the population. Müller, who has compared survey-data on religiousness in former communist Europe in the 1990s, registers only a moderate increase in church-attendance in the Orthodox countries, but finds evidence for the rise of a general attachment to and trust in the Orthodox Churches. He even speaks about 'a huge religious revival' in Russia (Müller 2008: 70; see also Inglehart and Norris 2004: 111–132, Greeley 1994). Furthermore, in all Orthodox countries the Churches have been able to re-establish themselves as religious actors in the public sphere and have gained a certain degree of political influence. This is particularly the case in Russia, where the Orthodox Church's status as one 'traditional church' on Russian territory is emphasized in the preamble to the law on religions from 1997, which restricts religious pluralism in Russia (Davis 1997).

Despite this evidence, however, Eastern Orthodoxy today appears not only as a religion on the rise, but also as a religion on the defensive. This point has been made by Ramet, who shows that in many cases the Orthodox Churches find themselves in a defensive and apprehensive position with respect to phenomena of societal modernization and Europeanization (Ramet 2006). Orthodox religion in Europe today is on the defensive at its borders – vis-à-vis the western world with its secular and pluralist values, and vis-à-vis other religions – but it appears equally defensive to the inside – vis-à-vis processes of modernization and secularization in the societies where it is rooted. The confrontation between Orthodox religion and secularism and religious pluralism is a double-confrontation: it affects the Orthodox Churches' external relations as well as their internal constitution and place in society.

This double-confrontation of Orthodoxy with secularism and religious pluralism is exemplified in a particularly clear manner by recent developments inside the Russian Orthodox Church. For the last decade, the Russian Orthodox Church has confronted actively the effects of modernization and globalization. In a move unprecedented in Orthodox history, the Patriarchy of Moscow issued, in 2000, a document entitled *The Bases of the Social Concept of the Russian Orthodox Church* (Russian Orthodox Church 2000), followed in 2008 by a document dedicated to the question of human rights, *The Russian Orthodox Church's Basic Teaching on Human Dignity, Freedom and Rights* (Russian Orthodox Church 2008). These documents lay out the Russian Orthodox Church's position on a variety of socio-cultural phenomena of modernity, encompassing a whole range of issues from state-church-relations and law to secularism, from culture to bioethics and human rights. The current Patriarch of Moscow, Kirill, elected to office in 2009 and former head of the Department for External Church Relations, was the chief responsible for both documents. It is apparent that he has made the confrontation of Orthodox religion with modernity a central theme of his patriarchy.

When *The Bases of the Social Concept of the Russian Orthodox Church* was published in 2000, many commentators interpreted the mere fact of its formulation as an important step of Russian Orthodoxy on its way towards a modern secular political order. Uertz, for example, wrote that 'the document contains important impulses for a constructive confrontation with the modern order' (Uertz 2004: 95); and Kostjuk interpreted the *The Bases of the Social Concept of the Russian Orthodox Church* as important step by the Russian Orthodox Church on its way towards becoming more modern. He pointed out that the formulation of the document constituted a leap into a modern regime of communication and self-positioning, but also observed that this modern impulse stood in tension with the predominantly conservative content of the text (Kostjuk 2004: 2001). Agadjanian also emphasized the ambivalence of the document between a pragmatic social and a conservative political agenda (Agadjanian 2003).

The Bases of the Social Concept of the Russian Orthodox Church addressed members of the Russian Orthodox Church and Russian society as a whole. Even though it found resonance also outside Russia and especially in the Catholic world (Uertz and Schmidt 2004), its main intended audience appeared domestic. With this document, the Church quite clearly reacted to the social upheaval of Russian society since the break-up of the Soviet Union, which had brought many freedoms, but also many social and economic problems and, in the eyes of the Church, moral decline. In the document, the Church offered guidelines for the Orthodox believer on questions such as abortion, contraception, euthanasia, genetic engineering and even environmental protection. Especially the political agenda of *The Bases of the Social Concept of the Russian Orthodox Church* constituted a novelty: the Russian Orthodox Church defined itself as independent from the Russian state and government. Drawing a lesson from the history of subordination under the Tsarist state and suppression by the Soviet state, the Church positioned itself as a potential counterplayer of the government and independent force in civil society (Bishop Ilarion [Alfeev] 2003). This commitment to a separation of church and state is, as I have shown elsewhere, not necessarily of a liberal nature (Stoeckl 2010), but it constituted a break with the long tradition of the symphonic model of church-state relations characteristic of Orthodox Christianity.

Rather than interpreting the document as evidence for a rise of Orthodox religion in Russia, I am inclined to interpret it as a gesture of self-defence. Orthodoxy in Russia today competes as much with other religions as with secularist worldviews; with the *The Bases of the Social Concept of the Russian Orthodox Church* it stakes its claims inside a heterogeneous and pluralist Russian society. The document represents as much a confrontation with modernity as an attempt at partial reconciliation. Notwithstanding the conservatism of its content, the mere fact that the Orthodox Church acknowledged and responded to questions of life in modern societies suggests that it is defending a position of relevance under conditions of secular and religious pluralist modernity.

The Russian Orthodox Church's Basic Teaching on Human Dignity, Freedom and Rights was published in 2008. It has the character of a final word in the ongoing debate about human rights inside the Russian Orthodox Church, manifest in speeches and interventions by high Church officials during the preceding years (Agadjanian 2008). Human rights enshrine freedom of conscience and equality of worldviews. From the Church's perspective, they are therefore an instrument that both protects religion – one must not forget that the Orthodox Churches behind the Iron Curtain suffered persecution and abuses that are not yet forgotten – and an instrument that challenges religion, because it proclaims the equality of faiths. It is precisely this double-impact of human rights on religion that emerges clearly from an analysis of the Orthodox document.

The Russian sociologist of religion Agadjanian speaks of an 'inward' and 'outward' orientation of the document. The 'inward-orientation' consists in providing a clear guideline to Church members on how to deal with human rights issues and how to use this legal instrument for the purpose of protecting the rights of the Church and its members (Agadjanian 2008: 15). Orthodoxy here appears in a minority position, as 'an institutional, social and moral *enclave*, which uses the human rights rhetoric to create and protect its own niche, its own modest space within the global multicultural universe.' (Agadjanian 2008: 18) In its 'outward-orientation,' in contrast, the document addresses the human rights discourse more generally and makes a distinctively Orthodox contribution to a national and international debate about human rights. Here Russian Orthodoxy appears as majority-voice that wants

> to remind the Russian society, the Russian state (and the international community, for that matter) that the Russian Orthodox Church has been a "formative factor" for the Russian cultural ethos, and therefore Christian anthropology, Christian vision of dignity and freedom, Christian version of rights, must define – at least in a certain degree – the public discourse of values and morality. (Agadjanian, 2008: 18)

The two documents are examples of how the Russian Orthodox Church deals with the double-confrontation with secularism and religious pluralism. This confrontation concerns the Church itself, its relation with believers, politics and society as a whole, and also the Church's external relations and its place in the world. What I want to do now is to interpret these documents from two different theoretical angles: a comparative-civilizational, and a postsecular multiple modernities perspective.

European Integration and Russian Orthodoxy:
A Comparative-Civilizational Multiple Modernities Approach

In a speech from 2006, the Patriarch of Moscow, at that time still Metropolitan of Smolensk and Kaliningrad, gave a motivation for the Church's engagement in the human rights debate. In his paper, read at the Tenth World Russian People's Council, a meeting that carried the title *Faith. The Person. The World. Russia's Mission in the 21st Century*, Metropolitan Kirill stated:

> There is an opinion that human rights are a universal norm. According to this view, there can be no Orthodox, Islamic, Buddhist, Russian or American concept of human rights since this would introduce relativity into the understanding of human rights, thus considerably restricting their functioning in international life. This is the thinking of many politicians and public leaders. Indeed, one can understand the desire to preserve the universal character of the concept of rights and liberties that does not depend on any variables. In fact, Orthodox people are among those who do not object to the existence of certain universal rules of behavior in the modern world. But these rules must be truly universal. The question arises here: Can human rights as set forth today really claim to be universal? (Metropolitan Kirill of Smolensk and Kaliningrad 2006)

This statement by Metropolitan Kirill, it seems to me, is predestined for interpretation from a multiple-modernities perspective. It presents *The Russian Orthodox Church's Basic Teaching on Human Dignity, Freedom and Rights* as one among competing codifications of human rights norms, comparable, perhaps, to the *Universal Islamic Declaration of Human Rights* (1981) or the *Bangkok Declaration of Human Rights* (1993). The basic idea is that the concept of human rights was generated and developed in western countries and might not be applicable in the same fashion elsewhere. 'It should be admitted', Kirill adds, 'that it succeeded in these countries, but also revealed its shortcomings'. Are western standards of human happiness applicable to all countries and all cultures? he asks. Do other civilizations not also have their positive experience of social life? (Metropolitan Kirill of Smolensk and Kaliningrad 2006). Kirill is not rejecting the idea of human rights; he is not denying the value of the concept as such. His statement does not have an anti-modern, pre-modern or 'fundamentalist' intent. Kirill is simply claiming that there can be multiple understandings of human rights and human happiness, and that the predominantly individualistic interpretation, which human rights have found in the west, might not be the most adequate elsewhere.

From a historical sociological perspective, the quote by Metropolitan Kirill confirms what the theory of multiple modernities, in the formulation of its chief representative, Eisenstadt, has always argued. The western trajectory of modernization must not be seen as the only possible pathway to modernity; instead, we find in the world a multiplicity of continually evolving modernities, each of which realizes a particular institutional and ideological interpretation of the modern programme according to specific cultural prerequisites (Eisenstadt and Schluchter 1998, Eisenstadt 2000a, 2000b, 2003). Religion represents one, if not the most important element among the cultural fundaments that shape the modernization-patterns of different societies. For Eisenstadt, religion does indeed constitute *the* main factor in the emergence of multiple modernities, since he sees multiple modernities rooted in earlier patterns of axial age civilizations, which, in turn, crystallize around religions (Eisenstadt 1986: 1).

The analysis of religion in Europe from this theoretical perspective pays special attention to the ways in which religions have shaped societies in the different parts of Europe. According to such a view, secularized Latin Christendom becomes the basis for the western pattern of modernity (Casanova 2006), whereas Orthodox Christianity and Islam in Eastern and South-eastern Europe give rise to markedly different societal and political developments. This deeper level of civilizational analysis of Europe is made clear by Spohn in his reply to Byrnes and Katzenstein's analysis of religion in Europe. Spohn criticizes the authors for not including a comparative-civilizational perspective in their analysis of European multiple modernities: '[...] following more strictly Eisenstadt's comparative-civilizational framework', Spohn writes, 'European multiple modernity should not be restricted, as the Byrnes and Katzenstein volume does, to the continuing salience of the religious realm in its manifold religious organizations and actors alone but also considered in its constitutive institutional and cultural role for the secular realm of politics, states, nations and collective identities [...]' (Spohn 2009: 360).

The Orthodox criticism of the western model of human rights could be interpreted as a form of resistance and consequently as an obstacle to a deeper cultural and political integration between the Orthodox East and Western Europe. The argument about the inadequacy of the western human rights discourse outside of the western cultural sphere, which the Russian Orthodox Church is putting forward, is by no means a singular case in the global religious-secular debate. As pointed out by Eisenstadt '[...] most contemporary religious movements take a markedly confrontational attitude to the west, indeed to anything conceived as western, seeking to appropriate modernity and the global system on their own, often anti-western, terms' (Eisenstadt 2000a: 22). Spohn observes that contemporary Europe is characterized by tensions between a Western European secular-cultural integration mode and an Eastern European revival of religion:

The post-war division of Europe in 1945 enabled the developing unification of Western Europe on the basis of Latin Christianity and strongly secularizing societies in confrontation with communist-atheistic Eastern Europe in the context of the global East-west conflict. This European constellation contributed to the pacification of the conflictive potential of religion on both sides of the Iron Curtain. In post-1989 Europe, however, the restoration of the structural and cultural pluralism of European civilization has been accompanied by the expansion of the Western European secular integration project to the East. This enlarging process of Europeanization has been confronted with growing opposition and tensions between the Western European secular-cultural integration mode and the Eastern European revival of nationalism and religion. In addition, the contemporary wave of globalization with growing immigration and intensifying inter-civilizational interactions has contributed to increasing tensions between secularized Latin Christian Europe, revived Christian Orthodox Europe and the Islamic civilization. (Spohn 2009: 362)

Spohn's interpretation of Orthodoxy in Europe privileges the external aspects of the Orthodox confrontation with secularism and religious pluralism; it sees Orthodox religion on the rise and in counter-tendency to Western Europe. The earlier-quoted statement by Kirill, at first sight, confirms this interpretation of a mounting contrast between Orthodox religion and western secularism.

The contrast between Orthodoxy and secularism, however, is, as I have tried to show above, in reality a double-confrontation. It takes place not only on the level of external relations of the Russian Orthodox Church, where the Church seeks to define its place in a global context, but also on the domestic level. The Orthodox Churches in Eastern Europe today operate in a social context that puts them on the defensive also in their domestic spheres. We can read the documents I have presented in support of the viewpoint that the Orthodox Christian tradition does indeed spell out a specific kind of modernity, but we should bear in mind that these documents rather *construct* such a modernity than actually *document* it. In other words, some caution is necessary when inferring from programmatic statements by officials of the Orthodox Church the existence of an Orthodox Christian civilizational sphere, which delineates a borderline relevant for European cultural and political integration. The comparative-civilizational multiple modernities perspective risks glossing over this difference.

Here, it seems to me, we should take very seriously some critical assessments of civilizational theory that also shed new light on the paradigm of multiple modernities. Knöbl points out that the strong claims of civilizational theory to cultural and religious path-dependency are problematic. 'It doesn't seem to be very plausible', he writes, 'to argue that individual and collective actors in different regions of a civilization and in very different periods of time were again and again reproducing the same civilizational arrangements by just drawing on the same intellectual and cultural resources […]' (Knöbl 2010, 93). In his view, the explanation of the durability and persistence of civilizational patterns requires an analysis of those mechanisms of power, authority, and control that guarantee the transmission of these very patterns. In this respect, Arnason's work on 'imperial formations' offers a new key for interpretation (Arnason 2003), because it highlights that civilizational patterns have to be supported by political power in order to stabilize, and that, in turn, power-holders are interested in preserving and expanding institutional arrangements (cf. Knöbl 2010: 93).

Looking at *The Bases of the Social Concept of the Russian Orthodox Church* and *The Russian Orthodox Church's Basic Teaching on Human Dignity, Freedom and Rights* from this perspective, what comes to the forefront is precisely the *political* nature of these documents. What political impact did the two documents actually have and how effective were they in shaping the discursive landscape on values and norms in Russia? Some evidence, especially the restrictive law on religions from 1997, which privileges the Russian Orthodox Church among the religious communities in the Russian Federation, supports a civilizational-imperial interpretation of the theological and political strategy of the Moscow Patriarchy, as does the appeal to the 'homeland' in one of the more controversial passages from *The Russian Orthodox Church's Basic Teaching on Human Dignity, Freedom and Rights*: 'One's human rights cannot be set against the values and interests of one's homeland, community and family' (Russian Orthodox Church 2008 summary of section III). Looked at from this perspective, the Moscow Patriarchy could be interpreted as acting in support of an imperial political strategy, inasmuch as its codification of social and human rights norms makes an attempt to set limits to ideological pluralism (see Arnason 2003: 5).

This analysis works for the field of Russian Orthodoxy and could be usefully applied to deepen the argument outlined in the last paragraph. It is, however, not equally applicable to Romanian, Serbian, Bulgarian, or Greek Orthodoxy, let alone to the Ecumenical Patriarchate of Constantinople and the Orthodox Diaspora Churches that belong to it. With regard to these churches, it would be much more difficult to argue from an imperial-civilizational perspective, or to lump them together into one type of Eastern Christian civilization. In terms of a multiple-modernities perspective on the religious situation of Europe, I would therefore subscribe to a criticism voiced by Wagner: '[…] there is a distinct risk that the analysis of multiple modernities, if based on the Axial Age debate, succumbs to the temptation of repeating the error of European social theory of much of the nineteenth and twentieth century, namely to inscribe the forms of modernity into compact and stable units similar to the national societies of former theorizing' (Wagner 2005: 100).

Orthodox religion feeds into a Europe of multiple modernities, and Russian Orthodoxy can be considered one example; but it is also this one example which brings to the forefront the difficulty of speaking about Christian Orthodox Europe as one civilization. Overtly strong claims to civilizational path-dependency run the risk of misrepresenting the religious situation in Europe. Below, I will therefore show how the postsecular multiple modernities approach re-locates conflict-lines from civilizational borders to secularist-religious tensions inside European societies, and also envisions a way of bridging these tensions.

European Integration and Russian Orthodoxy:
A Postsecular Multiple Modernities Approach

In Byrnes and Katzenstein's edited volume *Religion in an Expanding Europe*, Orthodox Christianity is called 'a self-consciously European religious tradition not very interested in undergoing Europeanization, as that process is currently defined' (Byrnes 2006, 296). The authors take a polemical stance to current secular definitions of Europeanization (see especially the chapter by Casanova in that volume) and argue, instead, that the return of religion 'is likely to demand new terms of coexistence with secularism' (Katzenstein 2006: 2). While from a comparative-civilizational viewpoint, the religious situation in Europe appears as a confrontation between western secular modernity and modernities informed by different religious origins and different secularization processes, Katzenstein draws our attention to the unsettled core of western secular modernity itself. The return of religion leads, from this perspective, not only to a confrontation with those modernities that are informed by different religious traditions, but also to a confrontation with the religious-secular identity of Western Europe itself: 'Religion continues to lurk underneath the veneer of European secularization. […] Legal and cultural Europeanization have left problematic and undefined the core of the European project. In the future religion may help fill that core by offering a focal point for political debate, engagement, and conflict' (Katzenstein 2006: 2). What I want to argue in the rest of this paper is that the moment we draw together in *one* theoretical framework the idea of a confrontation of multiple modernities *and* the observation that this confrontation leads to a re-definition of western modernity, we are shifting from a comparative-civilizational understanding of multiple modernities to a *postsecular* understanding.

The concept of postsecularism is introduced into the sociological and political-philosophical debate at a point in time when the revival of religion on a global scale and inside secular western societies raises questions about the relationship between religion and politics, which modern social and political thought had considered resolved through the process of secularization and its epiphenomena of separation of church and state, privatization of religion and gradual decline of religion (Casanova 2001). Within this broad debate, it was Jürgen Habermas (2006) who coined the term 'postsecular society' in order to describe a societal condition in which the continuity and presence of religion in the public sphere has become accepted normality. Even though postsecular positions have also been advanced by many other authors (for example: Rawls, 1997, Audi, 2000, Walzer, 2007), the focus in this paper will be on Habermas as key contributor to the philosophical debate on postsecularism over the last 15 years (Habermas 1996, 2008, Habermas and Mendieta, 2010).

Habermas's paradigm of postsecularity has two critical edges: the first concerns the religious citizen; the second the secular citizen. He formulates certain requirements for equal dialogue between the two. With regard to the secular citizen, this requirement is a postsecular consciousness and a principled openness to the religious argument. With regard to the religious citizen, a different kind of change in consciousness is required: a '"modernization of religious consciousness" as a response to the challenge religious traditions have been facing in view of the fact of pluralism, the emergence of modern science, and the spread of positive law and profane morality' (Habermas 2006: 13). This modernization consists in three steps for Habermas:

> Religious citizens must develop an epistemic attitude toward other religions and world views that they encounter within a universe of discourse hitherto occupied only by their own religion. They succeed to the degree that they self-reflectively relate their religious beliefs to the statements of competing doctrines of salvation in such a way that they do not endanger their own exclusive claim to truth. Moreover, religious citizens must develop an epistemic stance toward the independence of secular from sacred knowledge and the institutionalized monopoly of modern scientific experts. They can only succeed if from their religious viewpoint they conceive the relationship of dogmatic and secular beliefs in such a way that the autonomous progress in secular knowledge cannot come to contradict their faith. Finally, religious citizens must develop an epistemic stance toward the priority that secular reasons enjoy in the political arena. This can succeed only to the extent that they convincingly connect the egalitarian individualism and universalism of modern law and morality with the premises of their comprehensive doctrines. (Habermas 2006: 14)

This process of self-reflection of religious traditions under conditions of modernity is, in Habermas's view, the necessary pre-condition for including religions in the postsecular public sphere. He is also confident that such modernization is indeed taking place, pointing out the example of the Catholic Church, which theologically clarified its standpoint towards modern society with the Second Vatican Council. He adds that 'in the final instance it is the faith and practice of the religious community that decides whether a dogmatic processing of the cognitive challenges of modernity has been "successful" or not' (Habermas 2006: 14).

Habermas's understanding of religious modernization offers a new interpretative key for the self-positioning of the Russian Orthodox Church. We can read *The Bases of the Social Concept of the Russian Orthodox Church* and *The Russian Orthodox Church's Basic Teaching on Human Dignity, Freedom and Rights* in the light of the criteria for a 'modernization of religious consciousness' and study them with the aim of assessing the nature of this modernization. The Russian Orthodox Church looks back to decades of suppression, political collaboration, and theological and institutional neglect. What is at stake for Orthodox religion today is not only its response to modernization and globalization, but also a basic theological, intellectual and institutional recovery. The two documents are evidence that the Patriarch of Moscow has chosen to conduct this recovery in part in the modern language of social teaching and human rights.

Assessments as to whether these documents represent a genuine modernization or not differ (for a more negative assessment, see Agadjanian 2010, for a more positive one, see Thesing and Uertz 2001) and this chapter is not the place to settle the question once and for all. My point here is slightly different, namely that already by adopting the interpretative key of religious modernization within postsecular society, we are led to an important theoretical and methodological insight: the shift in perspective from a comparative-civilizational to a postsecular perspective restricts our conclusions; it makes us 'zoom in' on the Russian Orthodox Church as religious actor in the public sphere of the Russian Federation. In this way, not only does it become more difficult to generalize from one Orthodox Church to Eastern Christian civilization, but the inner make-up of Russian Orthodoxy and its place in rapidly modernizing Russian society also emerges much more clearly. The 'internal confrontation' of Russian Orthodoxy with secular society in Russia moves to the forefront; a confrontation in which *The Bases of the Social Concept of the Russian Orthodox Church* and *The Russian Orthodox Church's Basic Teaching on Human Dignity, Freedom and Rights* serve to stake the claims in a larger debate about values and norms. The 'multiple' of multiple modernities is, from this perspective, not situated along cultural-geographical borderlines, but corresponds to different actors and their respective standpoints on modernization and secularization.

This debate is not restricted to Russia; it concerns all European societies. A good example of the way in which the fault-lines of religious-secular debate in Europe shift from the border between East and west to the ideological front-line between religious conservatism and secularism, is the position of Metropolitan Ilarion, the present Head of the External Relations Department after Kirill's election as Patriarch. He considers the Catholic Church the chief ally of the Orthodox Church in the confrontation with 'militant secularism':

> Militant secularism, in its efforts to diminish the influence of religion, has been inspired first and foremost by an anti-Catholic pathos. The Catholic Church, in turn, is the chief opponent of secularism and liberalism in Europe today. [...] I am deeply convinced that the Roman Catholic Church is our main ally in Europe. (Bishop Ilarion [Alfeev] 2004)

The statement by Ilarion, at that time Bishop of Vienna and Austria and head of the Russian Orthodox Church's permanent mission to the European Union, makes clear that a Christian and a secular-humanist self-understanding of Europe are in serious conflict with each other; and that the opposing sides in this conflict cannot be framed in terms of 'East versus West'. Instead, on certain issues one is likely to find Moscow and the Vatican on the same side of fence. Multiple modernities, again, do not exhaust themselves at civilizational borderlines; they cross over borders and intersect on topics of concern, irrespective even of deep-rooted historical divisions.

A postsecular multiple modernities approach not only brings out these kinds of cross-civilizational affinities, the paradigm of postsecularity also envisions a way of bridging the gaps that result from religious-secularist debates. Postsecular political philosophy takes note of the rift between religious and secularist consciousness. It considers on equal footing religious doctrines and 'secularist secularism' and tries to scale down the disagreement between them in favour of a postsecular model of deliberation. This normative aspect of postsecular theory is relevant for a philosophical assessment of the confrontation between Russian Orthodoxy and secularism and of the arguments which Russian Orthodoxy brings forward in the global debate on human rights, values and norms.

Habermas's contribution to the debate about politics and religion is informed by his previous work on communicative action and deliberative democracy (Habermas 1993, 1996). What characterizes this work is the insistence on universalism as a valid category in modern political discourse. Universalism, and this is Habermas's most basic position, does not lie out there in 'principles from nowhere', nor do we need to abandon the idea of universality in the light of a multiplicity of moralities and beliefs: agreement on 'principles valid for all' can, instead, emerge in the process of communication and deliberation; they can be the fruit of a mutual learning process and general consent.

Habermas's appeal to universalism is an appeal in degrees. It depends on how we understand the 'all' in the 'principles valid for all'. In the initial formulation and intention of Habermas's philosophical work, this 'all' consisted of the members of a constitutional democratic state. It therefore comprised, necessarily, secular as well as religious citizens. From the normative starting point that only equal and democratic deliberation leads to the kind of universally agreed upon political ethic that should be characteristic of constitutional democracies, it is only logical that also the dialogue between the religious and secular citizen must take place under conditions of equality. This equality is threatened, however, when the secular public discourse renders it difficult for religious citizens to voice their arguments. Postsecularism is a response to this very particular problem. The main point lies in the assertion that not only religious citizens should be asked to translate their claims into the language of secular public discourse, but also the non-religious citizen is asked to play his part, that is, to scale down his secularist aspirations. Only in that case can we expect equal conditions of communication and the possibility of mutual comprehension.

Reading Habermas carefully we note that the normative desirability of postsecular deliberation is based on two kinds of reasoning: on the one hand, it follows structurally from the general theory of deliberative democracy; on the other hand, it follows philosophically from the principled openness of the communicative situation. We can never know beforehand which reasons will respond best to the complex reality of decision-making processes. The following long quote by

Habermas explains the normative-philosophical aspect of postsecularism very well:

> Religious traditions have a special power to articulate moral intuitions, especially with regard to vulnerable forms of communal life. In the event of the corresponding political debates, this potential makes religious speech a serious candidate to transporting possible truth contents, which can then be translated from the vocabulary of a particular religious community into a generally accessible language. [...] This requirement of translation must be conceived as a cooperative task in which the non-religious citizens must likewise participate, if their religious fellow citizens are not to be encumbered with an asymmetrical burden. [...] the secular citizens must open their minds to the possible truth content of those presentations and enter into dialogues from which religious reasons then might well emerge in the transformed guise of generally accessible arguments. (Habermas 2006: 10–11)

In recent writings, Habermas has taken the argument for postsecular society beyond the limits of a constitutional democracy and nation-state (Habermas 2001a, see also Kratochwil and Barbato 2009) and has made explicit the compatibility of postsecularism and the paradigm of multiple modernities:

> I consider the program of the group around Shmuel Eisenstadt and its comparative research on civilizations promising and informative. In the emerging world society [...] there are, as it were, by now only modern societies, but these appear in the form of multiple modernities because the great world religions have had a great culture-forming power over the centuries, and they have not yet entirely lost this power. (Habermas and Mendieta 2010)

Just as the western self-understanding of modernity emerged from confrontation with tradition, this dialectic between tradition and modernity repeats itself also in other parts of the world. 'There, too', Habermas adds, 'one reaches back to one's own traditions to *confront* the challenges of societal modernization, rather than to succumb to them' (Habermas and Mendieta 2010). Against this background, intercultural discourses about the foundations of a more just international order should no longer be conducted one-sidedly, rather, these discourses ought to take place under the symmetrical conditions of mutual perspective-taking, with the west as one participant among others (Habermas and Mendieta 2010). The pluralistic and multicultural society of Habermas's earlier writings is here expanded to comprise a 'world society' made up of different nations and cultural traditions. The philosophical paradigm of postsecularism offers itself as a theory of international relations (see Kratochwil and Barbato 2009).

Habermas's theory of a postsecular world society, which sees a world society of multiple modernities engaged in a deliberation about norms that can be considered overarching and universal, offers a valid interpretative key for the

Russian Orthodox position on human rights. Coming back to the statement by the Patriarch of Moscow quoted earlier, it should be stressed that in his speech in front of the Tenth World Russian People's Council, Kirill actually did more than simply propose that multiple conceptions of human rights should be considered valid: he expressed himself in favour of a *universal* conception of human rights. Perfectly in line with postsecular reasoning, Kirill appealed to fair rules of deliberation about rules and norms when he said: 'Orthodox people are among those who do not object to the existence of certain universal rules of behaviour in the modern world. But these rules must be truly universal. The question arises here: Can human rights as set forth today really claim to be universal?' (Metropolitan Kirill of Smolensk and Kaliningrad 2006). Kirill's statement resonates with Habermas's considerations on equality and universality:

> Independently of their cultural backgrounds all the participants intuitively know quite well that a consensus based on conviction cannot come about as long as symmetrical relations do not exist among them – relations of mutual recognition, mutual role-taking, a shared willingness to consider one's own tradition with the eyes of the stranger, and to learn from one another, and so forth. (Habermas 2001b: 129)

From a postsecular perspective, normative assumptions and self-definitions become exposed to critique and change. For western modernity, this means that it is confronted with alternative understandings of modernity not only at its borderlines, but also 'inside', with regard to its own normative self-definition. The question of human rights is a crucial topic in this respect because of its centrality for western self-understanding. While the example of the Russian Orthodox intervention in the human rights debate shows that in a postsecular world of multiple modernities concrete definitions of human freedom, rights, and agency are again open to debate, the conceptualization of postsecular deliberation formulated by Habermas makes clear that such a debate does not take place between sealed-off civilizational spheres, but has a transformative impact on the modernities at stake.

Conclusion

This chapter has introduced a distinction between a comparative-civilizational and a postsecular perspective within the paradigm of multiple modernities. I have argued that the first, comparative-civilizational perspective, helps us to understand modernization processes in large cultural-civilizational units; whereas the second, postsecular viewpoint, focuses on actors and cultural domains within civilizational units and on inter-civilizational crossovers. The two perspectives are complementary. The paradigm of multiple modernities offers the theoretical background for an analysis of different forms of modernity and pathways to modernization; the theory gains in precision when we distinguish a comparative-civilizational from a postsecular perspective and use both of these perspectives for explaining the place of religion in modern societies. Given the popularity of multiple modernities in present sociological and political theory, greater precision seems desirable in order to prevent the appeal to multiple modernities from becoming no more than a general catch-phrase for signaling plurality.

With regard to Europe, it becomes clear that we should look at European cultural and political integration both from a comparative-civilizational (imperial-civilizational) and a postsecular perspective of multiple modernities in order to explain differences as well as convergences, singular cultural constellations as well as inter-civilizational crossovers. The example of Russian Orthodoxy has been useful in clarifying the potential of the two perspectives with regard to explaining the role of religion in European integration. From a comparative-civilizational viewpoint, Russian Orthodoxy may appear as the 'other' to secular Western Europe (Neumann 1999); whereas from a postsecular viewpoint, it partakes in an ongoing process of defining the meaning of European political and cultural integration. Orthodox religion is undergoing a process of modernization that implies both a re-definition of its place inside the societies where it is traditionally represented, as well as its position in the larger European religious pluralist landscape. European integration, the overcoming of ideological divisions and the creation of shared institutions, is a process of defining common ground between Europe's multiple modernities, and it includes the re-negotiation of the place of religion.

References

Agadjanian, A. 2003. Breakthrough to Modernity, Apologia for Traditionalism: The Russian Orthodox View of Society and Culture in Comparative Perspective. *Religion, State and Society*, 31 (4), 327–346.

Agadjanian, A. 2008. Russian Orthodox Vision of Human Rights, in *Erfurter Vorträge zur Kulturgeschichte des Orthodoxen Christentums*, Vol. 26, edited by V. Makrides. Erfurt: Universität Erfurt.

Agadjanian, A. 2010. Liberal Individual and Christian Culture: Russian Orthodox Teaching on Human Rights in Social Theory Perspective. *Religion, State, and Society*, 38 (2), 97–113.

Arnason, J.P. 2003. *Civilizations in Dispute: Historical Questions and Theoretical Traditions.* Leiden: Brill.

Audi, R. 2000. *Religious Commitment and Secular Reason.* Cambridge, New York: Cambridge University Press.

Bishop Ilarion [Alfeev]. 2003. Arkhierejskij Sobor Russkoj Pravoslavnoj cerkvi 2000 goda: obsor osnovykh deyanij [The Council of the Russian Orthodox Church in the year 2000: an overview over the main issues], in *Orthodox Christianity and Contemporary Europe*, edited by J. Sutton and W. Van Den Bercken. Leuven, Paris, Dudley: Peeters, 249–270.

Bishop Ilarion [Alfeev]. 2004. *Christianity and the Challenge of Militant Secularism.* Public lecture delivered at the University of Melbourne, Australia, on 7 July 2004 [Online: *Europaica Bulletin*, 24 November 2004]. Available at: http://orthodoxeurope.org/page/14/52.aspx#5 [accessed 10 November 2005].

Byrnes, T.A. 2006. Transnational Religion and Europeanization, in *Religion in an Expanding Europe*, edited by P.J. Katzenstein and T.A. Byrnes. Cambridge: Cambridge University Press, 283–305.

Byrnes, T.A. and Katzenstein, P.J. (eds) 2006. *Religion in an Expanding Europe.* Cambridge: Cambridge University Press.

Casanova, J. 2001. Secularization, in *International Encyclopedia of the Social and Behavioural Sciences*, edited by N.J. Smelser and P.B. Baltes. Amsterdam, Paris et. al.: Elsevier, 13786–13791.

Casanova, J. 2006. Religion, European Secular Identities, and European Integration, in *Religion in an Expanding Europe*, edited by P.J. Katzenstein and T.A. Byrnes. Cambridge: Cambridge University Press, 65–92.

Davis, D.H. 1997. Editorial: Russia's New Law on Religion: Progress or Regress? *Journal of Church and State*, 39, 645–656.

Eisenstadt, S.N. 1986. Introduction: The Axial Age Breakthroughs – Their Characteristics and Origins, in *The Origins and Diversity of Axial Age Civilizations*, edited by S.N. Eisenstadt. Albany: State University of New York Press, 1–28.

Eisenstadt, S.N. 2000a. Multiple Modernities. *Daedalus*, 129, 1–29.

Eisenstadt, S.N. 2000b. The Reconstruction of Religious Arenas in the Framework of 'Multiple Modernities. *Millennium: Journal of International Studies*, 29, 591–611.

Eisenstadt, S.N. 2003. *Comparative Civilizations and Multiple Modernities.* Leiden, Boston: Brill.

Eisenstadt, S.N. and Schluchter, W. 1998. Introduction: Paths to Early Modernities. A Comparative View. *Daedalus*, 127, 1–18.

Foret, F. and Itçaina, X. 2011. Western European Modernities and Religion – A Perspective from Political Sociology, in *Politics of Religion in Western Europe. Modernities in Conflict?* edited by F. Foret and X. Itçaina. London and New York: Routledge ECPR Studies in European Political Science, 3–22.

Greeley, A. 1994. A Religious Revival in Russia? *Journal for the Scientific Study of Religion*, 33, 253–272.

Habermas, J. 1993. *Justification and Application. Remarks on Discourse Ethics.* Cambridge: Polity Press.

Habermas, J. 1996. *Between Facts and Norms: Contributions to a Discourse Theory of Law and Democracy.* Cambridge, MA: Cambridge University Press.

Habermas, J. 2001a. The Postnational Constellation and the Future of Democracy, in J. Habermas, *The Postnational Constellation.* Cambridge: Polity Press, 58–112.

Habermas, J. 2001b. Remarks on Legitimation through Human Rights, in J. Habermas, *The Postnational Constellation.* Cambridge: Polity Press, 113–129.

Habermas, J. 2006. Religion in the Public Sphere. *European Journal of Philosophy*, 14, 1–25.

Habermas, J. 2008. *Between Naturalism and Religion: Philosophical Essays.* Cambridge: Polity Press.

Habermas, J. and Mendieta, E. 2010. A Postsecular World Society? An Interview with Jürgen Habermas. *The Immanent Frame. Secularism, Religion, and the Public Sphere* [Online]. Available at http://blogs.ssrc.org/tif/2010/02/03/a-postsecular-world-society/ [accessed 8 August 2010].

Inglehart, R. and Norris, P. 2004. *Sacred and Secular. Religion and Politics Worldwide.* Cambridge: Cambridge University Press.

Katzenstein, P.J. 2006. Multiple Modernities as Limits to Secular Europeanization? in *Religion in an Expanding Europe*, edited by T.A. Byrnes and P.J. Katzenstein. Cambridge: Cambridge University Press, 1–33.

Knöbl, W. 2010. Path Dependency and Civilizational Analysis: Methodological Challenges and Theoretical Tasks. *European Journal of Social Theory*, 13, 83–97.

Kostjuk, K. 2001. Die Sozialdoktrin der Russisch-Orthodoxen Kirche: Schritt zur Zivilgesellschaft oder Manifest des orthodoxen Konservatismus? in *Die Grundlagen der Sozialdoktrin der Russisch-Orthodoxen Kirche. Deutsche Übersetzung mit Einführung und Kommentar*, edited by R. Uertz and J. Thesing. Sankt Augustin: Konrad Adenauer Stiftung e.V., 174–196.

Kostjuk, K. 2004. Die Sozialdoktrin – Herausforderung für die Tradition und die Theologie der Orthodoxie, in *Beginn einer neuen Ära? Die Sozialdoktrin der Russisch-Orthodoxen Kirche vom August 2000 im interkulturellen Dialog*, edited by R. Uertz and L.P. Schmidt. Moskau: Konrad Adenauer Stiftung e.V., 67–74.

Kratochwil, F. and Barbato, M. 2009. Towards a Post-secular Political Order? *European Political Science Review*, 1, 317–340.

Metropolitan Kirill of Smolensk and Kaliningrad. 2006. Human Rights and Moral Responsibility. Part I. *Europaica Bulletin* [Online], 97. Available at http://orthodoxeurope.org/page/14/97.aspx#3 [accessed 6 December 2009].

Müller, O. 2008. Religion in Central and Eastern Europe: Was There a Re-Awakening after the Breakdown of Communism? in *The Role of Religion in Modern Socities*, edited by D. Pollack and D.V.A. Olson. New York and London: Routledge, 63–91.

Neumann, I.B. 1999. *Uses of the Other. 'The East' in European Identity Formation.* Minneapolis: University of Minnesota Press.

Ramet, S.P. 2006. The Way We Were – And Should Be Again? European Orthodox Churches and the 'Idyllic Past', in *Religion in an Expanding Europe*, edited by T.A. Byrnes and P.J. Katzenstein. Cambridge: Cambridge University Press, 148–175.

Rawls, J. 1997. The Idea of Public Reason Revisited. *The University of Chicago Law Review*, 64, 765–807.

Russian Orthodox Church 2000. *The Bases of the Social Concept of the Russian Orthodox Church* [Online: Official Website of the Department for External Church Relations of the Moscow Patriarchate]. Available at: http://www.mospat.ru/en/documents/social-concepts/ [accessed 6 October 2011].

Russian Orthodox Church 2008. *The Russian Orthodox's Church Basic Teaching on Human Dignity, Freedom and Rights.* [Online: Official Website of the Department for External Church Relations of the Moscow Patriarchate]. Available at: http://www.mospat.ru/en/documents/dignity-freedom-rights/ [accessed 22 February 2011].

Spohn, W. 2009. Europeanization, Religion and Collective Identities in an Enlarging Europe: A Multiple Modernities Perspective. *European Journal of Social Theory*, 12, 358–374.

Stoeckl, K. 2010. *Political Hesychasm?* Vladimir Petrunin's Neo-Byzantine Interpretation of the Social Doctrine of the Russian Orthodox Church. *Studies in East European Thought*, 62, 125–133.

Thesing, J. and Uertz, R. (eds) 2001. *Die Grundlagen der Sozialdoktrin der Russisch-Orthodoxen Kirche. Deutsche Übersetzung mit Einführung und Kommentar.* Sankt Augustin: Konrad-Adenauer-Stiftung e.V.

Uertz, R. 2004. Menschenrechte, Demokratie und Rechtsstaat in der Sozialdoktrin – eine politikwissenschaftliche Betrachtung, in *Beginn einer neuen Ära? Die Sozialdoktrin der Russisch-Orthodoxen Kirche vom August 2000 im interkulturellen Dialog*, edited by R. Uertz and L.P. Schmidt. Moskau: Konrad Adenauer Stiftung e.V., 77–96.

Uertz, R. and Schmidt, L.P. (eds) 2004. *Beginn einer neuen Ära? Die Sozialdoktrin der Russisch-Orthodoxen Kirche vom August 2000 im interkulturellen Dialog*, Moskau: Konrad Adenauer Stiftung e.V.

Wagner, P. 2005. Palomar's Question. The Axial Age Hypothesis, European Modernity and Historical Contingency, in *Axial Civilizatoins and World History*, edited by J.P. Arnason, S.N. Eisenstadt and B. Wittrock. Leiden, Boston: Brill, 88–106.

Walzer, M. 2007. Drawing the Line. Religion and Politics, in M. Walzer, *Thinking Politically: Essays in Political Theory*. New Haven: Yale University Press, 147–167.

Chapter 6

A State Goddess in the New Secular Nepal: Reflections on the Kumari Case at the Supreme Court

Chiara Letizia

Introduction

In the last few years, Nepal has faced dramatic political change, putting an end to a two-century-old Hindu kingdom and establishing a secular republic under the leadership of a Maoist party.[1] In 2006 the Nepali Parliament proclaimed the country a secular state (*dharma nirapeksha rajya*)[2] and the Interim Constitution of 2007 reiterated Nepal's secular status. Following elections in 2008, the Constituent Assembly declared Nepal a secular federal, democratic republic, thanks to the political weight of the Maoist party (UCPN-Maoist) which won over 40 per cent of the electoral votes and formed a coalition government.

Challenges for secularism in Nepal appear manifold: the country, which still boasts a strong Hindu majority,[3] has seen an enduring symbiotic relationship between Hinduism and the monarchy (Sharma 2002). Since the eighteenth century, Nepali rulers have styled themselves and their culturally and ethnically diverse

---

1   This chapter presents findings from fieldwork research on secularism conducted in Nepal between September 2009 and April 2010, made possible by the generous support of the Post-doctoral Newton Fellowship of the British Academy. It is also part of a larger project to study the shaping of Nepali secularism through court cases, undertaken for the ANR Joint Programme on Justice and Governance in India and South Asia, directed by Gilles Tarabout and Daniela Berti. I am grateful to David Gellner for his comments on an earlier version of this chapter and to Philippe Gagnon for his kind help in editing it. This chapter also benefitted of the stimulating comments by the members of the Centre for the Study and documentation of religions and political institutions in Post-Secular Society (CSPS), University of Rome Tor Vergata.

2   The expression *dharma nirapeksha* (autonomous from/indifferent, impartial to dharma, i.e. 'religion'), was first used to render the English word 'secular' in the 42nd amendment to the preamble of the Indian Constitution. I have discussed elsewhere the uncomfortable feelings raised by this expression in Nepal (Letizia forthcoming).

3   Nepal Census of 2001 affirms that 80.6 per cent of Nepalese are Hindu, even if these figures are contested by minorities and are likely to change dramatically with the results of the 2011 census.

subjects as Hindu, and made Hinduism an essential component of national identity through a process of Hinduization.

Despite the declaration of a secular state, government interactions with religion have not diminished (CCD 2009: 1): the State is still involved in the management of trusts associated with Hindu gods and temples; government funds are still spent on Hindu religious festivals; slaughtering cows and 'causing religious conversion' (proselytizing) are still both outlawed;[4] many laws are based on Hindu norms and values; Hindu temples are found in government buildings, schools, military camps and courts; public holidays in the State calendar are mostly Hindu festivals; and the new President of the Republic has in many instances replaced the former Hindu king at public religious functions.

One such instance is the national festival of Kumari Jatra, which plays out publicly the long-lasting relation between the living goddess Kumari and the head of state. The Kumari is a child who lives a ritual life until puberty; during her annual festival, she is brought in a chariot in a three day procession around the city of Kathmandu. On this occasion, as a royal goddess, she formerly blessed the king by marking his forehead with a red *tika*, thus legitimizing his rule for one more year. With the advent of the republic, the Kumari now blesses the President instead. The continued role of the goddess may appear inconsistent with a secular republic, and has been perceived by some Nepali activists as a failure of the President in the exercise of his secular office. Nevertheless, for many others, it seems only natural that the head of the state should maintain this relationship with the goddess.[5]

If we consider the Kumari's presence in the public space as an inconsistency of Nepali secularism, a relic of a pre-modern past, we are implying that there is a model of secularism against which the secularity of that (or any) country should be judged. We are also taking for granted the postulated inevitability of secularization in the modernization process. More generally, considerations about the many challenges for secularism in Nepal assume and reify secularism as a part of a 'modernity package' that is challenging the deeply religious and traditional Nepali society.

---

4   While ethnic and religious minorities are still being indicted for the crime of cow slaughter (now justified on the basis that the cow is the national animal), the number of prosecutions against proselytization ('causing religious conversion', *dharma parivartan garaune*) has dwindled since 1990 and none have been found to have taken place since 2002. Resistance to the removal of these bans is strong, and they remained – even if the punishment were reduced – in the concept papers of the Constituent Assembly and the new draft Criminal Code presented to Parliament in 2011.

5   Chunda Bajracarya, a professor of Newar culture and one of the parties involved in the case studied in this chapter, explained: 'Kumari and the head of the State, whoever is the head of the state, are intimately connected. Now instead of the King we have the President. I think that the King should not be going to the Kumari: people have to feel that things have changed and that the political changes have occurred. The political change should change also the culture' (Interview, March 2010).

However, a recent debate in the social sciences has historicized the very notions of secularism and secularization and questioned their intrinsic association with modernization.[6] A review of the main arguments in this debate will be useful before returning to the Nepali case.

Secularism in the Social Sciences' Recent Debate

The three processes described by Casanova (1994) – a decline of religious beliefs and practices correlating with increasing modernization; the privatization of religion; and the differentiation of secular spheres (State, economy, science), understood as their emancipation from religious norms and institutions – are all interrelated in European history. Therefore, there is a general assumption that as 'components of a single general teleological process of secularization and modernization' (Casanova 2011a: 60), they constitute inevitable parts of the global modernization process. However, secularization is a contingent European dynamic and it relates only to the particular historical transformation of Western European Christianity; its generalization as a universal process correlated with modernization and transferred to other world religions and other cultural areas is highly problematic (Casanova 2009).

As early as the 1980s, the anthropologist T.N. Madan (1987) questioned the thesis that the historical *process* of secularization, which separated the two domains of 'the religious' and 'the secular' in Western society, with the former being confined to individuals' privacy, was a precondition of modernity everywhere. The debate has recently shifted to the religious and historical context in which secularism evolved, and has led to 'an unpacking of secularity as a religious-free neutral and universal development of European modernity' (Göle 2010: 43).

The work of Talal Asad (1993, 2003) and his anthropology of secularism have strongly contributed to deconstructing secularism, considering it as historically contingent and challenging the inevitability of the secular in the modern. Asad argues that the religious and the secular are neither immutable essences nor opposed ideologies, and that their mutual construction as interdependent concepts gain salience with the emergence of the modern State. While secular rationality was defining law, economic relations, and statecraft in the modern world, it was simultaneously transforming the conceptions, practices and institutions of religious life. Thus, secularism 'has historically entailed the regulation and reformation of religious beliefs, doctrine and practices to yield a

---

6   This debate started with Casanova (1994), Asad (2003) and Martin (2005), and has been well summarized by Cannell (2010). For a thorough multidisciplinary reflection and critique of secularism, see Calhoun, Juergensmeyer and Van Antwerpen (2011).

particular normative conception of religion (that is largely protestant Christian in its contours)' (Mahmood 2009: 836, 858).[7]

However, to acknowledge that secularism is a product of Western history specific to Latin Christendom does not imply that it is not suitable for non-Western civilizations. Rather, what needs to be considered is how the Christian Western European dynamic of secularization has been globalized and how religious traditions respond and are being reinterpreted, producing multiple formations of the secular in different historical and political contexts. These multiple secularisms should not be approached as replicas or 'deficient copies' of the Western original, but as distinctive formations, and the study of these distinctive formations can help relativize and challenge unreflexive notions of both religion and secularism.

Casanova (2010) suggests that secularism, a 'western essentialism', should first be deconstructed by emphasizing the various patterns of secularization *within* the West (Protestant/Catholic, European/American, etc.) to open up the way to a less Eurocentric and more comparative analysis of patterns of secularization in other secular modernities. In the same way, Bhargava suggests that scholars should attend to the histories of secularism and examine the transnational and historical development of the secular idea:

> Secularism too has a history made at one time largely by Europeans, then a little later by North Americans, and much later by non-western countries. Non-western societies inherited from their western counterparts specific versions of secularism but they did not always preserve them in the form in which they were received. They often added something of enduring value to them and, therefore, developed the idea further. (Bhargava 2010: 65)

The call to explore variations and different formations of secularism in multiple contexts is voiced in many recent publications (Jakobsen and Pellegrini 2008, Cady and Shakman Hurd 2010, Bubandt and Van Beek 2011). The aim is not merely to catalogue the variety of secularisms in the world, but to develop new concepts and identify practices at work outside the secular/religious opposition (Cady and Shakman Hurd 2010: 8) and to ethnographically test the secular/ religious opposition.

The term 'post-secular', used in recent years by a number of influential theorists like Casanova, Taylor and Habermas, expresses this need for a new thinking that transcends these terms, to coin new concepts and to find ways of accommodating religious claims in liberal institutions (Habermas 2008, Casanova 2009, Molendijk et al. 2010). Scholars are calling for a 'de-secularization' of our

---

7   The normative impetus internal to secularism reorganizes religious subjectivities in accordance with a liberal political rule that is retrospectively called 'a religiously neutral political ethic' (Mahmood 2006: 328). This is why secular consciousness cannot meet the challenges of increasingly plural societies where *different* forms of religious subjectivity need to be recognized and legally acknowledged.

secularist and modernist categories (Casanova 2009) to describe contemporary religious developments. Indeed, the categories that have been used until now, such as the 'de-secularization of the world', the 'return of religion' or the 'deprivatization of religion', all point to a simple reversal of a postulated previous process of secularization, and remain therefore within the same paradigm.

For Rosati, the postsecular encompasses two basic dimensions: the reflectivity of modernity and the reflectivity of religious traditions. The former points to an awareness of the limits of orthodox theories of secularization, while the latter represents 'their awareness to live in that common environment that is modernity (not only Western modernity)' (Rosati 2011: 247–8). The crucial point according to Rosati is that the reflectivity of religions should not be understood as a homogeneous process of individualization and spiritualization, and does not necessarily mean that religions must leave the public sphere. The model of secularity as a public space free from religious arguments, religious symbols and religious groups needs to be rethought (Casanova 2011b).[8]

The Nepali Case

Despite social scientists' deconstructions, secularism arrived in Nepal as a part of a modernizing project towards a 'New Nepal', with all the many features and assumptions that the recent debate would like to get rid of. The package, so to speak, has been delivered and is producing local responses, even though scholars may debate whether it should have been sent in the first place. While many researchers are questioning the use of the term 'secularism', the fact that local actors have been adopting and using this term compels us to study its local meanings and the strategies deployed in connection with it, taking into account the cultural, historical and political context of this use and adoption.

Rather than judging the secularity of Nepal on the basis of an abstract model of secularism, my research aims to study the ethnographic meaning of Nepali secularism, as I believe that empirically and ethnographically testing the western secular/religious opposition may contribute to its relativization and deconstruction. The ethnography of a non-Western context is particularly suited to helping us think beyond the secular/religious opposition, exactly because the local notion of 'religion' exceeds the western one constructed and regulated in opposition to the 'secular'.

Therefore, my research considers Nepali secularism's local history, its multiple understandings, and its recent shaping process. As will be shown below, these do not involve the separation of state and religion or the disappearance of religion from the public sphere. Does this simply mean that Nepal has not achieved a full

---

8   Casanova proposed that pluralist societies 'need to create neutral civic and political secular spaces in which all religious and non religious people can not only coexist peacefully but also partake in the same equal rights and freedoms' (2011).

secularism in its trajectory towards modernity? As there is not a single model of modernity (Eisenstadt 2000), nor a single model of secularism, such a question cannot be usefully answered. I suggest that we can instead turn our attention to discerning the development of a distinctive form of secularism with a distinctive way of defining relations between its multiple religious traditions and the state.

My fieldwork was concerned with the concept of secularism mainly in two ways: first, with an enquiry into the multiple understandings of secularism through interviews conducted mainly in the Southern plains (Tarai) districts,[9] and secondly, with the study of District and Supreme Court cases concerning the reform of religious traditions, to see if and how they contribute to shaping the fluid notion of secularism.

Secularism and Minority Rights: The Campaign of 1990

Even if secularism won the day in Nepal thanks to the political power of the Maoist party,[10] the declaration of secularism had also been a goal of the religious minorities and ethnic groups. The constitution of the Panchayat regime (1960–1990) defined Nepal as a Hindu kingdom. This regime denied ethnic, linguistic and religious diversity and used Hinduism as the cement of a nationalist and homogenizing project. In 1990, the People's Movement overthrew the Panchayat regime, providing the context for the rise of ethnic-based political identities. Organisations claiming to represent Nepal's diverse populations (who started to be collectively called as *janajati*) demanded that the new constitution officially recognize and protect ethnic, religious, and linguistic minority rights.

Buddhist leaders and ethnic activists formed a movement to demand a secular state. Abolishing the Hindu state, which maintained social and economic inequalities in favour of high-caste Hindus, was perceived as a way to achieve an inclusive society. For the activists, secularism would not banish religion from public life but would recognize religious diversity and bring an end to Hindu high caste domination. Far from a retreat from or rejection of religion, secularism was redefined as 'the institutional instantiation of freedom of religion and religious equality' (Leve 2007: 94).[11] This bid for secularism failed (the 1990 Constitution still declared the state Hindu), but it contributed to shaping the particular

---

9   I sought to catch glimpses of secularism from politicians, the legal community, the police, social activists, intellectuals and leaders of the religious communities: Hindus, Buddhists, Muslims and Christians.

10   Secularism had been part of the Maoist agenda since their 40-point demand submitted to the then Prime Minister Sher Bahadur Deuba on 4 February 1996 by Dr Baburam Bhattarai on behalf of the United People's Front Nepal, just before the launch of their People's War.

11   For example, the Theravada monk Aswagosh wrote: 'Secularism means that the state must be unbiased towards all religions. It does not mean that religion must be stopped' (Aswagosh 1994, quoted in Leve 2007: 94).

understanding of secularism in present-day Nepal as the principle whereby all religions are to enjoy equal rights and opportunities, leading to the abolition of the state-sponsored primacy given to Hinduism (Gellner 2001).

For example, it is telling that the first governmental step greeted as secular by the media and the public in 2007 consisted in the declaration of a number of Buddhist, Muslim, Christian Madhesi, Tharu and Kirant festivals as national holidays, in a calendar dominated by Hindu festivals.

A Multivocal and Sensitive Notion

Secularism emerged from my fieldwork as a multivocal and often sensitive concept, showing a potential for conflict in the way it was differently understood by different groups, religious minorities, and political parties.

Maoists welcomed secularism as a step towards the elimination of a deep-rooted feudalism based on Hinduism. For many Hindus, however, it was a despicable and uncalled-for measure leading to communal violence, encouraging Muslims to kill cows and Christians to convert everyone, thereby weakening Hinduism and the national identity. Muslims, in turn, saw it as a good opportunity to get the *shari'a* enacted as their community's own personal law and to receive more state support for their community's schools (*madrasahs*), while Christians, (mostly evangelical Churches) understood secularism as implicit permission to proselytize, despite the letter of the law.

Echoing the 1990s' vision, people belonging to religious minorities, *janajati*s and civil society understood secularism as the opportunity for all religious groups to receive equal recognition and as the freedom to choose and change their religion.

In fact, very few intellectuals outside Kathmandu legal circles understand it as the wall of separation between Church and State.

The Role of Judiciary in Shaping Secularism

The Interim Constitution of Nepal 2007 provided no model of secularism for the state to espouse, and the government conducted no information campaign after the declaration. Kattel (2010) notes that the political parties which put secularism in their manifestos for the CA elections did not explain the word either.[12]

With its place as yet unsecured in the still undrafted constitution, secularism has been taking shape beyond the Constitutional Assembly, through campaigns, demonstrations and incidents that result from the sudden disconnection between political power and Hinduism brought about by the Maoist government. These events have provided opportunities to launch a public debate reflecting on the

---

12   My interviews revealed that many politicians accepted secularism as a part of the Maoist agenda, and as a way to remove the religious basis of the monarchy, but did not give much thought to secularism *per se*, nor were they – belonging to the dominating Hindu high castes – at ease with this concept.

relationship between religion and politics. Some of these incidents ended up before the Supreme Court as Public Interest Litigation, a procedure enshrined in the constitution which has encouraged a growing judicial activism to challenge laws and practices inconsistent with human rights and the constitution. This has given judges the opportunity to rule on the relation between the government and religious traditions. My interest in such court cases stems from the realization that the judiciary may play a crucial role in defining the fluid notion of secularism.

In this chapter I present a court case that challenged the Kumari tradition in the name of child rights.[13] I will briefly go over the petition, the arguments of the parties and the court's verdict. This case allowed the judges and the public to reflect on the relationship between religion and the state, and provided some space and opportunity for a dialogue and debate among stakeholders to occur.

From the court papers and from my interviews there emerges a notion of secularism which started taking shape in 1990s and which acknowledges the importance of religion in the public space, recognizes the rights of religious groups, and involves the state in supporting and reforming religion. To describe it, I will draw on the notion of 'principled distance' proposed by Bhargava for India, and then read the court case from this perspective.

Before turning to the examination of the case, let me present briefly the Kumari goddess and her role for the Nepalese kings.

The Kumari and the Kings

Worshipping virgin girls as the Kumari is a very old Hindu practice. In Nepal, this cult had long been central to the Hindu-Buddhist culture of the Newars, the indigenous population of the Kathmandu valley.[14]

There are many Kumaris in the Kathmandu valley (at least 11, strictly connected with the Newar Buddhist monasteries) and their cult is not necessarily linked to kingship; but since the Malla period (fourteenth to eighteenth century), the cult of Kumari has served to legitimize Hindu kings: each of the three Malla kingdoms of Kathmandu, Lalitpur and Bhaktapur had its own royal Kumari. For Buddhist devotees, these Kumaris were a manifestation of Vajradevi, while for Hindus they were a manifestation of Durga-Taleju, the tutelary deity of the ancient Malla kings.[15] With the unification of Nepal, the Kumari of Basantapur in Kathmandu became prominent as the sole royal – and now national – Kumari. What follows concerns mainly this national Kumari, but many of the rules apply, with some

---

13   This case was first studied by Axel Michaels (2009), who kindly gave me his manuscript.

14   On Kumari, see Moaven 1974; Allen 1976 and 1996; Toffin 1993; Letizia 2003; Shakya and Berry 2005.

15   For the stories relating the origin of Kumari (mainly in connection with the goddess Taleju), see among others Hasrat 1970: 59; Mohaven 1974: 171; Lienhard 1978: 239–70; Slusser 1982: 311; Toffin 1993: 235.

variations, for the former royal Kumaris of Lalitpur and Bhaktapur. However, only the Basantapur Kumari must live apart from her parents in the 'Kumari House' near the ancient palace of the Malla Kings.

The Kumari is chosen from the Vajracharya-Shakya caste of Newar Buddhist priests. Starting as early as the age of two and until her first period, she is considered as a living goddess and conducts a life of ritual always dressed in red clothes. She does not attend a school but she is taught at home from a private preceptor. Newars and all Nepalis, Buddhist and Hindu alike, come to worship her regularly in the Kumari House,[16] and on the occasion of religious celebrations when she leaves her house on a chariot.

**Figure 6.1	Kathmandu Durbar Square, September 2009. Kumari Jatra Festival.**

Note: The living goddess Kumari is taken out on a chariot amidst the crowds for the first of three days of procession around the city.

Source: Photograph by the author 2009.

16	Kumari worship generally is particularly important for Newars, since no major ritual can be completed without it (Gellner 1992: 152–3).

**Figure 6.2   Kathmandu Durbar Square, September 2009. Kumari Jatra
            Festival.**

Note: A crowd of women stands on the stairs of Maju Deval temple, while awaiting the
chariot of the Kumari.

Source: Photograph by the author 2009.

On the last day of the Kumari chariot festival, as I have already mentioned, the
Kumari traditionally used to put a red mark – *tika* – on the king's forehead and
legitimated his right to rule for one more year. This tradition, started by King
Jaya Prakash Malla in the eighteenth century, was appropriated by the following
dynasty: when Prithvi Narayan Shah took control of Kathmandu in 1768 on this
festival day, he went straight into the Kumari House, he sat on the throne prepared
for Jaya Prakash Malla who had fled and took the tika blessing from the Kumari in
his stead. She thus legitimated the new king and the new dynasty.

The legitimating function of the *tika* was confirmed by stories about subsequent
kings of the Shah dynasty: it is said that King Tribhuvan in 1955 went to take
the *tika* accompanied by his son, the prince Mahendra. Even a goddess can make
mistakes, and the Kumari put the *tika* on Mahendra's forehead, instead of blessing
the king. The incident was considered inauspicious for the king: Tribhuvan died six
months later and Mahendra succeeded him (Anderson 1971: 135; Allen 1996: 12).

In 2006, King Gyanendra Shah presided over the Kumari festival for the last
time; in 2007, since the king had been stripped of his 'cultural rights', the first

prime minister and head of state under the Interim Constitution, Girija Prasad Koirala, took the king's place.[17] In 2008, Ram Baran Yadav was elected as the first president. Shortly after the election, he went to Kumari House to take the goddess's blessings. That year a new Kumari, Matina Shakya, was selected as the first republican Kumari. Since then she has blessed the president.

Despite the ten years of Maoist insurgency (1996–2006) and despite the People's Movement that overthrew the Hindu Kingdom, the space in front of the Kumari continues to serve as a legitimating space for every head of state, since the eighteenth century. Her role appears to have remained unquestioned. Indeed, Michaels (2009) affirms that when the Maoist leader Prachanda became prime minister, a flag was raised for some time on the Kumari house, on which one could read: 'the communist party salutes Kumari'.[18]

But some things have changed: the strong connection that linked the Kumari and the king has been severed. The Kumari selecting committee no longer verifies whether the Kumari's horoscope matches the king's,[19] and the royal priest (*rajpurohita*) is no longer involved in selecting a new Kumari. Instead, a committee of priests connected to the Taleju temple and the Kumari House has chosen the new incumbent. Their selection was not approved by the king, but by the president in the presence of a representative of the Guthi Samsthan – a state-controlled national trust funding Hindu religious institutions.

Moreover, in the last decade, a new legitimating source started challenging the authority and legitimating power of the living goddess, namely fundamental human rights. Already in September 2002, a member of parliament, Bidya Bhandari, asked for the abolishment of the Kumari tradition, arguing that it violated children's and women's rights. In 2004 the Committee for the Convention on the Elimination of Discrimination Against Women (CEDAW) made the same recommendation in a report to the UN General Assembly, lumping the Kumari tradition with other discriminatory practices and asking for its abolishment:

17　Nevertheless, the king also went to take the *tika* for the very last time, underscoring with this gesture the importance of the Kumari as a symbol of legitimization.

18　The Maoists adopted inconsistent attitudes towards religion during the 'People's War' (1996–2006) and beyond. They occasionally prohibited 'superstitious cults' and sometimes deliberately violated religious taboos, but also summoned shamans, worshipped deities, visited pilgrimage places, etc. Anthropologists have also showed how Maoists built their movement around symbols reinterpreting Hindu notions (Ramirez 1997, de Sales 2003, Lecomte 2006). The Maoist government after 2008 generally adopted an attitude of respect towards the religious beliefs of the masses (despite a few incidents such as the infamous decision of the then Maoist Prime Minister Dahal 'Prachanda' to break the tradition of appointing South Indian priests at the Pashupatinath temple). To the disbelief of Maoist cadres, in 2010 Prachanda worshipped a buffalo at a religious camp in Sunsari district, to appease the bad influence of Saturn.

19　But for Dr Chunda Bajracarya, the planets still are influential and will decide who is going to be president: only a president matching the Kumari would be elected, and only a Kumari fitting a president's horoscope will be chosen (Interview, March 2010).

The institution of dowry, *deuki* (dedicating girls to a god and goddess), *jhuma* (second sisters remain unmarried and spend their life in monasteries) *kumari pratha* (having a girl child as living goddess) and *badi* (practice of prostitution among young girls) (...) are contrary to the Convention and constitute discrimination against women. (CEDAW 2004)

The 'Kumari Case' at the Supreme Court

In 2005, a Newar human rights lawyer, Pun Devi Maharjan, filed a Public Interest Litigation (PIL) asking the Supreme Court to intervene to protect the fundamental rights of Kumaris (Maharjan 2005). The very fact that the powerful goddess legitimating the Kings of Nepal could thus be scrutinized in court as a human being deprived of human rights mirrors the political and symbolic transformation of the last years. The petition was filed under the 1990 constitution while Nepal was still a Hindu Kingdom, but the verdict was rendered in 2008, when the country had become a secular state. No explicit reference to secularism was made in this judgment; and yet this case allowed the judges to reflect on the relation between religion and the state and, as I will explain below, this judgement can be seen as a landmark case, setting a precedent for (a local definition of) secularism.

Petition and Arguments

Pun Devi sought a court order (*mandamus*) asking the government to stop unconstitutional activities carried out in the name of the Kumari tradition; to attend to the social security of ex-Kumaris; and to engage the Human Rights commission and the experts of the Newar community in the reform of the Kumari tradition (Bhattarai 2010: 112). The petition argues that the tradition of Kumari violated numerous legal provisions, including: Article 26(8) of the Constitution of Nepal, 1990, which prescribed the state's duty to safeguard the rights and interests of children; Section 14 of the Children Act, 1992, prohibiting that young girls be offered in the name of gods and goddesses for fulfilling a religious purpose; and the Convention on the Rights of the Child of 1989, to which Nepal is a signatory.

In her presentation of the facts, Pun Devi examines the various Kumari traditions, concluding that the young girls have been victims of exploitation and that many of their rights are being infringed (including their rights to personal liberty and freedom of movement and residence, freedom to go to school like other children, freedom to wear clothes of their choice, and so on). She claims that this has affected their physical and mental development, and that the institution of Kumari is a form of child labour. She observes that the state has made no provision to compensate the ex-Kumaris. As a result, says the petitioner, the life of Kumaris and ex-Kumaris is miserable.

Pun Devi did not seek to abolish this cult, but to reform it so that it may conform to human rights standards. Pun Devi's most effective argument during the hearings was that the restrictions on the rights of children becoming Kumari and the scarcity of funds they faced have already brought about the discontinuation of the custom in some places. She argued that unless the Kumari's human rights are fully guaranteed, the tradition could eventually die out. She suggests that for the tradition to earn more respect, it needs to be made more respectable through timely reforms and improvements.

International Western Supporters

Pun Devi Maharjan's petition received the support of the Center for Reproductive Rights (CRR), a non-profit legal advocacy organization based in New York and dedicated to defending and promoting women's reproductive rights worldwide. The CRR joined the pleadings in October 2006 and filed a report. But it went even further, calling for the elimination of the Kumari practice as 'an institutionalized form of discrimination against girl children' which 'results in violations of several basic human rights'. In her report, the legal advisor of the Center for Asia, Melissa Upreti, explained the Center's interest in the case:

> This case presents a unique opportunity for the Supreme Court of Nepal to determine whether in fact the right to freedom of religion and culture can prevail over the rights which are protected by international law and the Constitution of Nepal and, recognizing the important role of culture and religion in peoples' lives, to establish the scope of the state's positive obligations to protect these rights through a balanced approach that is consistent with constitutional principles and Nepal's obligations under international law. (Upreti 2006: 1)

Clearly, this report sought to pressure the Supreme Court to remind the government of its duties under international treaties.

The Reaction of the Newar Community

This case witnessed a public debate involving a petitioner who had placed religious freedom in the context of a (secular) set of fundamental rights versus the Newar community for which the tradition was a matter of identity. Newar community representatives invoked the right of religion, affirming that the Kumari tradition was its exclusive domain and should not suffer any 'outside' intervention.[20]

A group of Newar women also intervened in Court against Pun Devi's petition, contradicting her presentation of the facts. They argued that the petition failed to acknowledge the 'glorious prestige and honour of the Kumari culture (*kumari samskriti*)'.

---

20   As Gellner (2008: 90) noticed, 'many Newar activists responded that this is a Brahman-inspired attack on a key part of the Newars' heritage, an attack inspired less by genuine concern for child rights than by envy of the Newars' rich history and culture'.

In our interviews, Pun Devi refers to the criticism she received from her community, including Newari newspapers. According to some Newar journalists, her isolation has persisted.[21]

A strong opponent of Pun Devi, both in court and in publications, was Chunda Vajracharya, professor at Tribhuvan University and expert on Newar culture. In the book she edited, Chunda wrote that Kumari culture had been attacked by women's rights activists who didn't care for the dignity of religion and culture. She opposed her vision that Kumari is not a form of violence against women or children, but an ancient Newar tradition and culture, stating that every group has the right to protect its traditions (Vajracharya 2009: 4). Her main argument is that 'Kumari is our *culture* (in English); only we can change it, and nobody else can judge it' (Interview, March 2010). In November 2006, Chunda told the BBC that being Kumari does not affect the child's individual rights, arguing on the contrary that it elevates her status in society as 'someone divine, someone who's above the rest'.[22]

Her arguments were echoed by the father of present Kumari, Pratap Man Shakya, who also defended the traditional practices as privileges rather than exploitation:

> Kumari is a Goddess, not just an ordinary child and she owns the power of our state. Since she's a goddess, she gets special treatment. It's true, she is not going to school, but the school is coming to her. It's true, she does not live at home: but if she was going to a boarding school, she would not live at home either: are the boarding schools against human rights? (Interview, April 2010)

Newar activist Pabitra Vajracarya also justified the restrictions on Kumaris as the price of a high status:

> Let's take the example of President Obama. His case does not fit with human rights either. He cannot go wherever he wants, or go to cinema: if he goes, he has to go with security guards! Kumari is like a princess, and her status involves limitations to her life, exactly like a President, she cannot go wherever she wants. (Interview, September 2009)

---

21   But Pun Devi told me that while at first everybody was criticizing her, they eventually came round after she explained the reasons for her petition. This included Kumari and ex-Kumari families, who complained to her off-record about the plight of Kumaris, though none of them wanted to speak openly against the tradition or to support her endeavour.

22   She nonetheless agreed that 'some reform measures need to be put in place to ensure their right to education, sports and all-round social development as a child' (BBC 2010).

A Shakya-Vajracharya Tradition 'Attacked' by an Outsider

The respondents argued in court that Kumari is not only a Newar tradition, but in fact a tradition concerning only the high Buddhist Newar castes, the Shakyas and Vajracharyas from among whom the Kumari is chosen. This cast Pun Devi, a Maharjan (the caste of Newar farmers), as an outsider, something she refuted. Her first interview in 2009 started with these words: 'First of all, I'm of the same community as the Kumari and I worship her.' And she later added: 'Kumari tradition is not only their culture, it is *our* culture; Kumari tradition does not belong to only one community, because it receives our government's funds: it's a Nepalese tradition, of every Nepalese citizen. That's why we have to protect it.'

Pun Devi is actually somehow an outsider: as a lawyer trained to identify issues from the perspective of international human rights standards, she looks to her own community traditions with the critical 'external' outlook she gains from her Western-influenced, professional training. Like many Nepali lawyers engaged in judicial activism, she is a mediator and translator of the language of human rights.

The Committee's Report

After the hearing in October 2006, the court ordered the constitution of a committee of experts to study the issue and to submit a report within three months. This committee included the petitioner herself, Dr. Chunda Vajracharya as representative of the stakeholders, and Jal Krisna Shrestha as a coordinator. The coordinator presented the report of the committee to the Supreme Court in 2007 (Shrestha 2009), but both Pun Devi and Chunda Vajracharya felt that it was a 'one-side report' that did not take into account their vision, so they filed their own dissenting reports (later published in Vajracharya 2009).

The committee's report stated that though the Kumari parts with some freedoms, she gains some 'incomparable rights' and she leads a 'superior life' compared to other girls, characterized by pride, honour and divine power. The report did not admit to any human rights violations against Kumaris, and yet agreed that reforms in tune with the times were necessary and made recommendations to guarantee the right of education, freedom of movement and medical care.

Pun Devi disagreed with the report and presented her detailed research findings (based on her visits to many Kumaris and on the interviews with their families) citing several human rights issues in connection with education, freedom of movement, family environment, diet, dress, medical assistance, entertainment and marriage.

Decision[23]

The judgment strikes a delicate balance between the claims of Newars to their traditional religious rights, the position of the Hindu majority (to whom almost all judges belong and for whom the Kumari is a revered tradition), the importance of the Kumari as a national deity, and the claim that the state has a national and international legal duty to uphold human rights. A key aspect of this decision is the court's general conclusion about the primacy of social reforms based on human rights over traditional religious practices:

> If any custom or tradition has caused any infringement to the fundamental rights [...] this Court is competent to enforce the enjoyment of rights thus infringed. This court may also issue an order prohibiting such custom or tradition by law. In case of conflict [...] religion must yield to provide space for social reforms. Religious practices cannot be an impediment to social reforms. [...] The State may prohibit traditional practices and dogmas if they tend to create impediments to any human rights. (Bhattarai 2010: 130)

The existence of state values that are independent from and prevailing over those of the religious tradition is an essential prerequisite of the notion of secularism. Without referring to the principle of secularism, the court thus established one of its cornerstones and helped to secularize the newly declared secular state, by distinguishing the domain of the religious (practised by communities) and the domain of human rights (protected by the state).

The court did not, however, find that a violation of human rights was inherent to this Kumari tradition. Clearly sympathetic, the court noted that no written documents existed for imposing the rules applied to Kumaris. Those rules are applied only on the basis of 'oral traditions and beliefs', and so they were held not to be inherent to the Kumari tradition: any member of the Newar community could become an agent of change in traditional practices (and for example send Kumari to school). The court also refuted the allegation of child labour and took great pains to distinguish 'child labour' from 'Kumari work' (that is, sitting on her throne to be worshipped) and to identify the latter as an essential part of a particular Hindu and Buddhist devotion.

The judges rejected the findings of the CEDAW committee and underscored the value of the Kumari tradition for Newars and for the country, pointing out that the practice is deeply connected with the religious rights of the majority who follow the Hindu and Buddhist religions, and that 'without the presence and participation

---

23   The verdict was rendered on 16 August 2008 (2 Bhadra, 2065 B.S.) by Justices Bala Ram K.C. and Tapa Bahadur Magar, and published on the Supreme Court journal (Maharjan 2008); it has been republished by the National Judicial Academy in both English and Nepali, in a collection of landmark decisions of the Supreme Court on gender justice (Bhattarai 2010).

of Kumari, it would be impossible to hold certain festivals, worships and cultural activities of the followers of the Hindu and Buddhist religions of Kathmandu, Lalitpur and Bhaktapur' (Bhattarai 2010: 132).

The court acknowledged that *past* Kumaris, due to confusion and backwardness, may have been deprived of their fundamental rights and held that the state must help and support them. In the judge's view, it is the duty of the State to promote its religious and cultural customs and the state should appreciate the Kumaris' contributions to the cultural and religious life of the nation, and thus make arrangements for their social security.

With these fine distinctions, the judgment avoids the labelling of the Kumari tradition as a discriminatory practice and as an infringement of child rights, while leaving space for change and reform. Moreover, the court recognized the need to support and promote the Kumari cult.

Finally, the court ordered that a new expert committee be formed, to render its report within one year, with a view to conducting an extensive study of how Kumari rights can be promoted in compliance with the Constitution and international human rights. The court also issued a *mandamus* to the government, ordering it to implement the report of the committee once it is submitted.

The Role of the Committees

The committees appointed to study the tradition constitute a very interesting aspect of this and other cases. In the committee, the Newar community representatives, at first fiercely opposed to any intervention in their custom, were co-opted by the court to study and reflect on their own tradition. This has given members of the Newar community an opportunity to examine their own tradition with 'secular eyes', and compare it with secular human rights values. In their decision, the judges affirm that the members of the community can be the agents of change in their traditional practices. Such committees offer an example of the potentially constructive role played by the court in shaping new understandings of the religious tradition, as a powerful forum for raising awareness and negotiating reform.

Pun Devi noted that in the end, the court didn't decide, but passed the responsibility to a committee and the government, postponing the whole thing by a year.[24]

It is also true that in this way, the court used a strategic detour, on one side denying that the Kumari tradition conflicted with human rights, and on the other admitting a need for reforms and delegating to a committee the sensitive determination of the nature and extent of such reforms. A decision ordering the

---

24 Moreover, court-appointed committees often fail to produce their reports, or reports are just not implemented: the committee report of this case has yet to be submitted and it seems unlikely to be forthcoming unless a petition is filed to seek the enforcement of the court decision.

constitution of a team of experts is quite a common feature of cases dealing with sensitive issues opposing powerful and conflicting interests. Such committees with members representing all stakeholders were also formed in the cases concerning the Pashupatinath temple, in order to decide how its managing trust would be severed from the state's control (Letizia forthcoming), and in the conflict raised around Christian and Kirant burials in the Slesmantak forest, contested by the Hindus (Mulmi 2011). These committees give parties a precious opportunity to negotiate, identify pragmatic solutions, and practice (post-)secularism.

Religion and Culture

A court case involving religious traditions and confronting them with human rights, inevitably entails defining what is of the religious domain and what is not, what can be changed and what cannot be questioned. This can lead to a 'religionization' of the state and of the courts called to decide in matter of tradition, ritual details, and so on.

The debates inside and outside the court give rise to a question that exceeds the ambit of this case: the distinction between religion (pure, not involving any discrimination *per se*) and culture or tradition (which may have been affected by some social evils and can be modified according to the modern times).

The petitioner offers a clear view of this distinction. She draws a line close to the core Kumari practices, considering them 'religion', that cannot be touched, and considering the rest 'culture', which must be changed to enable the custom to survive. She distinguishes between the belief in the Kumari (this is *dharma*, 'religion'), and whatever is done in the Kumari tradition (which is *samskriti* 'culture' or *parampara, ritirivaj* 'custom, tradition'). For her, the state cannot interfere in matters of religion, but can interfere in cultural practices that infringe upon human rights. According to the petitioner, the core part of tradition and its very existence cannot be questioned, is unchangeable and so to speak out of history. But the surrounding traditions and practices are cultural products and can be modified according to historical changes.

This duality seems to apply to the very nature of Kumari, who as a living goddess is both divine and human, and her human part requires human rights. In her report, Pun Devi quotes the opinion of a Newar scholar who affirms that the Kumari tradition seeks to protect a divine power (*daivi shakti*), and this divine power must not be affected; but the divine power is not present in the child for 24 hours, so that when Kumari is in her human condition, she should enjoy human rights, and tradition should be modified accordingly (Maharjan 2009: 50).

It seems to me that the court judgement echoes the same mindset. The court did not find fault within the Kumari tradition *per se*. Instead, it ascribed the past problematic situations to confusion and backwardness. The court adopted the view that social ills allegedly emerging from the religious tradition were in fact, upon closer inspection, to be distinguished from true religion. In the end, the opposition between (true) religion – which does no wrong – and (undesirable) cultural elements – wrongly identified with religion – is very close to Pun Devi's views.

The Role of the State

The lack of concern on the part of the government in this case is particularly telling. The government attorney simply dismissed the whole thing, saying that 'the government has no direct involvement or participation in the matters relating to the custom of Kumari'. One could take this to mean that the state is maintaining its secular distance, but even without considering the annual ritual involving the president, it is an incredible statement, considering that the state does finance the Kumari cult: it provides monthly allowances to Kumaris and ex-Kumaris through the Guthi Samsthan, and additional allowances for maintenance and education through the Kaushi Tosha Khana, an office of the finance ministry that manages the pensions of civil servants in Nepal. The Kumari of Kathmandu is also supported by Kathmandu municipality.

The verdict calls the state into play to improve the financial support to Kumaris. The fact that the state provides financial support to this religious custom is never made an issue. Actually, no one involved in the court hearings paused to consider whether secularism precluded the continued financing of the Kumari tradition by the state. State involvement here was not only assumed as normal by all the parties involved, but much of the case was about the existence of a state duty to support Kumaris in order to 'appreciate their contributions to the cultural and religious life of the nation'.

That secularism could not possibly mean the removal of state funding was clearly manifested in the outrage of Newar community during Indra Jatra in 2008, when the Maoist Finance Minister announced in his budget speech a cut of government funding for religious festivals (a decision quickly revoked after intense popular protests).

To sum up, the court:

- recognized the Kumari tradition as an integral part of the Newar culture, and explicitly considered Newars as 'agents of change in their traditional custom and practices in tune with times';
- affirmed the principle that the state retains a duty to support and promote a religious tradition considered valuable for the 'social, cultural and religious life of the nation';
- assumed that a court can engage with religion to enact social reform and to ensure compliance with constitutionally recognized human rights;
- established the primacy of human rights over religious tradition, and yet this primacy does not mean religion should shrink away from the public sphere.

From this case emerges a rather unusual form of secularism that ascribes to the state an active role in both supporting and reforming religious traditions. Thus a conclusion from this case could indicate that Nepali secularism is developing in a direction quite different from the neutral stance and no-relation policy which is generally seen as a mark of secularism in the west.

A Distinctive Form of Secularism?

The case and fieldwork data discussed in this chapter point to a distinctive form of secularism in the making, which (a) is understood as religious freedom and religious equality (as in the 1990s campaign) of both individuals and groups; (b) gives importance to religious groups in the public sphere (e.g. the recognition of minorities' festivals in the calendar was saluted as a secular step, or the Muslim understanding of secularism as an opportunity to apply their personal laws); and (c) ascribes to the state an active role in both enhancing and reforming religious traditions, as has been evidenced in the Kumari case.

I suggest that the normative reflections of Bhargava on an (idealized) Indian form of secularism and his notion of 'principled distance' (2010: 63–105) could be relevant as conceptual framework to describe this form of secularism.

'Principled Distance' and 'Contextual Secularism'

Bhargava argues that Indian secularism has to differ from the classical liberal model, which dictates strict separation between religious and political institutions, and recognizes individuals and beliefs but not groups and practices (Bhargava 2010: 25–6). The circumstances of India (and the same can be said for Nepal) – which include an enormous diversity of religious communities, social practices emphasized over individual beliefs, and many discriminatory religious practices in need of reform – dictate that religious freedom must also include the right of religious communities to carry out their own practices, and that equality of citizenship applies also to the religious groups to which citizens belong. In the absence of a unified religious organization, reform within Hinduism can hardly be initiated without the help of the state.

Bhargava introduces the notion of 'principled distance', which entails a flexible approach to the matter of state intervention in the religious domain or its abstention from it. The state has secular ends and is institutionally separate from religion, but it can engage with religious issues at the level of law and social policy. Whether the state intervenes or not depends on what strengthens religious liberty and equality of citizenship (Bhargava 1998: 536; 2010: 87–96). This form of secularism accepts religion as a resource that 'manifests itself as individual belief and feeling as well as social practice in the public domain' (Bhargava 2010: 88).

Bhargava's reflections shed light on possible ways in which secularism might be shaped in Nepal through a contextual moral and legal reasoning freed from the rigid application of a Western concept, thus reducing the potential for fundamentalist reactions and mistrust between communities. Such secularism could both accommodate potentially conflicting and competing religious diversity, and allow for collective and individual religious rights which occupy both the private sphere and the public scene. It could also allow the state to intervene in religiously sanctioned discriminatory practices. The Kumari case indicates a blueprint as to how religious traditions can be analysed, questioned, reinterpreted, and yet also upheld by the judiciary as a response to the challenges of state secularization.

I suggest that this distinctive form of secularism could find more acceptance in Nepal 'by embodying the idea of respectful transformation of religions'. This would be in keeping with 'a venerable tradition of religious reformers, who tried to change their religions precisely because they meant so much to them' (Bhargava 2010: 91). As shown in the Kumari case, the notion that religious traditions must accept the challenge of modern times is widely accepted and allows for substantial reforms to take place without hurting the 'religious feelings of the people' that are recurrently invoked by fundamentalists.

The Kumari case seems to fit with Bhargava's model. It constitutes a precedent to qualify the principle that would separate the state from the religious sphere, authorizing 'interference' in an ancient and respected tradition in order to promote social reforms and compliance with constitutionally recognized human rights, and also affirming the state's duty to support religion.

The Supreme Court recognized the Kumari tradition as an integral part of Newar culture, and acknowledged the religious right of Newar community, asking representatives of that community to research whether reforms should be undertaken, and to advise the court accordingly.

This case does not blur the institutional limits of state and religion: both the court and the government have secular ends, and yet they are not simply establishing the primacy of human rights over religious tradition: they engage with religion to promote social reforms and human rights compliance. Moreover, this primacy does not involve a shrinking of religion's presence in the public sphere. The petition was filed not to abolish the tradition, but to ensure its survival, as it is considered valuable both for the Newar community and the 'social, cultural and religious life of the nation'. It ended in a rather peaceful acknowledgement by the community of the necessity of such reform.

The limits of this emerging secularism, however, have only just begun to be outlined and tested, and they will certainly be tested further if real inclusivity is implemented. The Kumari case deals with the Hindu-Buddhist religious traditions of the majority of the population, and is associated with national pride: court cases involving the relationships between religious minorities and the state will certainly modify and shape the notion further. The Kumari case has been debated among the high-caste Hindus who dominate the legal and political fields, but a truly inclusive policy which allowed a significant number of persons belonging to religious and ethnic minorities to occupy positions of authority at the Court and in the government would naturally lead to a more effective separation between Hinduism and the state.

Finally, the Kumari case did not extend to any consideration of whether the president's receiving a *tika* from the Kumari might amount to a failure to exercise his secular office, a situation that will be certainly questioned when a Muslim president celebrates the festival of Eid in his capacity as Head of State.

Conclusions

A Human being Deprived of Rights or Still a Sacred Source for Political Power?

Through the petition of Pun Devi, new agents such as lawyers and judges enter the Kumari tradition, a space previously managed by priests and devotees. The Kumari's religious power is partly reduced to 'tradition and cultural values', and the devotion and worship she receives is translated by the petitioner as a social problem to be examined and corrected on the basis of legal norms (she reads the Kumari *puja* as child labour). This leads to what Axel Michaels (2009) calls the 'politische Ohnmacht', or political impotence of the Kumari: under the scrutiny of the judges and the committees, she loses the power based on the belief that she is a goddess and that, as such, she is above all rules and norms.

In the legal language of the petition, the Kumari is transformed from a powerful goddess, legitimizing Nepalese kings, into a human child deprived of human rights. And this is what moved Pun Devi to file the case. In her words: 'I filed a case to protect her right, arguing that before being a Kumari she is a human being.' On the face of it, a stark contrast is being presented between medieval mysticism and modern rights-based rationalism. However, as with the claim of Pun Devi herself to belong to the community of worshippers of the Kumari, and the identification of particular cultural practices as being distinct from eternal religious verities, we are shown here a strong case of the South Asian penchant for versions of modernity that do not exclude the cosmological and religious genealogies of the past (see Bubandt and Van Beek 2011).

The source of legitimation of political power in present Nepal is not the Goddess's blessing but elections and democratic appointments based on constitutional provisions. In theory, there is no need for political leaders to take the Kumari's blessing, attend the worship of Gods (*pujas*), visit temples or pay their respects to Hindu *babas*. But just as in the past, religious events, religious leaders and religious institutions are being courted not only because they enjoy wide public trust and can exert a great deal of influence, but also because many politicians are religious – Maoists included. The symbolic appeal of the Kumari is such that, in the end, the judges fully recognized the Kumari's national importance as a legitimate, state-sponsored institution.

After the massacre of the royal family in 2001, King Gyanendra faced a serious popularity crisis, having been crowned just after the massacre and, at the same time, having being held responsible for it by many Nepalis. A key legitimating moment for Gyanendra came during the festival of Kumari Jatra, and the media underscored the powerful meeting of the 'new Kumari and the new king'.[25] Thus, Gyanendra followed the example of King Jaya Prakash Malla, who founded the Kumari Jatra in a critical time of his reign and Pritvi Narayan Shah, who marked the beginning of his dynasty with the *tika* of the Kumari.

Hausner (2007) and Gellner (2010) have shown how Gyanendra tried to rule as a Hindu king connecting with the Gods, and that his five-year reign (2002–2006) was a time when Hinduism was consciously promoted by the regime to gain legitimation. In 2007, citizens and the media were watching attentively whether and how King Gyanendra visited and was received by the Kumari, 'to assess whether the monarchy would be invested with ritual power' (Hausner 2007: 137). The space in front of the Kumari is still present and powerful, and cannot be left empty; as Nepali anthropologist Mukta Tamang once put it, 'it is important that the President go there, and does not leave the place to the king'.[26]

In the last two years, the former king participated in a considerable number of religious festivals, temple inaugurations, and fire sacrifices, while around him many supporters chanted slogans calling for the return of the monarchy. This has been taking place mostly in the South, where the Hindu right wing from both Nepal and India support him most. Anti-secular voices increased in the wake of a weakening of the constitution drafting process, and conservative forces became more active through religious and political action, asking that secularism and monarchy be put to a referendum.

The symbolic challenge that the king poses for the president appeared clearly in March 2010, when President Yadav and former king Gyanendra both visited Janaki Mandir in Janakpur for the celebration of Ram Nawami. To avoid a clash, the President's visit was hastily rescheduled. Only two hours apart, they entered the temple for the *puja*, and were treated pretty much in the same way: both covered by the same honorific parasol and accompanied by the temple's Mahanta.

That Kumaris are still dangerously able to mark the 'wrong forehead' and legitimate someone who was not supposed to be, seems to be suggested by a move on the part of the government in 2010, requesting the former king not to leave his residence to participate to a function celebrating ex-Kumaris in Basantapur. *The Nepali Times* reports that Gyanendra was forced to cancel his

---

25 Writes a (definitely pro-king) journalist in the Kathmandu Post: 'The people heaved a sigh of relief when the Kumari offered her blessing to the King without hesitating, indicating a prosperous future.' (…) 'Those who know the tradition believe that this annual meeting between the King and the Goddess will only consolidate the monarchical system in the country. They have the verdict: when the new Monarch meets the new Living Goddess, the country prospers' (Bishwakarma 2001).

26 This remark was made by Dr Tamang following his lecture Identity and Capability: the current debate on constitution making in Nepal, held at SOAS, London on 10 November 2010.

visit to the Kumari Ghar at the eleventh hour, apparently due to security reasons (*The Nepali Times* 2010).

The Nepali Times suggests that the government's move to prevent former king Gyanendra from attending this function shows that he is not a commoner just yet. I would say that it is the Kumari's symbolic and political importance that has not yet ended. The programme had been organized by the World Youth Hindu Federation (WYHF) and the event was an opportunity to associate Kumaris, Hindu religion and the monarchy, as made clear by welcome banners that read 'His Majesty King Gyanendra', with his portrait on either side of the function's gate.

It may be that the legitimizing role of the Kumari is only transitional, for a secular government that has yet to find its stability and is still waiting for a constitution; but even at the cost of becoming a child capable of being deprived of her rights, the child goddess remains a significant state-sponsored practice, acknowledged under the officially secular legal regime.

The analysis of this case and of the processes shaping secularism in Nepal supports the view that a model of secularity as a public space free from religious arguments, religious symbols and religious groups is unlikely to be implemented, and that Nepal is following its own alternative pathway to modernity, which involves building a 'post-secularism' through dialogue and debates of a pragmatic nature.

I see Nepal as a postsecular laboratory, where western notions of secularism and modernity are but one factor among many, and where the state's policy and the judiciary must walk a tightrope, upholding secular values and yet balancing the Hindu majority traditions and the claims of minorities for social, political *and* religious recognition.

References

Allen, M. 1976. Kumari or 'virgin' worship in Kathmandu valley. *Contributions to Indian Sociology*, 10/2, 293–316.

Allen, M. 1996. *The Cult of Kumari: Virgin Worship in Nepal*. Kathmandu: Mandala Book Point (1st ed. 1975 Kathmandu: INAS).

Anderson, M.M. 1971. *The Festivals of Nepal*. London: Allen and Unwin.

Asad, T. 1993. *Genealogies of Religion: Discipline and Reasons of Power in Christianity and Islam*. Baltimore, MD: Johns Hopkins University Press.

Asad, T. 2003. *Formations of the Secular: Christianity, Islam, Modernity*. Palo Alto, CA: Stanford University Press.

BBC 2010. Nepal 'goddess' inquiry ordered. Available at: http://news.bbc.co.uk/1/hi/world/south_asia/6105808.stm.

Bhargava, R. 1998. *Secularism and its Critics*. New Delhi: Oxford University Press.

Bhargava, R. 2010. *The Promise of India's Secular Democracy*. Delhi: Oxford University Press.

Bhattarai, A.M. 2010. *The Landmark Decisions of the Supreme Court, Nepal on Gender Justice.* Lalitpur: National Judicial Academy.

Biswakarma, K. 2001. When the new Monarch meets the new Living Goddess. *The Kathmandu Post*, 2 September.

Bubandt, N. and Van Beek, M. 2011. *Varieties of Secularism in Asia. Anthropological Explorations of Religion, Politics and the Spiritual.* New York: Routledge.

Cady, L.E. and Shakman Hurd, E. (eds) 2010. *Comparative Secularism in a Global Age.* New York: Palgrave Macmillan.

Calhoun, C., Juergensmeyer, M. and J. Van Antwerpen (eds) 2011. *Rethinking Secularism.* New York: Oxford University Press.

Cannell, F. 2010. Anthropology of secularism. *Annual Review of Anthropology*, 39, 85–100.

Casanova, J. 1994. *Public Religions in the Modern World.* Chicago and London: University of Chicago Press.

Casanova, J. 2009. 'Exploring the post-secular: Three meanings of "the secular" and their possible transcendence'. Paper presented at New York University, 22–24 October.

Casanova, J. 2010. 'Religion and globalization'. Paper presented at Max Planck Institute for the Study of Religious and Ethnic Diversity, Gottingen, 5 May.

Casanova, J. 2011a. The secular, secularizations, secularisms, in *Rethinking Secularism*, edited by C. Calhoun, M. Juergensmeyer and J. Van Antwerpen. New York: Oxford University Press, 54–91.

Casanova, J. 2011b. 'The return of religion to the public sphere: A global perspective'. Paper presented at Blackfriars, University of Oxford, 21 January.

CCD 2009. 'State and Religion'. Nepal Participatory Constitution Building Booklet Series N.1- Kathmandu: Centre for Constitutional Dialogue.

CEDAW. 2004. Report of the committee on the elimination of discrimination against women 30th/31st session. *General Assembly Official Records* A/59/38 par. 208–209. New York: United Nations. Available at: http://daccess-dds-ny.un.org/doc/UNDOC/GEN/N04/462/77/PDF/N0446277.pdf?OpenElement [accessed: 5 January 2011].

De Sales, A. 2003. The Kham Magar country: Between ethnic claims and Maoism, in *Resistance and the State: Nepalese Experiences*, edited by D.N. Gellner. Delhi: Social Science Press, 326–57.

Eisenstadt, S.N. 2000. Multiple modernities. *Daedalus*, 129(1), 1–29.

Gellner, D.N. 1992. *Monk, Householder, and Tantric Priest: Newar Buddhism and its Hierarchy of Ritual.* Cambridge: Cambridge University Press.

Gellner, D.N. 2001. Studying secularism, practising secularism. Anthropological imperatives. *Social Anthropology*, 9, 337–40.

Gellner, D.N. 2008. I. Whittaker *Living Goddess* (a film). *Himalaya*, 28(1–2), 89–91.

Gellner, D.N. 2010. 'What is left of Hinduism in the Federal Republic of Nepal?' Majewski Lecture, Oriental Institute, Oxford University, 15 November.

Gellner, D.N. 2011. Belonging, Indigeneity, Rights, and Rites: The Newar Case, in *The Politics of Belonging in the Himalayas: Local Attachments and Boundary Dynamics*, edited by J. Pfaff-Czarnecka and G. Toffin. Delhi: Sage, 45–76.

Göle, N. 2010. Manifestations of Religious-Secular divide, in *Comparative Secularism in a Global Age*, edited by L.E Cady and E. Shakman Hurd, 41–53. New York: Palgrave Macmillan.

Habermas, J. 2008. Notes on post-secular society. *New Perspectives Quarterly*, 25(4), 17–29.

Hasrat, B.J. 1970. *History of Nepal as Told by its Own and Contemporary Chroniclers*. Hosiarpur: Dev Datta Shastri.

Hausner, S. 2007. Pashupatinath at the end of the Hindu state. *Studies in Nepali History and Society*, 12(1), 119–40.

Jakobsen, J. and Pellegrini, A. 2008. *Secularisms*. Durham, NC: Duke University Press.

Kattel, S. 2010. Nepalma dharmanirapeksatako bahas [Debate on secularism in Nepal]. *SOCH*, 3(1), 2–4. Kathmandu: Society for Humanism.

Lecomte-Tilouine, M. 2006. 'Kill one, he becomes one hundred': Martyrdom as generative sacrifice in the Nepal People's War. *Social Analysis*, 50(1), 51–72.

Letizia, C. 2003. *La Dea Bambina. Il Culto della Kumari e la Regalità in Nepal*. Milano: FrancoAngeli.

Letizia, C. forthcoming. Shaping secularism in Nepal. *European Bulletin of Himalayan Research*, 39.

Leve, L. 2007. 'Secularism is a human right!' Double-binds of Buddhism, democracy, and identity in Nepal, in *The Practice of Human Rights: Tracking Law Between the Global and the Local*, edited by M. Goodale and S. Engle Merry. Cambridge: Cambridge University Press, 78–113.

Lienhard, S. 1978. Problèmes du syncrétisme religieux au Népal. *Bulletin de l'Ecole Française d'Extrême Orient*, 65(1), 239–70.

Madan, T.N. 1987. Secularism in its place. *The Journal of Asian Studies*, 46(4), 747–59.

Maharjan, P. 2005. *Nivedanapatra* [Petition]. Pundevī Maharjan vs. Govt. of Nepal, Office of Prime Minister and Council of Ministers et al., writ n. 3581, 23 Vaiśākha, 2062 BS (6 May 2005).

Maharjan, P. 2008. (2065 B.S.). Pun Devi Maharjan vs. Govt. of Nepal, Office of Prime Minister and Council of Ministers and Others. Nepal Kanun Patrika (NKP), 50 (6), 751–76.

Maharjan, P. 2009. (2065 B.S.). Jivit devi kumariharuko manavadhikar sthiti: Anusandhan prativedan [The situation of the human rights of living goddess Kumari: A research report] (2008), in *Kumari Sarboccama* [Kumari at the Supreme Court], edited by C. Vajracharya. Bauddha: Stela Tamang, 36–50.

Mahmood, S. 2009. Religious reason and secular affect: An incommensurable divide? *Critical Inquiry*, 35, 836–62.

Martin, D. 2005. *On Secularization: Towards a Revised Theory*. Aldershot, UK: Ashgate.

Michaels, A. 2009. Macht und Ohnmacht einer lebenden Göttin – Die Kumārī im politischen Wechsel Nepals, in *Handlung und Leidenschaft. Jenseits von actio und passio*, edited by K.P. Köpping, B. Schnepel and C. Wulf. Berlin: Akademie Verlag, 164–76.

Moaven, N. 1974. Enquête sur les Kumari. *Kailash – A Journal of Himalayan Studies*, 2, 167–87.

Molendijk, A., Beaumont, J. and Jedan, C. (eds) 2010. *Exploring the Postecular: The Religion, the Political and the Urban*. Leiden and Boston: Brill.

Mulmi, A.R. 2011. Nepali indutva. *Himal Southasian*. Available at: http://www.himalmag.com/component/content/article/4546-nepali-hindutva.html [accessed: 1 January 2012].

Ramirez, P. 1997. Pour une anthropologie religieuse du maoïsme népalais. *Archives de Sciences Sociales des Religions*, 99, 47–68.

Rosati, M. 2011. Review of Exploring the Postsecular. *Tijdschrift voor Economische en Sociale Geografie*, 102(2), 125–249.

Sharma, S. 2002. The Hindu state and the state of Hinduism, in *State of Nepal*, edited by M.D. Kanak and R. Shastri. Kathmandu: Himal Books, 22–38.

Shakya, R. and Berry, S. 2005. *From Goddess to Mortal: The True-Life Story of a Former Royal Kumari*. Kathmandu: Vajra Publications.

Slusser, M.S. 1982. *Nepal Mandala: A Cultural Study of the Kathmandu Valley*. Princeton: Princeton University Press.

Shrestha, J. 2009. Kathmandau Upatyakama Pracalit Kumari Pratha Visayaka ek Prativedan [a report on the current Kumari tradition in Kathmandu Valley], in *Kumari Sarboccama* [Kumari at the Supreme Court], edited by C. Vajracharya. Bauddha: Stela Tamang, 51–60.

The Nepali Times. 2010. 21 September, available at: http://www.nepalitimes.com/blogs/thebrief/2010/09/21/impious/ [accessed: 13 December 2010].

Toffin, G. 1993. *Le Palais et le Temple: La Fonction Royale dans la Vallée du Népal*. Paris: CNRS Editions.

Upreti, M. 2006. Report of Center for Reproductive Rights, 28 October, in the Nepal Supreme Court file records for Writ Petition n. 3581 (quoted in Maharjan 2005).

Vajracharya, C. 2009. *Kumari Sarboccama* [Kumari at the Supreme Court] Bauddha: Stela Tamang.

Chapter 7

Big Man of the Big God: Nigeria as a Laboratory for Multiple Modernities

Enzo Pace

Introduction

The theoretical paradigm of multiple modernities was put forward by Shmuel Eisenstadt (2000; Sachsenmaier, Riedel, Eisenstadt 2002) as an alternative to classical modernization theory, according to which the western program of modernity was the only possible pattern of modernization to be adopted in all societies.[1] One crucial element of the classical 'only-one-pattern-of-modernity' theory was the structural differentiation between the political and the religious spheres. From a multiple modernities perspective, this structural differentiation loses its central importance. When we look at what is happening outside the west, we find many examples that suggest that the process of modernization of state and society is not only compatible with the persistence of religious attitudes and behaviours of people, but actually needs religion in order to morally support the rapid social change that the program of modernity usually provokes. As a result, since Eisenstadt's seminal works first appeared, the idea of multiple modernities has spread rapidly across the social sciences to explain patterns of modernization and secularization in non-western contexts. Many scholars have focused on China, India, South Korea, and Latin America (particularly on those countries with an upsurge of Neo-Pentecostalism). Less attention has been paid, however, to sub-Saharan Africa, perhaps because of recurrent stereotypes we have cultivated in the west. Public opinion tends to consider this continental area undeveloped, dominated by corrupted dictatorships, torn by violent inter-ethnic and religious conflicts, devastated by famines, epidemics, infant mortality and so on. All these representations are partially true, but in spite of these phenomena, over the past ten years Black Africa has seen a process of economic growth and modernization. Nigeria provides a good example of this process. The rapid social change occurring

---

1   The title has been drawn from a paragraph of a book by Ogbu Kalu, African Pentecostalism (2008), a seminal work that has helped me to understand the phenomenon of the Pentecostalism in Africa outside Eurocentric stereotypes. Kalu was a prominent scholar on Pentecostalism at the McCormick Theological Seminar in Chicago (USA). He passed away in 2009 (he was born in Ohafia, Nigeria, in 1942), and his scientific contribution is still alive. I would like to pay homage to him with this chapter.

in this big African country depends not only on structural factors, mostly linked to the exploitation of the *black gold*, the oil resources located in the Niger Delta in the South East, but also on the role played by religion.

My aim in this chapter is to analyse the function of religion in the process of modernization in Nigeria, on the basis of an ongoing research project with my colleague Annalisa Butticci that focuses on the structures and dynamics of pastoral leadership in Pentecostal and Charismatic African churches in Ghana, Nigeria, and in the Italian Diaspora (Pace and Butticci 2010). This study addresses the centrality of leadership formation and its circulation from African points of origin to missionary destinations, to Europe, and back to Africa. It enquires into the different narratives and discourses shaped by post-colonial African contexts and the neo-colonial migrations of the African Diasporas that informed visions of Pentecostal leadership. The project deals with the effectiveness of pastoral leadership and its impact on the popularity and spread of Pentecostal and Charismatic churches, as well as launching inquiries into the organizational structures of their religious communities (cf. Pace and Butticci 2010). This is a relatively new phenomenon, which represents not only the emergence of a new type of Christianity all over the world (Jenkins 2002), but also an open-air social laboratory to grasp the reconfiguration of the relation between modernity and religion. In short, we are facing a Christianity of the Third Generation (CTG). Building on the findings of the research, this chapter argues that Nigeria's laboratory represents a case study for analysing the resurgent *power of religious imagination* and its coherence with the values, lifestyles, and socio-economic mobility of individuals in a modern post-colonial society.

The focus on pastoral leadership stems from the insight that the growth and wealth of the Pentecostal movements in Africa and in the African Diasporas owe a great deal to the peculiar charisma of Pentecostal pastors. The question is how religious leaders create and communicate new symbolic universes with which their congregations engage diverse religious, economic, social and political contexts. Their power of communicating the gospel and their ability to translate and transform social, economic and political uncertainty into moral, social, and spiritual action are two of the main aspects that define their charisma. Their lives and experiences of multiple belongings, cross-cultural experiences, and cross-religious trajectories are emblematic of the worldwide Pentecostal movements within which they work. In this sense, the churches they are leading are structurally not only a transnational organization but also market-oriented in socio-religious terms (Corten and Marshall-Fratani 2001, Freston 2004, Währisch-Oblau 2008). This means that, in many cases, religion is a source for creating an *authorized language* useful both for ritual and social action in a free market of denominations and various non-Christian traditions (Islam, traditional cults, Hinduism and Buddhism). In Nigeria, like in other African societies (Ghana, Uganda, Kenya, South Africa, Ivory Coast and so on), the Christianity of Third Generation represents a way of being modern, of accepting the values of the liberal economy without cutting off the religious roots that shape the collective consciousness.

In this sense, the Christian framework is deeply intertwined with the deep roots represented by so-called traditional religions (cults of spirits and deliverance from the evil) (Bediako 1992, Kalu 2008).

The theoretical assumption recognizes religions as means of communication (Pace 2011) and sites whereby stored collective memories are mobilized into social actions by the transfer of energies accumulated in liturgy. By doing so, the pastors make their spiritual and charismatic gifts available to their congregations as they create social networks and universal communities, a *bolding* social capital, in Putnam's (2001) terms, that stimulates social mobility and the culture of entrepreneurship. I focus precisely on *religious leaders as entrepreneurs* in a free religious market. In the literature this corresponds to what Kalu (2008) defines as "Big Men of the Big God" who made – and still make – the history of African Pentecostalism both in Nigeria and in the European Diasporas. Names like Adeboye, Ashimolowo, Adelaja and Olukoya have been the subject of several studies, and national and international magazines write about their power and influence in African and European societies. Additionally, most of these studies focus on the new configuration of the sacred space. The leaders founded mega-churches, inventing a new repertoire of ritual actions. This fact provides a rationale for further research on religion as communication, including the organization of the sacred space, as well as the semiotics of the sacred within the urban space.

The combination of the entrepreneurship profile of the religious pastors of the Pentecostal and Charismatic churches in Nigeria along with the construction of big spaces for prayer and deliverance converge in the argument I would like to present, namely that multiple modernities in Nigeria means, on one hand, the invention of a *competitive Christianity*, more coherent with the social expectations of many people of becoming modern *via* religion, and, on the other, the process of *de-localization and mobility* of belonging.

After a short presentation of the socio-demographics features of Nigeria, and brief sketch of the evolution of Christianity in the country, with a particular focus on the post-colonial era, I discuss the typology of religious leadership that emerges in the Pentecostal environment and its social impact on the process of modernization as defined above.

Nigeria: Socio-demographic Aspects and Religious Geography

Nigeria is a federal republic that gathers 36 States (see Figure 7.1). The story of this very big country has been shaped by British colonialism. In 1886 the United Kingdom inaugurated its rule in the region by creating the Royal Niger Company. It was the first step towards a protectorate in 1902, and then to an exploitation colony in 1914. The Nigerian people gained their independence in 1960. Since 1966 the political conflicts between the various leaders, representative of the dominant ethnic groups, were at the root of a recurrence of state and military coups (in 1966, twice in a short period; in 1970, just after the end of the civil war against the secession of the Igbo movement which proclaimed the independence of the Republic of Biafra in the South; and in 1983 when a military regime seized power until 1989). The fuel of these conflicts was, not only in metaphoric sense, the oil boom in the 1970s, when oil companies started to exploit the black gold in the area of the Niger Delta. The heritage of the British colonization was one important source of the conflicts, because under British rule the southern part of Nigeria (both the Yoruba land in the west and the Igbo land in the south-east) started to develop more rapidly than the Hausa- and Fulani-dominated north.

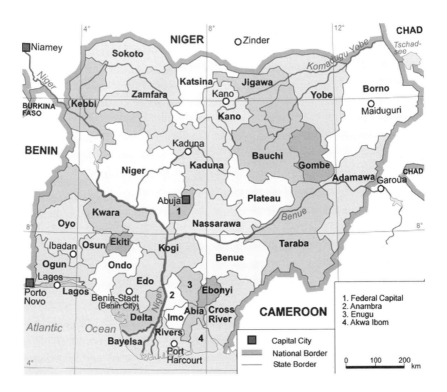

Figure 7.1   The Federation of Nigeria with its 36 States

Source: http://commons.wikimedia.org/wiki/File:Nigeria_political.png. Permission is granted to copy, distribute and/or modify this document under the terms of the GNU Free Documentation License, Version 1.2 or any later version published by the Free Software Foundation.

A big country indeed, with a land area of 923,768 square kilometres and 162 million inhabitants (180.7 per square kilometre). The majority of the population is rural (52 per cent), and in 2011 GDP reached $2,589 per capita. It is also a mosaic of cultural and linguistic groups (250), but the most prevalent are the so-called

Big Three: Hausa-Fulani in the north, Yoruba in the south-west, and Igbo in the
south-east. Abuja, the Federal capital (population 1.3 million), is in the middle of
the country, a sort of truce area between the Muslim Hausa-Fulani part in the north
and the Christian Yoruba-Igbo part in the south. Actually it is an artificial division,
because in the past there was a migration from the south to the north of many Igbo
people, and in the most important northern cities, like Kano, Katsina, and more
recently Jos, the coexistence of the Igbo (called non-natives by the native Hausa)
with Hausa and Fulani has been deteriorating. Religious difference sometimes
hides political and economic conflicts, particularly concerning the battle for the
land (Pase 2011). The most crowded area is Lagos with 15.6 million people.

In the midlands, the ratio between Muslim and Christian is more balanced
than in the other part of the country. The official figures concerning the religious
differentiation of the Nigerian people are as follows:

Table 7.1   Religions in Nigeria

Muslims	Christians		Traditional religions
50.5%	Protestants	15.0%	**1.3%**
	Catholics	13.6%	
	New Pentecostals	19.6%	
	Total	**48.2%**	

In spite the apparent irrelevance of traditional religions, the ancient cults of the
spirits persist. According to the Nigerian theologian, Bolaji Idowu:

> It was a serious mistake that the Church took no account of the indigenous beliefs
> and customs of Africa when she began her work of evangelization. It is now
> obvious that by a misguided purpose, a completely new God who had nothing to
> do with the past of Africa was introduced to her peoples. Thus there was no proper
> foundation laid for the Gospel message in the hearts of people and no bridge built
> between the old and the new; the Church has in consequence been speaking to
> Africans in strange tongues because there was no adequate communication, In
> consequence, the Church has on her hands communities of believers who, by and
> large, live ambivalent spiritual lives. (Bolaji Idowu 1973: 427)

While both Catholic and Protestant Churches have been relatively unable to
understand the religious memory of the Africans, African Pentecostalism (in its
various manifestations) seems a system of belief that is able to grasp the universe
of religious meanings of the people. In this sense, Kalu is right when he writes:

> The Pentecostal experience broke out without missionaries or any foreigners
> and often to the consternation of missionaries who deployed the colonial

government's clout to contain the flares … African Pentecostalism did not originate from Azusa street (*the mythical place in Los Angeles where the narrative of the Pentecostal movement traditionally starts: remark by the author*) and is not an extension of the American electronic church. (Kalu 2008: viii)

Roughly speaking, Pentecostalism seems to me a way by which Africans are trying to reformulate their Christian experience using the symbolic resources of their respective indigenous cultures. It is therefore important to pay attention to the three waves of the spread of Christianity in Nigeria and other African countries, from the first evangelization up to now. Figure 7.2 sums up this process.

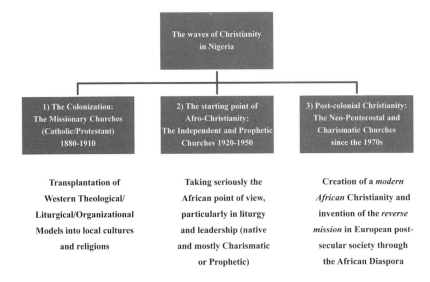

Figure 7.2   The waves of Christianity in Nigeria

The third wave started in the 1970s, and because of its intrinsic mobility, changed in the following decades, and perhaps in every generation. The sharp transformation within the Pentecostal movement occurred in the 1980s, when a new kind of leadership arose: pastors who are able to "perform as movie stars and virtuoso healers" (Kalu 2008: xii).

Pentecostalism thus indeed became a label that covers a variety of *religious imagination and invention*, using media language to enter the popular culture, abandoning the rhetoric on poverty, mercy, humility and asceticism, and preferring to recast the story of the Gospel as liberation theology, empowerment for social and economic success, hope, prosperity and so on. Those who are able to incorporate in their performance the popular culture, rooted in the traditional religions, the promise of spiritual liberation and social promotion, and the language of the media that transforms a rite in a theatrical performance, emphasizing extraordinary personal gifts in the big auditorium or city of prayer, become suddenly new religious leaders. They differ from either Catholic priests or Protestant pastors, but also form the prophetic figures which animated the Independent Churches in the second wave. Gifford (2004: 23–4) notes that in many African societies people are aware of the "paradigm shift": everyone knows where the prayer centres are, their all-night services, their crusades, conventions and Bible schools, the new mega-churches, the posters that advertise the deliverance sessions, and above all everyone knows the new religious superstars. As a rule, scholars tend to label this phenomenon Pentecostalism, but I am conscious that it is insufficient to grasp the socio-religious dynamic occurring in the area. Omenyo (2002) is right when he notes that we are facing a Pentecost outside Pentecostalism. Therefore in order to explore to what extent this new kind of religious leaders and their new kind of churches represent a good example to test the concept of multiple modernities, below I focus on the leadership profiles.

Pop-religion and Pentecostal leadership

According to Ojo (2006), a religious leader is one who occupies a leading position and is involved in directing humans and materials towards the achievement of goals set either by the religious groups or the leader himself. A combination of personality traits and the activities performed by religious leaders are important in any consideration of religious leadership. Charisma may be responsible for the founding of the religious group, but entrepreneurial skills are needed to keep things going.

These leaders, described as "creative visionaries" (Miller and Yamanori 2007), which I prefer to define as "virtuosi of improvisation" (Pace 2011), are the products of the social contexts in which operate. Their charisma is socially grounded in both their origin and Diaspora contexts. Elsewhere, I have depicted these men and women as extraordinary religious leaders with a mobile personality able to move and change the symbolic boundaries of the believing system, inventing a new means of communication that, on one hand, mobilizes the symbolic resources – pre-existent in the system and in its relation with the socio-religious environment – and, on the other, transforms the available and received patterns of symbols into a new moral shape. They also offer new definitions of social identity to a people which perceives its identity to be at risk.

The Pentecostal movement both in the African Continent and in the Diaspora owe a great deal to the diverse leadership of these pastors. In Nigeria, Ojo (2006) has discussed how Pentecostal churches have launched movements to combat the postcolonial stasis. In Ojo's words:

> Pentecostal and Charismatic movements developed within a milieu of political instability, economic recession and social tension. In the midst of these uncertainties and deteriorating living conditions many Nigerians turned to the religious sphere to find answers to their problems. Such an ever-present reality of the supernatural is central to the world-view of Africans. Therefore, the successes of the movements rest on their ability to the felt needs of millions of Nigerians. Certainly, the discourse of change and solution provided much relevance against the failure of the centralized state. (Ojo, 2005: 235)

Ojo argued also that the charisma of the Pentecostal pastors is closely associated with the power of the spoken word, and these religious leaders are often accepted as the custodians of the divine spoken word. They offer a specific location to structure individual expressions (feeling, emotions, and the utopia of "a new world is possible") of the sacred into a relatively friendly chain of communication that it seems a reliable means of recognizing, and steering divine intervention in the everyday life. Many of these leaders are conscious of their connections to the global world as part of the indices of their success.

They have often travelled to the western world, often invite western Pentecostal leaders to preach at the programme, and occasionally maintain residential apartments in the west (Ojo 2006). They engage in intensive *religious transactions* across national borders and international networks. The transactions in the circular trade between Africa, America and Europe are informed by specific forms of reciprocity of exchange as well as gift-economy that include interchanging of spiritual gifts, salvation goods, economic and social resources, people, and ideas.

In our previous study on Nigerian and Ghanaian Pentecostal churches in Italy (Pace and Butticci 2010), we described how for most of the women and men pastors, the leadership experience starts within the existing religious communities. In the Diaspora these women and men find themselves involved in a new spiritual life that turn them into "born again" Christians and eventually pastors. Their life stories are marked by an articulated narrative of migration, inter-cultural and inter-religious relations and by an extraordinary art of crossing social, religious, cultural, and national borders. Their familiarity with crossing borders is traceable to their multi-religious families, their multi-ethnic social relationships, their crossing trajectories of class and status both in their origin and destination society, and their creation of transnational religious spaces. They find themselves, on one hand, in a condition that empowers them to act as leaders and exercises power on people who belong to different classes, status, and ethnic groups, while on the other they experience daily racism, economic, social, and religious marginalization.

One of the most remarkable features of the Nigerian and Ghanaian Pentecostal and Charismatic Diaspora in Italy is the increasing number of women pastors. These women pastors are often a novelty in the context of Italian society. One of the most remarkable anomalies about these female pastors is their religious leadership in a Catholic country such as Italy, where women are not allowed to have any role as priests or religious leaders. They have to confront the widespread racist stereotypes of black women and discrimination both by officialdom and in matters of church leadership. These women pastors challenge and provide dissonant lifestyles that transcend the traditional roles they are ascribed as domestic workers, street sellers, migrants, mothers, and wives. As Lawless (1988: 73) notes: "What a better example, then, of the woman re-scripting her life and refusing to accept the stance of female as muted than the woman preacher?"

In Nigeria, although women predominate numerically, men dominate the leadership of Pentecostal and Charismatic organizations. Leadership in the areas of preaching, counselling, and giving administrative direction is almost the exclusive right of men. Whenever women are given leadership opportunities, they are usually in such undefined areas as "leaders of choruses", "directors of nurseries", "director of welfare departments", "women fellowship", and so on. However, a few exceptions (Hachett 1990, 1993, Olajubu 2004, Shootill 2008, Bateye 2009) have illuminated the interactions between charismatic Christianity and gender, as well as the leadership roles of female pastors and pastors' wives. In this sense, Pentecostalism is a sort of cultural battlefield for equality between women and men: what is happening under the sacred canopy of many Pentecostal churches is an anticipation of the process of modernization of gender relations.

Another important element involved in the process of modernization *via* Pentecostalism relates to younger generation. Pentecostalism appears as a proxy-language at the intersection of generational units living in the information society and the transformation of the social environment: the third wave enhances the Nigerian younger generation (particularly those who are well educated, brought up on university campuses) to develop the ethics of success and entrepreneurship *via religion.*

Focusing on the exercise of leadership and charismatic power by pastors, one the most important aspect I would like to highlight is precisely their strategy to empower communities and groups as well people's responses and reaction to their charisma, promoting:

a. social mobility of younger generation;
b. re-orientation in equality of gender relations;
c. religion as a *brand* in a higher differentiated market of salvation goods.

One of the main features of the charisma of the new Christian leaders is their appropriation of religious emotional power. Their ability to lead regimes of the emotions is an incredible source of power for these charismatic pastors. They regularly gather large followings in their public religious outings – crusades, anointing services, breakthrough seminars, healing services, Holy Ghost nights/ festivals, special women deliverance sessions, etc. – through their perceived faith healing powers.

The liturgical space – in Durkheimian terms – works as *le fait social*, the social dimension of the sacred performance in which the actors are able to create a new *social images of themselves*. In the sacred space, the leaders often present themselves as successful entrepreneurs, offering themselves a model to be followed. Their lifestyle and their material world define their public images. Their creative attempt to construct their own style is shaping a new "aesthetic of African Pentecostal Pastors" made by a perfect synthesis of spirituality and public culture (Meyer 2007, 2010).

From this point of view I will try to reconstruct four ideal-types of leadership among the variety of pastors I have met during my field research in Nigeria (see Figure 7.3)

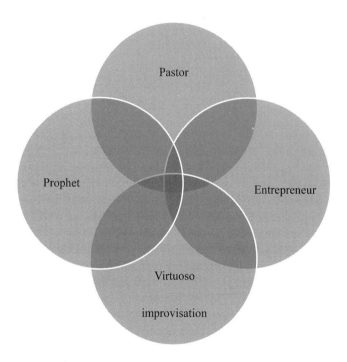

Figure 7.3   The multiple creativity of the charismatic profile of leadership

The typology depends on two symbolic axes of the religious discourse which arose in various Pentecostal churches. The first originates from the centrality of the Bible. It measures the distance of the new leadership from the Protestant roots. The more relevant the Bible in the rite and in everyday life, the closer the community to the Protestant tradition. The less relevant, the more we are facing a post-Protestant experience: the Bible is only a pre-text (not a sacred text) for the exercise of the power of communication by a new Charismatic leadership. This axis is symbolically vertical: the transcendental foundation of the (human) power of communication.

The horizontal axis concerns the feeling of belonging to a community, the socio-religious solidarity that the ethic of Christian brotherhood feeds as a rule. The individuals' behaviours oscillate between two opposite poles: at one end, they tend to take part in religious services without any personal engagement to the internal life of the church, at the other are those who feel themselves to be not only members but also missionaries of the new church. At the first pole, the individualization of religious choice prevails, at the second, solidarity is the predominant ethical perspective that make sense of the social action. In the middle, of course, there is a variety of religious supply-sides (by churches or faith healers) that offers a mixed combination of individualization of believing along with a soft strategy of involving people in moral issues.

Through the intersection of the two symbolic axes, we can ideally mark the boundaries of four type of leadership that emerge in the Nigerian socio-religious laboratory. As Kalu notes in general for the African continent, but it is true particularly for countries like Nigeria

> ... the explosive growth of African Pentecostalism intensified in 1990s through a vigorous evangelization program and thereby created a very complex environment ... but what about the aftermath of growth? Growth can be traumatic. One example of this growth is its impact on ministerial formation as the movement sought to mobilize the personnel to match its passion for evangelization ... Elijah's Mantle became a dominant imagery; the altars of the Old Testament legitimized the formation of new churches and ministries under new leadership that had not tasted formal theological training. The models of ministerial formation became scrambled ... The emphasis on the leadership of the Holy Spirit created conditions in which people could declare the Spirit called and gave them vision. No one could query the authenticity. (Kalu 2008: 123–4)

It is necessary to keep in mind the level of the abstraction of each type, but in the Nigerian case, the four boxes depicting the different elements that characterize the four Pentecostal leadership represent a good approximation to the real context we have observed in our field research. Just to give an example, arriving in Kano, a capital of the Hausa-land in the north, a big city of about five million inhabitants, including the metropolitan area, one realizes that even though the majority of the population are Muslims, since 1990 there has been a proliferation of new Pentecostal churches. Many are concentrated in an urban area called the *foreigners' city* (*sabon gari* in Hausa language), close to the Old City where the Mosque, the Palace of the Emir and a big market are located. The name means that the residents are considered not indigenous to Hausa land. They are formally Nigerian citizens, but do not enjoy the same rights as Hausa citizens. Historically in the northern part of Nigeria, this discriminatory attitude toward non-Hausa people has originated from the question of land ownership (Pase 2011), reinforced by the Muslim emirs and sultan in the nineteenth century, and not really opposed by the British rule. The construction of the railway under the British Protectorate in the 1920s attracted many workers from the south, particularly from Yoruba and Igbo lands. Many of them became resident in Kano, and a large majority are Christian, members of various denominations, mostly Pentecostal. Within five minutes' walking distance, around the Sabon Gari market of Kano, there are a huge number of churches with sometimes incredible names (like the Locust Army of Jesus Christ), and within five minutes' driving distance there are eighteen different churches. Pentecostal effervescence means in this case a missionary fervour reinforced by the liturgical creativity that brings the impact of the gospel into the everyday life of the people, transforming the urban segregation into a citadel of faith where people, in spite the various religious belonging, are free and proud to be Christian in a city dominated by Hausa Muslims – a sort of micro and multi-Christian Jerusalem on the hill. With the introduction of Shari'a in 2000 in many northern states of Nigeria, including Kano, riots and clashes between groups of Muslims and Christians increased. Sometimes religion hides political and economic conflicts, particularly concerning the exercise of rights over real estate by the so-called non indigenous population.

That is the situation in Kano and in other cities in the northern part of Nigeria (from Kaduna to Jos). However the proliferation of churches we have depicted concerns the whole Nigerian society.

In Table 7.2, below, I have summed up the four types of leadership; my intention is to show the consistency of each type to *modernity*. The definition I suggest to manage this complex notion – modernity – is based on two assumptions: *individualization of believing* (Tschannen 1992) and *deterritorialization* (Deleuze and Guattari 1972) *of belonging* (the disconnection of ties between religious practices, culture and space).

Table 7.2   The four types of Pentecostal leadership

Type of leadership	Bible	Community	Religious context
Pastor	Centrality	Strong belonging	*Closer to Protestant Tradition*
Prophet	Centrality	Strong belonging	*Inventing new church*
Virtuoso	Less centrality	Individualization and weaker belonging	*New church in old skins*
Entrepreneur	Quite absent	Individualization, no compulsion to belong	*Promotion of salvation goods*

While the figure of the Pastor (closer to the Protestant tradition) cares that the people should be familiar with the sacred text and thus shapes the liturgical action according to the centrality of the sacred word that creates a spiritual and cognitive communality among the believers (the born-again Christian), the Virtuoso and the Entrepreneur tend to finalize their liturgical performance to show the presence of the extraordinary power of the Spirit during the service. In the Virtuoso of improvisation – who reinvents rituals of the traditional religions, disguising them under the Christian symbols – the Bible is often only a pre-text for another text: deliverance from the evil, representing dramaturgically the spiritual warfare between Jesus and the Devil. The Virtuoso exercises charisma in exorcising those who are possessed by evil spirits, being a faith healer who is interested in demonstrating his/her extraordinary gift on some individuals in front an astonished mass of believers who fill a big auditorium or a city prayer.

The difference between this kind of leadership and the Entrepreneur is precisely the role of the audience during the liturgical performance. In the former – the Virtuoso – apart from the miracles and faith healing performed by the leader, there is more chance and time for those present to participate by singing and dancing, hearing the sermon or hanging on every word of the leader – shouted very often at the top of his/her voice – and so on. In the latter – the Entrepreneur – however, there is only a "one man show", and those present are the choreography of an exhibition of the extraordinary personal gifts of the leader.

Each ideal-type tends to come up with a peculiar organization model, a spiritual/moral message, a redefinition of the gender and generation relations, an ethics of work and family life. The impact on the social environment depends precisely on the combination of vertical/horizontal dimensions: the greater the communitarian involvement of members, nourished by an intensive biblical education/study, the stronger the creation of *bolding* (social) capital in an urban district, that can be mobilized at local, national and transnational levels. In contrast, in the case of entrepreneurship, the attitudes of people are closer to the Putnam's idea of "bowling alone": in this case the supply-side indeed plays a crucial role in mobilizing "religious clients" looking for a *good promoter of salvation goods*.

To sum up, we are facing a modern morphology of the sacred in an urban environment (particularly in the mega-city), and one of the most dynamic factors that promote the change of the urban landscape is the merging of the two new kinds of Pentecostal leadership.

In order to illustrate better the crucial differences between this new kind of leadership and the previous one (Pastor and Prophet), let me provide some examples. In the case of the prophetic profile, many scholars have pointed out the relevance of the prophetic movement, which anticipates some elements of modern Pentecostalism in Africa. Roughly speaking, we can frame the figure of the Prophet in Africa according to the classic Weberian notion of charisma: on one hand, he/she opposed indigenous gods and traditional rites of exorcism and on the other, criticized the missionary methods used by Catholic and Protestant churches, particularly when both tried to replace the indigenous culture with another (Euro-

Christianity) without any efforts to understand the mentality of the people. The worldview of the indigenous people was removed, ignored, and in many cases dismantled by the missionaries: the local gods became idols on the periphery of the cognitive maps of the people. Recognizing the dignity of the pre-Christian point of view, the African prophets tried to confront the Bible message, particularly those parts of the sacred text that emphasize the power of the Spirit (Mary 2000, 2005, 2008, Mary and Laurent 2001, Lanternari 2003).

Such is the case of William Wade Harris (1865–1920), who first led a religious movement openly against French colonial rule in Liberia and Ivory Coast, and then a new church, after his imprisonment by the French army, which persecuted him because of his liberation message for the oppressed, particularly among those who bore the traces of slavery and human trafficking in their memory. He was student at a Methodist school in Cape Palmas (Liberia). Liberia was a land where since 1822, encouraged by a philanthropic American society, many Afro-Americans had returned *home*, escaping from the last remnants of slavery in the USA, hence the name. Arriving in Liberia, they suddenly realized that the promised land was under the rule of a new *white boss*, the French and British colonies. Against the European domination, Harris led a social protest, and because of his opposition to French rule in the region, he was imprisoned. In jail he claimed he experienced a vision of the Archangel Gabriel, who announced to him that he had been appointed as prophet by God to prepare the way for Christ as saviour of the African people. Released after two years, he started, as itinerant preacher, to convert people from Liberia to Ivory Coast up to the Gold Coast (Ghana), promoting a Christian revival out of the historical churches, particularly the Catholic church, which was (and is up to now) the dominant one in the region. Because of recurrent persecutions, he appointed twelve apostles in 1915. After the death of the prophet, they were able to establish a new denomination in Ivory Coast and the Gold Coast. At the same time, other prophets, following the example of Harris, exported his church model all over Africa. Changing the content, many of them adopted prophetic status to cope with both colonial domination and the *white Christianity* associated with it. The most notable figures include Simon Kimbangu (1889–1951) who created the Kimbanguist church (very popular until today in Zaire) (Desroche 1969, Martin 1975, Asch 1983, Mokoko Gampiot 2004), and Garrick Sokari Daketima Braide (1885–1918) who was active in the Niger Delta, transplanting the Kalabari traditional religions into Christian prophetic message (Tasie 1978, Wariboko 2010).

Though most of the prophetic leaders lived in the last century, this does not mean that these figures have disappeared from contemporary African society. From July to December 2006, for instance, Nigerian newspapers reported the story of Emeka Ezeogu, 'King' of the Christian Praying Assembly based in Lagos, who convinced some members to set fire to themselves so as to attain paradise. He was arrested, sentenced to death and hung after a lengthy trial (Ojo 2005). He undoubtedly exercised a charismatic power over the members; he was a visionary prophet who restored some voodoo rituals within a Christian frame.

All these prophets were more or less critical of the first attempt made in Africa by Protestants to create independent churches, therefore caricaturized as "white garment churches" or *mademoni* (Kalu 2008: 64), like *Aladura* (literally "praying people", in Yoruba land in Nigeria) or *Zionists* (particularly in South Africa) or *Abaroho* (in East Africa) (Peel 1968, Anderson 2000, Asamoha-Gyadu 2005). As Kalu notes:

> A wave of African indigenous churches arose all over Africa at the different time before the First World War and especially during the influenza epidemic of 1918 ... The earliest or classical churches emerged from mainline churches by recovering the pneumatic resources of the translated Bible ... Soon differences among various groups appeared, based on the dosage of traditional religion in the mix: some messianic leaders claimed to be one or the other of the Trinity; the revivalistic promoted the ideological significance of indigenous religion by privileging the resonance with Christian symbols; the vitalistic tapped the occult powers; and the nativistic were virtually indigenous cults operating with Christian symbols and paraphernalia. Thus many forms operated beyond the pale of Christianity. (Kalu 2008: 30)

Sometimes, Puritanism and evangelical fundamentalism occurred within the boundaries of mainstream denominations, and in some new independent churches. Through these two theological positions some independent churches leaders clearly rejected traditional and cultural ingredients that have been used in others new denominations without any censorship.

The turning point for the emergence of a new type of leadership is customarily fixed around the 1980–1990s. Van Dijk, a prominent scholar of neo-Pentecostalism in Africa, has pointed out that:

> During the early 1970s the populace of some of the townships of Malawi's largest city, Blantrye, witnessed the emergence of a new religious phenomenon. Young boys and girls, referring to themselves as *aliliki*, preachers, began to attract crowds by conducting large revival meeting. These young people, some of them still in their teens, travelled from one place to another, and in fire and brimstone sermons strongly denounced the sinfulness and evil of everyday urban life. (Van Dijk, 1992: 55)

This new stratum of the younger generation, mostly undergraduates and graduates of the most important universities, from middle and upper classes, sometimes stimulated by professors who opened a new church just within the campus, indeed represents one of the sharpest sociological indicators of the modernization process *via religion* that is occurring in many African countries, from Nigeria to Burkina Faso, from Benin to Congo, as Corten and Marshall-Fratani (2001) have documented.

In Nigeria, in particular, almost all the founders of new Pentecostal and Charismatic churches are young, acting as promoters of salvation goods, specializing in modern techniques in performing the *power of the spoken word:*

> The sermons they preach, the instructions they give to the associates, the revelations they claim to receive are manifestations of that charisma. Moreover, these religious leaders regularly gather large followers in many of their public religious outings – crusades, anointing services, breakthrough seminars, healing services, Holy Ghost nights/festivals, etc. through their perceived miraculous powers Also associated with the charisma is their personality as successful managers of their organizations. The Nigerian religious leaders often present themselves as successful entrepreneurs and are conscious of various marketing techniques they use to keep their organizations going. Many of these leaders are conscious of their connections into the global world as part of the indices of their successes. They often travelled to the Western world, often invite Western Pentecostal leaders to preach at the programmes, and occasionally maintain residential apartments in the West. Charisma may be responsible for the founding of the religious group, but entrepreneurial skills are needed to keep things going. (Ojo 2006)

Every Sunday morning, in the city of Ile-Ifé, in the university campus of Obafemi Awolovo (a prominent political leader who died in 1987, who contributed to modernizing the Nigerian State after the independence), a huge number of people convene. They are undergraduates; they are not coming for the classes, as the university is officially closed; rather, they are coming to attend a religious service organized by various denominations, mostly Pentecostal. Every open public space is occupied by the *flock* of believers, which are called to perform a collective rite shaped by sacred symbols and, at the same time, by a spectacle not very far from the talk-shows they can see on TV. In the same public space this younger generation exhibit a vibrant passion for the sacred, representing publically a modern style to believing and belonging. "Our mass is more funny", a young boy told me when I asked the difference between the rite he was participating in and the service occurring in another corner of the campus very close to us. The idea of religion as empowerment and communication materialized in front of me. And it was reinforced when I attended a religious service of the church *Sanctuary of Hope*, inaugurated by a professor of Biology and Medicine of Ile-Ifé University in 1997. After the rite I talked with him, and he told me his story, which started with the creation of the Spokesman Communication Service 10 years before opening the church:

> ... the Spokesman Communication Ministries came as a result of direct revelations ... This was supported by several words of prophecy. God revealed to me that I has been called, 'to communicate truth and bring hope to this generation with aim of healing the desolate of this generation' ... It is worthy

to note here, that at that stage of the ministry the thought was that the ministry would only be evangelical and taking the word from place to place. The house fellowship was to remain a house fellowship while members will remain as members of their local churches. I was actually antagonistic to founding a church but members of the ministry mounted pressure. Despite the pressure, I felt God has not called me to start a church. One Sunday morning in Bristol, I saw a vision. In that vision, I was in Oduduwa hall Obafemi Awolowo University, Ile-Ifé. With the hall packed full and God said, 'This is your church', after that I dismissed the vision. I was later invited to worship at the new covenant church by a friend. I later joined the church and became a regular member of the church, giving messages regularly and handling bible studies. After about two years the Lord said to him, 'I have called you to establish a church what are you doing?' (interview conducted by the author in Ile-Ifé, April 25, 2010)

This university professor shifts from the class to mass without any problem, performing different roles: a good teacher and scientist, on one hand, and on the other, a modern preacher who is able to *communicate* a word that seems to empower a younger generation who want to be modern *via religion*.

These two stories provides concrete examples of the new religious imaginary stimulated by Pentecostal religiosity and, by and large, by a new stratum of religious leadership which is no longer in debt either to European theology or to historical Black African Churches. It is, to quote again Matthew Ojo, a fine scholar of Ile-Ifé University, the era of jet-age pastors (Ojo 2005: 245). The leaders of the Pentecostal and Charismatic movements are definitely breaking new ground here. The modernization in this case directly affects the lifestyle of the leaders. They have to prove their ability to obtain success and to transmit this energetic vision of the world to the followers. Because of this transformation of religious leadership into entrepreneurship skills, the new churches are coping with the *classical* problem of the succession of charisma in a new way: not by adopting the traditional pattern experimented in the African prophetic churches (from the father to the son, by *jus sanguinis* rule), but rather by the recruitment of the best managers brought up with the leader. For example, in the Redeemed Christian Church of God there is a strong continuity between Josiah Akindayomi, the founder, and Enoch Adeboye, the successor, a continuity that goes beyond casual resemblances. As noted by Ukah:

While Josiah developed an authoritarian personality as a prophet, Adeboye has constructed a public image as the oracle of God and figure of power, attracting overwhelming reverence from his followers. As Josiah was the bearer of covenant from God, Adeboye is a bearer of the word of God, the physical voice of God among human beings. The church constructs a linkage of Josiah as Moses (and Elijah) and Adeboye as Joshua (and Elisha) thereby claiming the existence of a continuity with both leaders. (Ukah 2003: 45)

Conclusion

In the Nigerian laboratory we can observe a modern religious form of believing and belonging, in terms of, on one hand, the *individualizing of believing*, and on the other the *de-territorializing of belonging*. From the point of view of economics of the *signs*, aesthetics and architecture of symbols, what we see here is the tendency to build mega-churches, big structures (auditoria able to host thousands and thousands people), malls of the spirit, *non-lieus*, according to Augé (1992), that sometimes entails extensive travel to reach the service or the performance of the leader every week or the minor activities during the week.

The theoretical framework of multiple modernities in this case is a useful tool to depict the social change occurring under the sacred canopy for three reasons. Firstly, *multiple* refers to the peculiar dimension of the Pentecostal movement: instead of execrating any form of syncretism, Pentecostalism gives new meanings to the religious code oppressed and repressed over the past three centuries (Meyer 1999). These *traditional* religious codes regain dignity in the frame of Pentecostal Christianity. The latter adapts itself to the former, not vice-versa like in the past. Roughly speaking, Pentecostalism is telling us that the dichotomy between tradition and modernity is not appropriate in understanding the socio-cultural change occurring in sub-Saharan States.

Secondly, *modernity*, in the context of a social effervescence of the sacred indicates the opposite pole to archaism, an open-air social laboratory in which people experience a new kind of solidarity – in Durkheim's terminology – the writing of a new social pact: freedom of religion, religious diversity and public role of the religions, reconstructing the social order devastated by the corruption of the post-colonial leadership, and the accumulation of social injustice (Falola 1998).

The term *multiple modernities*, then, highlights the peculiar religious landscape in Nigeria (and to some extent in other sub-Saharan African states). The example of Africa shows how "being modern" does not necessarily imply "being secular", as classical modernization theory would have it. Instead, people enter the program of modernity *via* religion. They experience the religious deregulation as a process of modernization that feeds into an entrepreneurial mentality and promotes social mobility of the younger generations. The outcomes are, on one hand, a higher level of religious mobility of individuals, which implicitly reflects the free choice of believing and belonging, and, on the other, the facility for them to move freely in a religious field without any institutional obstacles. Religion, in this sense, plays a crucial function in promoting a cultural program that is modern without being secular.

References

Anderson, A. 2000. *African Reformation*. Trenton: African World.
Asamoha-Gyadu, K. 2005. *African Charismatics*. Leiden: Brill.

Asch, S. 1983. *L'Eglise du Prophète Kimbangu.* Paris: Khartala.

Augé, M. 1992. *Non-lieux.* Paris: Seuil.

Bateye, B.O. 2008. Paradigmatic Shift: Reconstruction of Female Leadership Roles in the New Generation Churches in South-western Nigeria, in A. Adogame et al. (eds), *Christianity in Africa and the African Diaspora: The Appropriation of a Scattered Heritage.* London: Continuum.

Bediako, K. 1992. *Theology and Identity.* Oxford: Regnum Books.

Bolaji Idowu, E. 1973. *African Traditional Religion. A Definition.* London: SCM Press.

Corten, A., Marshall-Fratani R. (eds) 2001. *Between Babel and Pentecost.* Bloomington: Indiana University Press.

Deleuze, G. and Guattari, F. 1972. *Capitalisme et schizophrénie.* Paris: Minuit.

Desroche, H. 1969. *Dieux d'homme.* Paris: Mouton.

Eisenstadt S.N. 2000. Multiple Modernities. *Daedalus* 129(1), 1–30.

Falola, T. 1998. *Violence in Nigeria: The Crisis of Religious Politics and Secular Ideologies.* Rochester: Rochester University Press.

Freston, P. 2004. *Evangelical and Politics in Asia, Africa and Latin America.* Cambridge: Cambridge University Press.

Gifford, P. 2004. *Ghana's New Christianity: Pentecostalism in a Globalizing African Economy.* Bloomington: Indiana University Press.

Hachett, R.I.J. 1990. Enigma Variations: The Religious Movements in Nigeria Today, in A.F. Walls, W.R. Shenk (eds),. *Exploring New Religious Movements.* Elkhart: Mission Focus.

Hachett, R.I.J. 1993. From Exclusion to Inclusion: Women and Bible Use in Southern Nigeria, in I. Wollaston and J. Davies (eds), *Sociology of the Sacred Texts.* Sheffield: Sheffield Academic Press, 225–59.

Jenkins P. 2002. *The Next Christendom: The Coming of Global Christianity.* Oxford: Oxford University Press.

Kalu, O. 2008. *African Pentecostalism.* Oxford: Oxford University Press.

Lanternari, V. 2003. *Movimenti religiosi di libertà e salvezza.* Roma: Editori Riuniti.

Lawless, E.J. 1988. *Handmaidens of the Lord: Pentecostal Women Preachers and Traditional Religion.* Philadelphia: University of Pennsylvania Press.

Martin, M.L. 1975. *Kimbangu: An African Prophet and His Church.* Grand Rapids: Eedermans.

Mary, A. 2000. *Le bricolage africain des héros chrétiens.* Paris: Cerf.

Mary, A. 2005. Metissage and bricolage in the Making of African-Christian Identities, in *Social Compass* 3, 281–94.

Mary, A. 2008. Africanité et christianité, in *Archives de Sciences Sociales des Religions* 143, 9–30.

Mary, A. and Laurent, J.P. (eds) 2001. Prophètes, visionnaires et guérisseurs de l'Afrique subsaharienne contemporaine, in *Social Compass* 3, 307–438.

Meyer, B. 1999. *Translating the Devil.* Trenton: African World.

Meyer, B. 2007. Pentecostalism and Neo-Liberal Capitalism. *Journal for the Scientific Study of Religion* 20, 2, 5–28.

Meyer, B. 2010. Aesthetic of Persuasion: Global Christianity and Pentecostalism's Sensational Forms. *South Atlantic Quarterly* 9, 741–63.

Miller, D.E., Yamanori T. 2007. *Global Pentecostalism: The New Face of Christian Social Engagement*. Berkeley: University of California Press.

Mokoko Gampiot, A. 2004. *Kimbanguisme et identité noire*. Paris: L'Harmattan.

Ojo, M. 2005. Religion, Public Space, and Press in Contemporary Nigeria, in T. Falola (ed.), *Christianity and Social Change in Africa*. Durham, NC: Carolina Academic Press, 233–52.

Ojo, M. 2006. *The End-Time Army. Charismatic Movements in Modern Nigeria*. Trenton: African World Press.

Olajubu, O. 2004. *Women in the Yoruba Religious Sphere*. Albany, NY: State University of New York.

Omenyo, C.N. 2002. *Pentecost Outside Pentecostalism*. Zoetermeer: Boeckcentrum.

Pace, E. 2011. *Religion as Communication*. Farnham: Ashgate.

Pace, E. and Butticci, A. 2010. *Le religioni pentecostali*. Roma: Carocci.

Pase, A. 2011. *Linee sulla terra. Confini politici e limiti fondiari in Africa sub sahariana*. Roma: Carocci.

Peel, J.D.Y. 1968. *Aladura*. London: Oxford University Press.

Putnam, R. 2001. *Bowling Alone*. New York: Simon & Schuster.

Sachsenmaier D., Riedel J. and Eisenstadt S.N. (eds) 2002. *Multiple Modernities*. Piscataway, NJ: Transactions Publishers.

Shootil, J.E. 2008. *Gender, Social Change and Spiritual Power*. Leiden: Brill.

Tasie, G.O.M. 1978. *Christian Missionary Enterprise in the Niger Delta*. Leiden: Brill.

Tschannen, O. 1992. *Les theories de la secularisation*. Genève-Paris: Droz.

Ukah, A.K. 2003. Advertising God: Nigerian Christian Video-Films and the Power of Consumer Culture, in *Journal of Religion in Africa* 33, 203–31.

Van Dijk, R. 1992. Young Born-Again Preachers in Post-Independence Malawi, in P. Gifford (ed.), *New Dimensions in African Christianity*. Nairobi: All Africa Conference of Churches.

Währisch-Oblau, C. 2008. *The Missionary Self-Perception of Pentecostal/ Charismatic Leaders*. Leiden: Brill.

Wariboko, N. 2010. *Ethics and Time*. Idaho Falls: Lexington Books.

Chapter 8

The Modernity of New Societies: South Africa, Brazil and the Prospect of a World-Sociology

Peter Wagner

Just Another BRIC in the World?

The question of "multiple modernities" is a major challenge to socio-political thought, but it is also a topic of current journalistic and political debate. Indeed, as we will briefly discuss below, there are reasons to assume that the multiplication of modernities was first of topical concern before it became an intellectual challenge. Today, BRICS has become an acronym of everyday use in newspapers and political discourse. It refers to Brazil, Russia, India, China, and South Africa together, and its use often just means to signal that the current world is composed of more bricks than only those two or three of the times of the Soviet Union and the Third World and that its stability accordingly requires a more nuanced architecture. Sometimes, however, it is insinuated that these bricks are not of the same kind and that building with them can be difficult. At that moment, the question of multiple modernities arises, even though it is not always recognized.

Moving one step closer, the bricks are of very different kinds indeed. In the centre, RIC are traditionally seen as long-established civilizations. They are natural rocks, which may have undergone some polishing, but nevertheless always remain what they are. This image is conveyed, among others, by the author who gave the inspiration to the debate about multiple modernities, the late Shmuel Eisenstadt. One can have considerable doubts about the adequacy of this image. The impact of extended periods of socialist re-organization or of colonial rule on socio-cultural relations is highly underestimated in the view that the multiplication of modernities mainly arises from the encounter of crystallized civilizations and their stable "cultural programmes" with European modernity after 1800 (for a critique of the civilizational approach to the study of modernity, see Wagner 2011a). To understand better why this approach became the centre of the debate about varieties of modernity, we need to briefly reconstruct the context of its emergence.

Until the late 1960s, modernization theory had provided sociology with a comprehensive and rather consistent approach to the comparative analysis of contemporary societies and their transformations over time from the alleged onset of modernity, in Europe and North America slightly more than two centuries ago, onwards. From the 1970s onwards, however, this theory became discredited by the combined onslaught of renewal in social theory, which reintroduced agency and creativity against any notion of self-propelled evolution; of the linguistic and micro-historical turns, which questioned the possibility of grasping large-scale social phenomena and their long-term continuity; and of postcolonial studies and dependency and world-systems theory, which emphasized western domination, instead of lags in "development", as the cause for divergence in societal trajectories. Forceful as it was, the interim outcome of such critical debate was the abandonment of any comprehensive attempt at analyzing entire social configurations and their historical trajectories. Comparative-historical sociology was in disarray (for a more detailed discussion, see Wagner 2003).

By the end of the twentieth century, though, the concept of "multiple modernities" and its associated research programme had arisen to redress the situation. The novel approach returns to the comprehensive ambition of modernization theory by proposing to study societies comparatively across the globe over an even much longer time-span, namely from the so-called axial age in the middle of the first millennium BCE onwards. At the same time, it addresses constructively some of the main criticism directed against modernization theory. Against the assumption of a unilinear logic of evolution and, thus, convergence of societal trajectories, it posits the persistent diversity of modern social configurations. Against the postulate of western normative and/or functional superiority, it develops the idea of plural forms of modernity without a conceptually predetermined hierarchy of achievements. Against the idea of structural-functional determination, it posits the interpretative engagement of human beings with the world, producing cultural programmes that give underlying interpretative patterns to social life. In sum, as mentioned above, the current diversity of modernities is seen to emerge from the encounter of historical cultural collectivities, often referred to as "civilizations", with the commitment of modernity to autonomy and mastery as it most pronouncedly, but not without ambiguities, was elaborated in Europe. In its transformation towards modernity, each underlying cultural programme retains some specificity, thus there is no reason to assume convergence, but rather persistent diversity. Rightly, this approach has been seen as reviving comparative-historical sociology (see some of the contributions to Arjomand 2012 for further elaboration).

In the light of its achievements and the intellectual constellation in which it arose, some of the shortcomings of this approach appear as a surprise. Defying or ignoring the novel emphasis in social theory on agency, on contexts of action and speech and on the event of colonialism, its concepts of "modernity" and "cultural programme" presuppose too high degrees of commonality and continuity: commonality of interpretative patterns across often very large collectivities; and continuity of the underlying cultural programme over very long stretches of time (for related critiques, see Smith 2009 and now Delanty and Mota 2012). As a consequence, disputes within a collectivity over its way of being-in-the-world as well as more than merely gradual transformations of interpretative patterns tend to be lost out of sight.

The observation that the most elaborate approach to the study of the variety of modernities shows such strong deficiencies can probably be explained by the conjunction of two facts. On the one hand, the most sophisticated intellectual critiques of modernization theory proved unable to reconstruct a historical sociology of large-scale social configurations (see Wagner 2010 for more detail). On the other hand, events in the world called for a return of such a sociology. Two such events stand out. First, the rise of the Japanese economy to outcompete the supposedly most advanced economies of the west, in particular, that of the US, showed that no cultural background in Protestantism was required to achieve high levels of "rationalism"; and organizational analysis of Japanese capitalism suggested furthermore that the "rationality" of economic action in Japan was different from the one prevailing in the west. Second, the Iranian Revolution of 1979 occurred in a society that had been considered to have advanced more than others on the linear path of modernization. However, the revolution not only newly established a political regime that is based on religious commitment, but found numerous followers in its own and other societies. This, too, is something that should not have occurred according to modernization theory's implicit philosophy of history. In the absence of a more compelling approach, both these events were taken far too easily to lend themselves to an interpretation from a civilizational perspective, pointing to the long isolation and thus relative cultural homogeneity of Japanese society and to allegedly characteristic political features of predominantly Islamic societies.

In our view, the socio-cultural transformations in Japan and Iran over the past half century require a different approach, but its development is neither within the competence of this author nor the objective of this article. We referred to the events in these societies only to signal that the plausibility of the "multiple modernities" approach owes more to a constellation in which "Old World" societies underwent major transformations in a context of global interconnectedness in which convincing alternative perspectives to analyze these transformations were not at hand rather than to its own strengths. To comparatively analyze varieties of modernity more appropriately, one needs to introduce the insights from the critiques of modernization theory more explicitly; and to do this, it is more fruitful to leave the "Old World" with its inclination for civilizational analysis behind, and look at situations in which the conflictive creation and re-creation of socio-political arrangements catches the attention rather than continuity, consensus and commonality.

If informed by conceptual debate, there is no problem with topicality in social analysis. Let us thus move from RIC to the B and S of BRICS and consider the rise of two "new societies" in global consciousness, Brazil and South Africa, as a challenge to the idea of multiple modernities. To do so succinctly in a short essay, this chapter will need to remain programmatic, rather than going into much detail, and will draw its inspiration from an approach that preceded the "multiple modernities" debate but is largely forgotten, namely Louis Hartz's *The Founding of New Societies*, published in 1964, which offers a multi-author comparative analysis of the US, Latin America, South Africa, Canada and Australia, held together by Hartz's own "theory of the development of new societies".[1]

The reasoning will proceed in four steps. First, it will be argued that the constitution of "new societies" is an occurrence that interrogates our understanding of modernity and requires widening it. Second, we will explore ways in which "new societies" are "modern", and maybe modern in a particular way. One of these particularities, arguably the most important one, thirdly, is what has been called "the racial encounter" (Hartz) or "the colonial encounter" (Talal Asad). Throughout these sections, Brazil (sometimes Latin America in general) and South Africa will be referred to as key examples, and they will be contrasted to the US as a northern variant of a "new society" and with the "tradition of modernity" (Derrida 1989) that prevailed in Europe. Finally, it will be suggested that recent developments in the South – some of those that provide reasons why B and S exist within BRICS – show a radicalization of modernity that will have an impact on the North and will need to be centrally taken into account in a future world-sociology of modernity.

Modernity and the Constitution of Societies

Among the many incoherences of the sociological theories of modernity, one in particular has found little critical attention. Modern societies, it is usually suggested, emerge from a radical rupture with the social configurations that precede them. Furthermore, those societies are seen as placing the freedom of the human beings and the rationality of their actions at their centre. Thus, the creation of modernity should be a moment of constitution of new societies. At the same, time, however, the emergence of modern society was explained by characteristics of the preceding society: class struggle in feudalism and the rise of the bourgeoisie; centralization of political power; Protestantism and new individualism. Thus, modern society no longer appeared as constituted in human social action, but as evolving from social conditions to which human beings could only give a twist.[2] Its emergence was to be explained against the background of, and conditioned by, that which preceded

---

1   I discussed Hartz's approach in an earlier essay, which can be consulted for more detailed conceptual elaboration (Wagner 2012a). The current essay aims at applying the insights from the former to comparative analysis. It draws on research within the project 'Trajectories of Modernity', funded by the European Research Council under the European Union's Seventh Framework Programme (FP7/2007–2013) as Advanced Grant no. 249438, in which the comparison of Brazil and South Africa with European modernity is central. It has benefitted from discussions with the members of the research group for which I am grateful.

2   Political theory committed the opposite error. In social contract theory, it hypothesized the creation of the modern polity by individuals with little history and social bonds.

it. As a result from the so-called agency-structure debate in the 1970s and 1980s, the "constitution of society" (Giddens 1984) in the interactions of human beings became a key theoretical concern, but there have been very few analyses that followed up on that notion.

The centrality of civilizational analysis in the current study of modernity confirms this impression. However, as alluded to above, the issue can possibly be re-opened by distinguishing different societal situations. With his term "new societies", Hartz suggests that there is a founding moment in rather recent history and that the constellation at this moment of founding is the key to understanding the emerging society. Rather clearly, he works with a distinction between the "New World" and the "Old World", the only partial exception being South Africa at the very edge of the "known world" before European expansion. These societies have also been called "settler societies", referring to the fact that Europeans left their native territory and settled elsewhere. But we should bear in mind that all these terms speak from the European perspective: there was no "new" world that had not been known; and the Europeans did not settle on uninhabited territory. The sociology of "new societies" has often, though implicitly and mostly thoughtlessly, been a sociology of elites, considering only the actions of the settlers of European descent as giving shape to the new forms of socio-political life (an issue to be taken up again below).

Such criticism notwithstanding, such sociology captures an important difference that has escaped the more general sociology of modern societies: there are societies in the world that can impossibly be analyzed by any, even "soft", logic of continuity and historical determination because they emerge from relatively recent encounters between different population groups, from the spatial displacement that at least one of those groups experienced, and from the invasion of their territory by alien and unknown people that marked the life of the other groups. At some point, in some cases earlier and in others later, these events culminated in a moment of conscious founding of society and related institution-building, often dominated by the European settlers, or one group among them.

For Latin America, this is the period of declarations of independence in the early nineteenth century, which in the particular case of Brazil means the founding of a monarchy that will be transformed into a republic at the end of the nineteenth century. In South Africa, too, there are two such moments. The founding of the Orange Free State and the South African (Transvaal) Republic by the settlers of Dutch descent occurred in the middle of the nineteenth century. These polities co-existed with native African polities, in particular the Zulu kingdom and the Xhosa chiefdoms, and with the Cape Colony, part of the British Empire and dominated by the settlers of British descent, on the territory of what is now the Republic of South Africa. After the South African War, the Union of South Africa was founded under British domination in 1910.

Furthermore, many of these societies have undergone a recent re-founding that not least aims at creating a condition of equal freedom for all residents on the territory of these societies and, importantly, correcting historical injustice.

For South Africa, this re-founding occurred with the end of the apartheid regime, which was based on formal exclusion of the population of native African descent from citizenship and from numerous rights associated with the former, after a protracted liberation struggle led for most of the twentieth century by the African National Congress (ANC). In 1994, a new Constitution was passed and the ANC has won all political elections since by large majorities. In Brazil, the re-founding is a slightly more gradual process beginning with the end of military dictatorship in 1985 and accelerating with the election of the Workers' Party (PT) candidate, Luiz Inácio Lula da Silva, as president of the republic in 2002. His election was preceded at local and regional level by increasing critical involvement of the citizenry in policy-making, recently referred to as "insurgent citizenship" (Holston 2008). The democratic persuasiveness of the reformist agenda is confirmed by the recent election of Dilma Rousseff, the PT candidate, to succeed Lula as president.

Brief as these notes have been, they do suggest, we claim, that such history of "new societies" requires a sociology that does not start out from a constituted society and sees it transforming but instead analyzes the constitution of society and its re-constitution at later moments through the actions and interactions of its members. For this reason, Louis Hartz's approach was and remains useful, despite its limits that we will discuss later. The starting-point in Hartz's analysis, namely, are human beings, more precisely groups of European settlers who move across space, leaving the societies behind in which they grew up towards lands unknown to them in which they make new *experiences*. At the outset, thus, there is no "Brazil" or "South Africa", there is only people who are socialized in one context and move to another one the experience of which they will need to interpret, because they are "self-interpreting animals" (Taylor 1985: ch. 2). They relate to each other and the world by means of language through which they assign meaning. They acquire the tools of *interpretation* during socialization, and they carry these tools with them when arriving at new shores that present unprecedented issues to them, and also, we add, when they encounter others whose existence was unknown to them. Pierre Bourdieu (1990, and other places) called "habitus" the sedimentation of a set of registers for action within the body of a human being during socialization. If this human being mainly encounters situations that are similar to the habitus-creating ones during his or her later life, the reproduction of society is the likely outcome, according to Bourdieu. In turn, the confrontation of such habitus with situations that differ from those that created it requires creativity when using the tools at hand for interpreting novel challenges, and thus is a major source for social change. This is, according to Hartz, what characteristically happens to the European settlers, and "the founding of new societies" is the outcome of this confrontation of a particular European habitus with a novel situation.

Against this background, Hartz distinguished types of "new societies" according to the time of first settlement and the socio-cultural characteristics of the settlers. The settlement of Southern America was enacted by feudal groups from Spain and Portugal; the USA and what Hartz calls Dutch South Africa were settled by bourgeois groups during the period of the European Enlightenment; and the settlement of "British South Africa" coincided with the rise of the workers' movement in Europe and therefore had a "radical" taint. Feudalism, Enlightenment and radicalism are, in Hartz's terminology, "fragments" of the European societal self-understanding.

Up to this point, one may see here nothing but a conceptually slightly more nuanced version of the history of European expansion. Hartz, though, underlined strongly that the emerging societies were 'new' in the sense of having particular self-definitions that were highly distinct from European self-understandings, that they were indeed having "a major problem of self-definition" (Hartz 1964: 11) because it is intolerable to be a "fragment", a part without a whole. Even though their cultural resources are European, they need to be extended and enlarged to become a whole that as such did not exist in Europe. The members of the new societies draw on the inherited resources but need to rework them because they are incomplete. For this reason, to paraphrase Charles Taylor, new societies are *self-interpreting societies* par excellence, and in each case their self-definition is highly different from any societal self-understanding that one finds in Europe.

The Modernity of "New Societies"

One may say that to be modern means to be engaged in self-interpretation; and if this is so and one follows the above characterization, then new societies are modern by force of circumstance. But we need to explore the particular modernity of new societies in some more detail.

Modernity, as we have argued elsewhere (Wagner 2008, 2012b), is about the commitment to govern one's own lives and create one's own laws for living together, and this commitment demands self-interpretation and self-questioning. More specifically, one can also argue that such a commitment arose in a particularly pronounced way during the European Enlightenment – even though this period is neither the earliest nor the only one in human history to which one can trace such self-understanding. Interestingly, Hartz connects the two propositions and, thus, made it possible to see the distinct self-understandings of new societies as varieties of modernity. At one point, Hartz is remarkably clear about this question, suggesting that "the Enlightenment fragments", i.e., the United States, British Canada, and Dutch South Africa, "embody modernity itself" (Hartz 1964: 45). Hartz thus uses the familiar understanding of modernity as arising in eighteenth-century Europe with Enlightenment thinking that emphasizes both personal freedom and popular self-government. In contrast to standard views, however, he suggests that European thinking always operated in a context of opposing this view to the preceding feudalism and to the subsequent socialist thought that radicalizes the Enlightenment. Europe, thus, never embodies "modernity itself", but brings modernity forth within intellectual and political contexts in which the key tenets of modernity never stand alone. This, though, they do in the Enlightenment fragments in which "the whole of the culture" which embraces individualism and democracy can "unfold as it could not unfold in Europe" (Hartz 1964: 40).

A brief digression on the United States of America may be permitted. Hartz's earlier book on the American liberal political tradition had provided the model for the above notion, arguing that Lockean individualism was the core component of the US self-understanding because it was imported by bourgeois Enlightened settlers who shed the feudal past of Europe and did not know about the later radicalization of Enlightenment thought with the rise of the European working-class (Hartz 1955). In a way, thus, the US are more modern than Europe could ever become, and Hartz (1964: 40) asserts that "the European traveler immediately sees" this feature, thus referring to views of the United States that discover pure or radical modernity in the New World in ways in which modernity could not exist in Europe. If we look at European writings about the US in the early twentieth century, that is, after the rise of the US economy to world-market competitiveness and the decisive presence of the US military in the First World War, we see how the authors recognize a modernity that is different from the European one, in many respects superior to the latter, but at the same time normatively more problematic. It is in these writings, we may suggest, that the topic of multiple modernities first arises, at least in Europe, and it arises because of the emergence of a "new society" (see Wagner 1999).

From such an angle, how should one understand the modernity of new societies that are not, or not predominantly, informed by the Enlightenment self-understanding? In Hartz's view, the feudal and radical fragments do not embody modernity, but they stand in particular and well defined relations to it, the former as rejection of the Enlightenment spirit, the latter as, indeed, its radicalization. Hartz seems to recognize the force of the need for self-interpretation and asks whether a feudal fragment, even devoid of its European roots, "will not in the end produce an Enlightenment out of its own resources" (Hartz 1964: 27). But he answers the question in the negative by resorting again to the discussion of actors and their world-interpretations: "The migration in both the Canadian and South American cases was primarily military, clerical, and rural. Feudalism itself, so to say, shrank. [...] The feudalism of the fragments was not only divorced from the seeds of the urban European Enlightenment, but was made more doctrinaire by a kind of clerical aristocracy" (ibid.). While this may be true of early colonization, here Hartz seems to be trapped by his concept of fragment and to underestimate the capacity for re-constitution against the lasting and determining impact of the original constitution of new societies. Thus, for Hartz, the fragments exist as rather coherent interpretative frameworks without resources for self-generated change. They determine social life, which thus becomes much more conservative than the European social settings left behind.

There is much compelling evidence for this view in *The Founding of New Societies*. However, there is also neglect as well as problematic interpretation of some evidence. Two examples need to suffice. First, one may object that the declarations of independence and constitutional developments in the early nineteenth century, which led to the foundation of the Latin American states as we know them, were clearly shaped by the liberal-revolutionary stimulus from France. Hartz cannot fail to notice this, but surprisingly here abandons his emphasis on self-understandings in favour of an analysis of interests and power of the dominant groups, thus suggesting a purely instrumental recourse to the revolutionary ideology. Recent research has strongly argued the opposite. Carlos Forment (2003) has argued that there is a tradition of "democracy in Latin America" since the early nineteenth century, which is distinct from the one famously investigated by Alexis de Tocqueville for the North, but not necessarily deviant or incomplete for that reason. More recently, Aurea Mota (2012) has reconstructed the "attenuated liberalism" that informs constitutional law in Latin America from the nineteenth-century and thus addresses social and cultural issues of which European political thought was aware, too, but had greater reluctance to explicate them formally. To give a last example, recent work by Francisco Ortega (2012) on Latin American political actors in the early nineteenth century shows a much greater awareness of the heterogeneity of the new societies than the one confessed by their North American counterparts. Hartz underplays the role of the explicitly constitutional moment in the founding of Latin American new societies, in the early nineteenth century, in favour of the world-interpretations the early settlers had.

While this may be seen as a mis-dating of the moment of founding, our second example concerns the underestimation of the possibility of re-founding at later moments. Thus, Hartz (1964: 32) argues that "the Perón-Vargas tradition of authoritarian labor organization" in Latin America needs to be understood against the background of Catholic traditionalism and emerges in "a situation in which the masses have not been effectively activated by liberal influence". This is an interpretation in line with the idea of fragment closure and lack of other cultural resources, such as Enlightenment or radical ones. However, it seems more persuasive to suggest that these examples exemplify a major transformation of Latin American modernity, one that proceeds in parallel with the European organization of modernity from the late nineteenth century onwards and draws on some similar interpretative elements while dealing with the novel situation of an organizing working class (as Larrain 2000 and 2007 and Domingues 2008 have argued). We recognize here the limits of the argument that reside in assumptions about fragment isolation and about absence of novel problems of such kind that interpretative creativity is required.

Understandings of Modernity in the Face of the Encounter with the Other

In more general terms, both the persuasiveness and the limits of Hartz's perspective reside in the ambiguity inherent in his view of the "fragments" and their contexts. On the one hand, the idea of "the fixity of a fragment" leads to a determinism in his reasoning that contrasts with his focus on experience. On the other hand, there is the insight that a fragment cannot exist on its own and that "the energies arising out of its breakdown" (Hartz 1964: 28) create a kind of imposed dynamism that does not exist in this form in the "Old World". The context of fragment breakdown is the new situation of the settler in the "New World", and the key component of this situation is what Hartz calls "the racial encounter".

When referring to the "racial encounter" Hartz anticipates Talal Asad's (1995) use of the term "encounter" that was meant to avoid the one-sided view of colonialism as absolute domination, and he does so with similar intent. He deploys a double comparative agenda, distinguishing first between the European fragments as such and secondly exploring variations within the fragments, which are often "derived from the impact of [Latin American,] African and aboriginal cultures, non-western in character". This two-step process leads first to a reflection in terms of concept formation and use. Hartz is aware of the potential objection that "the European ideological categories" of feudalism, liberalism and radicalism may impose a straight-jacket on the comparative analysis. He insists, though, that their value does not lie in fitting completely, "but that they give us a point of analytic departure". In general, "one can view every situation in which the West meets the non-West as a situation involving two fragments", and he considers the "analytic" priority he gives to the west as – rather too – harmless: "If we adopt the Western norm for certain analytic purposes, the distortion of that norm by the non-Western fragment will measure perfectly, from its own angle, the degree of compromise which it itself has been forced to make." Even though this statement sounds open enough, we today, more informed by postcolonial writings, are less convinced that this approach does "not in any way limit the examination of American history from the standpoint of the Iroquois or the Cherokee" (Hartz 1964: 28, for all quotations).

Hartz himself did not analyze how categories from the colonized populations actively shaped the outcome of the "encounter" with Europeans; he only showed himself open to that possibility. Otherwise he only took the effect of the presence of non-European populations for modifications of the "European categories", or the "Western norm", into account. Along those lines, though, his comparative observations on colonial modernity are significant.

Hartz introduces distinctions between the fragments according to the ways in which they dealt with the unexpected presence of human beings on the territory on which the Europeans settled (see in general Mbembe 2001). He strongly underlines the significance of "an experience so great as that involving the Indian and the African", which required that "the most heroic effort [was] to be made to extract from the European ideologyes the message that they contained for the racial relationship" (Hartz 1964: 49). The most simple – and, one should add, not at all "heroic", despite its mythification in US movies and military jargon – "method for implementing the Western ideologies" was extermination. The effects of such violence will haunt the settler modernity that employs it, for two reasons. Because the elimination is never complete, "alienated native populations [...] raise peculiarly agonizing problems" at the margins of the new societies. Furthermore, the settlers' persistent "hunger for labor" leads to the importation of slaves there where the native populations are almost exterminated, "and with the slave a more permanent, and hence more complicated relationship has to be worked out'" (Hartz 1964: 50, all quotations). This second observation, in particular, suggests a lasting dependence of the settlers – or of Europeans in general – from non-Europeans, an insight peculiarly absent from both modernization theory and the multiple modernities approach.

Those more permanent relationships differed significantly between the feudal culture, on the one hand, and the liberal and radical ones, on the other. For present purposes, we may also say that they differ between a Catholic and a Protestant interpretation. We moderns like to see our own self-understanding as normatively superior to others, including the feudal one from the European past, which were or are based on unjustifiable hierarchies. The history of slavery, more specifically, tends to see feudal-minded Latin Europeans as clinging to slavery at a historical moment at which the Enlightened British were advocating, and more and more imposing, a ban on slavery, thus opening the avenue to historical progress. Hartz's comparative sociology draws a different picture, observing that "the racial relationship was in one crucial sense easier for the feudal cultures than for the liberal or the radical", because the former had at hand "a concept of status which could be revamped for the purpose", which "the Enlightenment culture did not" have (Hartz 1964: 50).

Given that European feudal society was a hierarchical order distinguishing between status groups into which people were born, the European settlers in Latin America could avail themselves of conceptual means that served for including other, new members into the same social structure (see Elliott 2000). The native Americans, and later the African slaves, entered the order at the bottom rank, but they were included into a concept of common humanity that also drew on Catholic Christian belief, as most famously exemplified by Bartolomé de las Casas. As a consequence, "the Latin-American fragments, by absorbing the African like the Indian into their status system, indeed by creating that system out of their ranks, were saved from the oscillations of egalitarian morality" (Hartz 1964: 57). Those oscillations stem from the fact that the Enlightenment is committed to the "norm of equality" (Hartz 1964: 58) applied to all – known – human beings, on the one hand, but was transferred to a context in which other human beings were unexpectedly encountered, on the other. To use again Hartz's own words: In the Enlightenment culture "a human being was entitled to full equality, so that if he was to be enslaved in any way, his very humanity had to be denied" (Hartz 1964: 50). Thus, the liberal – and also the radical – fragment lacks the possibility of gradation within the ranks of human beings that the feudal fragment has. It has to include or to exclude. Therefore, its "battles over race are fought out in terms of the moral extremes which that norm imposes on human relationships, in conscience if not always in fact" (Hartz 1964: 58). In practice, this often meant, as in the Southern United States and Dutch South Africa, a temporarily successful combat against "the full egalitarian outcome of the Enlightenment faith through definitions of the Negro as property or as an inhuman species of race" (Hartz 1964: 60).

Democracy as the equal liberty to participate in collective self-determination is the political commitment of the Enlightenment. Within the liberal fragment, this commitment is best exemplified by the Orange Free State and the South African (Transvaal) Republic, two Afrikaner states in South Africa that rushed ahead – in the standard view of the history of political modernity – to adopt manhood suffrage much earlier than European polities. They did so, though, by limiting such political equality to the white population while at the same time heavily relying on black labour for domestic services and agriculture. Thus, in Hartz's words, we are "talking about the Greek democracy of a white community made even more egalitarian by the fact that a group of Negroes flourish beneath it" (Hartz 1964: 59).

The Radicalization of Modernity from the South

Hartz writes at a moment when the apartheid regime is firmly in place in South Africa, but he considers change to be imminent and, for instance, predicts that the new generation of South Africans of Dutch descent (Afrikaners) "will challenge the idea that the Afrikaner has devised the only way of racial life" (Hartz 1964: 22). He writes shortly after the Cuban revolution and at the high point of decolonization in Africa leading to the emergence of numerous new independent states. He suggests that the established elites in the fragments will not be able to maintain their hegemony, and that their own new generations will have a different outlook on the world and demand change. If we look at the end of apartheid in South Africa and the emergence of "insurgent citizenship" in Brazil and other Latin American societies in this light, we recognize the force of this emergent world-sociology, written at the time of the Sharpeville massacre in South Africa and even before the temporary elite entrenchment of the military dictatorships in Latin America. Today, the change that Hartz could only point to in suggestive, but also vague terms has clearly started to happen. To demonstrate this, we will conclude with some observations about the past two decades that point the further elaboration particular interpretations of modernity in the South, distinct from the North. For reasons of brevity, we will focus on South Africa (the following draws on Wagner 2011b).

Emerging from a period during which self-determination was interpreted as the domination of a minority over the majority, South African modernity today is strongly committed to free and equal democracy in its attempt at re-directing socio-political organization away from apartheid exclusion and oppression. In the history of European modernity, the emphasis on collective self-understanding was based on some idea of the unity of the people – often specified as the nation – that concealed the underlying tension between the multitude of human beings of which any collectivity is composed and the supposed emergence of a common will as required by the concept of popular sovereignty. In South Africa, this tension is plainly evident since democratic South Africa emerges from domination of its majority population by a minority population group that, though, remains a part of the re-defined collectivity (see Chipkin 2007). The tension is visible in former President Thabo Mbeki's characterization of South Africa as a society of two nations, one black and one white, or of the association of the use of Afrikaans with the history of oppression, thus singling out one of the two predominantly white language communities as the former oppressor.[3] In turn, the creation of the term "rainbow nation" by Archbishop Desmond Tutu, a key figure in the transition, was meant to symbolize current unity in diversity, thus a situation in which different cultural orientations can co-exist without threatening the basic commonality – of a "nation" – that is required for forming and sustaining a democratic polity. The symbol of the rainbow was meant to go together with the practices of the Truth and Reconciliation Commission (TRC) that was charged with reviewing past violence and injustice and to design and implement measures for compensation. Despite the achievements of the TRC, as impressively narrated by Antjie Krog (1998), both the terms "rainbow" and "reconciliation" are currently rather used as something that is still to be accomplished and for which considerable requirements are by far not met.

The current democratic condition of collective self-determination, second, was reached at least partly as a result of a struggle that was seen as national liberation on the model of similar struggles in other former colonies in Africa (for a discussion of the reasons for the end of apartheid see Lipton 2007). The agent of struggle was the ANC-based alliance, which for this reason is seen – and sees itself – as the key agent of future collective self-determination. ANC has repeatedly gained the absolute majority in post-apartheid elections, even coming close to a two-thirds majority that would allow changes to the Constitution. The only exception is the province of the western Cape and some municipalities including the city of Cape Town, which currently are governed by the Democratic Alliance (DA), a party that emerged from white opposition to apartheid and sees itself as a civic-liberty-minded opposition to lasting uncontrolled one-party rule. Thus, South Africa faces a political situation that in one respect is similar to other African polities after the end of colonization: the agent of national liberation becomes the organized site for collective self-determination, thus marginalizing the role of elections and parliament in what comes close to being a one-party democracy (for a discussion see Chabal 2009), in contrast to European democracies, and retaining a strong substantive pre-determination of the scope of collective action, in contrast to the standard liberal understanding. In contrast to other African polities, however, the dominant party is itself an alliance in which considerable difference of opinion and relatively pronounced public debate exist, and furthermore, the successful presence of the DA in particular allows for persistent opposition politics and at least the regional elaboration of a government alternative (for a recent overview of South African party politics see Butler 2010). Thus, we recognize here a

---

3   For a demonstration of how lived experience may differ from political analysis of oppression see Dlamini 2009.

particular positioning of the South African polity between a republicanism that allows a strong substantive direction of political action but can be criticized as a "tyranny of the majority" (Tocqueville), on the one hand, and, on the other hand, a liberalism that emphasizes individual autonomy in terms of both civil rights and pursuit of opportunities, but can be criticized for neglecting the current impact of past oppression and exclusion and for aligning itself too easily with current global economic ideology.

This latter possibility leads, thirdly, to the particular relation between political equality and social solidarity that exists in South African debates and practices. As has been argued, the viability of democracy may depend on relations of trust within the citizenry that are also the source for solidarity, that is, as the willingness to support others in need on the assumption of similar commitment to the polity and thus trust in the fact that oneself would also find support if in need (Offe 1998; for a broader discussion of changing forms of solidarity see Karagiannis 2007). Rather than an option that can be more or less strongly pursued, the reduction of inequality through organized solidarity may thus be a pre-condition for sustaining South African democracy. Apartheid was a political regime of exclusion that sustained an economic regime of exploitation and impoverishment, identifiable through wage differences between black and white workers, infrastructural underprovision of townships and lack of concern for rural regions that were merely considered as a flexible reservoir for labour (see Seekings and Nattrass 2006 for a long-term analysis). As a consequence, apartheid South Africa combined political dominance by a minority with extremely high social inequality. Anti-apartheid struggle focused on political inclusion as the most visible and most easily identifiable feature of apartheid, but the expectation was that a change towards an inclusive democratic political regime would also quickly improve the living conditions of the majority. This, though, has clearly by far not happened to the expected degree, and discontent with the persistence of poverty and inequality, including now high inequality within the black population due to the creation of groups of successful black businesspeople and politicians, is high. The commitment to political equality remains uncontested, and there is even some broad agreement about the need for redistribution to remedy past injustice. However, domestic redistribution raises fears about lowering the opportunities of the formerly privileged groups, especially with regard to future generations. And the strategy of solving distributive problems through growth, rather successfully employed by North European social democracies during the 1950 and 1960s, faces today a less favourable international environment for varieties of economic policy.

This brief discussion of current key issues in South African society has focused on three socio-political questions that have in general accompanied the history of modernity but for which South Africa shows a strong particularity. First, the idea of collective autonomy requires a collectivity capable of deliberating about its own rules and laws, and this is particularly difficult when such collectivity emerges from a former situation in which a minority oppressed and excluded the majority of the same collectivity. Second, any modern polity needs to determine the relation between individual autonomy and collective autonomy, between the freedom to self-determine one's own life and the freedom to collectively shape the conditions in which good lives – in variety – can be lived. Debates over the past decades have led to an emphasis of the former over the latter in the west. This turn may be problematic in its own way in western societies, as this author would hold. For South Africa, it is highly plausible to sustain that the creation of the conditions for living good lives needs so considerable collective effort that any easy acceptance of the "Western turn" to prioritize individual self-realization seems precluded. This applies in particular, thirdly, to conditions of poverty as prevail for almost half of the South African population and for conditions of highly unequal access to the benefits that a society is basically capable to provide, such as healthcare and basic and higher education, as they suggest that this society does not exist as a collectivity of responsibility.[4]

For a long time, in contrast, west European modernity – to limit ourselves to this part of the global North – assumed not only to have solved all the above issues but to have institutionalized the solutions so that they would be forever safely available. The solutions are, first, the democratic nation-state, in which the homogeneity of the nation paves the way for the emergence of a general, collective will in popular sovereignty; second, the liberal constitutional state of law, which combines the commitment to individual liberty with constitutional guarantees, thus eternalizing the liberal achievement and limiting the power of potentially tyrannical majorities; and thirdly, the welfare state institutionalizing social solidarity by redistributing the surplus generated by the smoothly managed functioning of a market economy.

Today we can see that these developments have neither provided general solutions nor permanent achievements whose superiority resides in their conceptual foundations, but we can recognize them as historical responses to problems arising in particular form in European settings. The temporary nature of these solutions can be gathered from two further observations, a historical one and one on the current situation. Historically, the solutions were basically all already at hand when European modernity transformed into the totalitarianisms of the post-First World War period. Some of their elements were even used for this transformation, such as the ideas about the unity of the nation and the historical role of working-class solidarity. Others, such as the ideas of individual rights and constitutional guarantees, were insufficient to defend the achievements of modernity in Europe at that moment in history. Today, again, one cannot be too sure about the permanent nature of the features of European modernity. The reach of the general will in its national expression is questioned both by infra-nation-state movements and the process of European political integration. The relation between individual and collective autonomy is at stake anew when the position of one's own collectivity in the global context needs to be determined. Furthermore,

---

4   It shall just be noted that, mutatis mutandis, these three issues are similarly relevant for the current constellation of Brazilian modernity.

the emphasis on individual liberty reaches conceptual limits in novel debates about cultural rights, ethical issues, and about the ecological sustainability of a way of living in which consumption is seen as a major expression of individual self-realization. Thirdly, the "European social model" is under strain due to heightened global competitiveness that limits the surplus to be distributed. In such a situation of Northern crisis and Southern determination to address long-neglected issues, we see, first, a new diversity of forms of modernity emerging and, second, may find that the Southern varieties prove to be more apt to address the challenges of the time.

References

Arjomand, S. (ed.) Forthcoming. *Social Theory and Regional Studies*. New York: Stony Brook Press.

Asad, T. 1995. *Anthropology and the Colonial Encounter*. New York: Prometheus.

Bourdieu, P. 1980. *Le Sens Pratique*. Paris: Minuit.

Butler, A. 2010. The African National Congress under Jacob Zuma, in *2010: Development or decline?* edited by J. Daniel et al., *New South African Review*, no. 1. Johannesburg: Wits University Press, 164–83.

Chabal, P. 2009. *Africa: The Politics of Suffering and Smiling*. Scottsville: University of KwaZulu-Natal Press.

Chipkin, I. 2007. *Do South Africans Exist? Nationalism, Democracy and the Identity of "the People"*. Johannesburg: University of the Witwatersrand Press.

Delanty, G., Mota, A. Forthcoming. Brazil and the multiple modernities framework. *Proto-Sociology*.

Derrida, J. 1989. *Of Spirit: Heidegger and the Question*, trans. G. Bennington and R. Bowlby. Chicago: Chicago University Press.

Dlamini, J. 2009. *Native Nostalgia*. Johannesburg: Jacana.

Domingues, J.M. 2008. *Latin America and Contemporary Modernity: A Sociological Interpretation*. London: Routledge.

Elliott, J.H. 2000. The discovery of America and the discovery of man, in *Facing Each Other. The World's Perception of Europe and Europe's Perception of the World (An Expanding World*, vol. 31, part I), edited by A. Pagden. Aldershot: Ashgate.

Forment, C.A. 2003. *Democracy in Latin America 1760–1900*. Chicago: University of Chicago Press.

Giddens, A. 1984. *The Constitution of Society*. Cambridge: Polity.

Hartz, L. 1955. *The Liberal Tradition in America*. New York: Harcourt, Brace, and World.

Hartz, L. 1964. *The Founding of New Societies. Studies in the History of the United States, Latin America, South Africa, Canada, and Australia*. San Diego: Harcourt, Brace, Jovanovich.

Holston, J. 2008. *Insurgent Citizenship: Disjunctions of Democracy and Modernity in Brazil*. Princeton: Princeton University Press.

Karagiannis, N. 2007. Multiple solidarities, in *Varieties of World-making*, edited by N. Karagiannis and P. Wagner. Liverpool: Liverpool University Press, 154–72.

Krog, A. 1998. *Country of my Skull. Guilt, Sorrow, and the Limits of Forgiveness in the New South Africa*. New York: Random House Broadway.

Larrain, J. 2007. Latin American varieties of modernity, in *Varieties of World-making*, edited by N. Karagiannis and P. Wagner, 41–58.

Larrain, J. 2000. *Identity and Modernity in Latin America*. Cambridge: Polity.

Lipton, M. 2007. *Liberals, Marxists and Nationalists. Competing Interpretations of South African History*. New York: Palgrave Macmillan.

Mbembe, A. 2001. *On the Postcolony*. Berkeley: University of California Press.

Mota, A. 2012. Researching Brazilian modernity. Programme-paper within the research project "Trajectories of modernity". Barcelona.

Offe, C. 1998. Demokratie und Wohlfahrtsstaat: eine europäische Regimeform unter dem Streß der europäischen Integration, in *Internationale Wirtschaft, nationale Demokratie*, edited by W. Streeck, Frankfurt/M: Campus, 99–136.

Ortega, F. In preparation. *"Born of the Same Womb, Different in Origin and Blood". Social Fragmentation and the Making of Latin America 1760–1860*.

Seekings, J. and Nattrass, N. 2006. *Class, Race, and Inequality in South Africa*. Durban: University of KwaZulu-Natal Press.

Smith, J. 2009. Civilizational analysis and intercultural models of American societies. *Journal of Intercultural Studies*, vol. 30, no. 3, 233–48.

Taylor, C. 1985. *Philosophical Papers*, vol. I. Cambridge: Cambridge University Press.

Wagner, P. 1999. The resistance that modernity constantly provokes. Europe, America and social theory. *Thesis Eleven*, no. 58, 35–58.

Wagner, P. 2003. As intellectual history meets historical sociology. Historical sociology after the linguistic turn, in *Handbook of Historical Sociology*, edited by G. Delanty and E. Isin. London: Sage, 168–79.

Wagner, P. 2008. *Modernity as Experience and Interpretation*. Cambridge: Polity.

Wagner, P. 2010. The future of sociology: Understanding the transformations of the social, in *History and Development of Sociology*, edited by C. Crothers. UNESCO online Encyclopedia.

Wagner, P. 2011a. From interpretation to civilization – and back: Trajectories of European and non-European modernities. *European Journal of Social Theory*, vol. 14, no. 1.

Wagner, P. 2011b. Violence and justice in global modernity: Reflections on South Africa with world-sociological intent. *Social Science Information/Information sur les sciences sociales*, vol. 50, October.

Wagner, P. 2012a. World-sociology beyond the fragments, in *Social Theory and Regional Studies*, edited by S. Arjomand. New York: Stony Brook Press.

Wagner, P. 2012b. *Modernity: Understanding the Present*. Cambridge: Polity.

Index

Abou El Fadl, K. 25, 27–8, 30–31, 35
Abû Zayd, N. 24–5, 35
Ackerman, B. 33
Adams, S. 2, 15
Agadjanian, A. 10–11, 14, 79, 90–91, 93,
    99–100, 107, 111
Agamben, G. 84, 93
Agos 64–5, 76
Akhiezer, A. 80, 94
AKP (Justice and Development Party)
    67–8
Alexander I, Tsar 80
Alexander II, Tsar 80
Allen, M. 122, 124, 138
ANC (African National Congress) 168,
    175
Anderson M.M. 124, 138
Anderson, A. 157, 160
An-Na'im, A.A. 27–8, 35
apartheid 168, 174–6
Arendt, H. 34, 36
Arjomand, S. 164, 178
Arnason, J.P. 2, 15, 104, 111
Asad, T. 117, 138, 166, 172, 178
Asamoha-Gyadu, K. 157, 160
Asch, S. 156, 161
Assmann, J. 17
Atatürk, K. 9, 62–8, 77
Audi, R. 105, 111
Augé, M. 160–61
Augustine 60
axial civilizations
    and modernity 86, 164
    and reflectivity, *see* Reflectivity and
      axial civilizations
    and religions 7, 86
Azimi, S. 55–6, 60

Baker, C. 4, 15
Barbato, M. 109, 113

Bateye, B.O. 151, 161
Bauman, Z. 44
Beaumont, J. 4, 15, 65, 75, 141
Beck, U. 6, 15
Beckford, J. 71, 75
Bediako, K. 145, 161
Bellah, R. 6, 15, 35
Berdiaev, N.A. 90, 94
Berger, P. 74–5, 87, 94
Berkes, N. 68, 75
Berry, S. 122, 141
Besançon, A. 90, 94
Bhargava, R. 12, 15, 78, 118, 122, 134–5,
    138
Bhattarai, A.M. 126, 130–31, 139
Bishop Ilarion [Alfeev] 99, 107, 111–12
Biswakarma, K. 137, 139
Böckenförde, E.-W. 32, 35
Boesche, R. 24, 36
Bolaji Idowu, E. 147, 161
Bourdieu, A. 44, 85, 88, 91, 94, 168, 178
Brazil 163, 165–8, 174, 177
Bubandt, N. 136, 139
Buddhism
    and consent 25
    and common good 23
    and equality of human beings 27
    and human rights 31
    and individuality 28
    and multiple modernities 7
    in Nepal, *see* Nepal and Buddhism
    and pluralism 25
Burke, E. 31
Butler, A. 175, 178
Buttici, A. 144, 150, 162
Byrnes, T.A. 97, 105, 112

Cady, L.E. 118, 139
Calhoun, C. 1, 6, 12, 15, 60, 86, 94, 117,
    139

Çamuroglu, R. 44, 60
Cannell, F. 117, 139
Casanova, J. 2, 5, 15, 74, 87, 94, 102, 105,
        112, 117–19, 139
Castoriadis, C. 84
Catherine the Great 80
Catholicism
    and modernity 5
    and modernization 106
    and secularism 107
Çayir, K. 70, 75
Chabal, P. 175, 178
Chakrabarty, D. 29, 36
Chang, W. 27, 36
Cheng, C. 28, 36
China 39, 81, 88, 93, 143, 163
Chipkin, I. 175, 178
Christian, D. 80, 94
Christian orthodoxy
    and civilizational analysis 97–8,
        102–104, 107
    and democracy 98
    and political culture 5
    and post-communist revival 98, 103,
        106
    in Russia, *see* Russian Orthodox
        Church
    in Turkey 65–6
Çinar, A. 70, 75
Cizre, U. 67, 75
Clarke, G.L. 69, 75
colonialism 145–7, 156, 163–4, 166, 170,
        172
complementary learning process,
        see postsecular (society) and
        complementary learning process
confucianism
    and consent 26
    and individuality 28
    and pluralism 33
    and political culture 7
    and the priority of rights 30–31
Confucius 24–5, 27, 31, 36
Connolly, W. 86, 94
Corten, A. 144, 158, 161
Cosmopolitanism 6
CSPS (Centre for the Study and
        Documentation of Religions and

Political Institutions in Postsecular
        Society) 1, 115

Dagi, I. 61, 76
Danilevsky, N. 81
Davie, G. 3, 13, 15, 71, 74, 76
Davis, D.H. 98, 112
Davison, A. 62, 68–9, 76, 78
Davutoglu, A. 61, 76
De Maistre 31
De Sales, A. 125, 138
Delanty, J. 164, 178
Deleuze, G. 154, 161
Della Dora, V. 65, 76
democracy
    agonistic 32–3
    consociationalist 34–5
    and collective self-determination
        174–6
    and common good 7, 22–4, 26, 30, 34
    and consent 19, 24–6, 29–30, 32
    deliberative 108
    and democratic ethos 7, 23, 33–4
    and equality of citizens 108, 174–6
    liberal 170–71, 176–7
    multiple democracies 17–40
    and pluralism 24–6, 29, 33–4
    and political conflict 176
    and priority of rights 30–32
    and protestantism 7, 17–18, 22–3
    and religious tradition 109
de-privatization of religion, *see* postsecular
        (society) and de-privatization of
        religion
Derrida, J. 166, 178
de-secularization 4, 90, 118–19
Desroche, H. 156, 161
Diamond, L.J. 22, 36
Dink, H. 9, 64–7, 76
Diotallevi, L. 68, 76
Dlamini, J. 175, 178
Domingues, J.M. 171, 178
Dostoyevsky, F. 10, 81
Dressler, M. 61, 76
Durkheim, É. 13, 16, 32, 57, 83, 151, 160
Duso, G. 20, 36

Eisenstadt, S.N. 2, 7, 15, 16–20, 35–9,
    75–6, 81, 83–6, 94, 102, 109, 112,
    120, 139, 143, 161–3
Elliott, J.H. 173, 178
enlightenment
    fragments 168–70, 172–4
    and racial encounter 166, 172–3
    religious 87, 95
    secular 87
Esposito, L. 68–70, 78
Europe 10, 43–4, 49, 60, 67, 80–84,
    87, 89–90, 92, 97–8, 102–105,
    107, 111, 117, 144, 163, 166–7,
    169–170
Ezbudun, E. 67, 77

Falola, T. 160, 161, 162
Ferrara, A. 6, 7–8, 10–11, 16–17, 22, 36,
    97
Fiorenza, F. 87, 94
Forment, C. 171, 178
Foret, F. 97, 112
Foucault, M. 84, 94
Frank, K. 69, 78
Fraser, N. 56, 60
Freston, P. 144, 161
Fukuyama, F. 18–19, 36

Gellner, D.N. 121, 123, 127, 137, 139–40
Giddens, A. 83, 94, 167, 178
Giesen, B. 62, 65, 76
Gillespie, G. 86, 94
Gifford, P. 149, 161
Göle, N. 4, 9, 16, 42, 46–7, 59–61, 70,
    75–7, 117, 140
Gorski, P.S. 6, 16
Greeley, A. 98, 112
Greve, A. 65, 76
Grigoriadis, I.N. 70, 76
Guattari, F. 154, 161
Gülalp, H. 61, 76
Gülen, F. 70, 78

Habermas, J. 3–6, 11, 16, 22, 32, 36, 56,
    60, 68–9, 71, 74, 76, 91–2, 94,
    105–106, 107–110, 112–14, 118,
    140
Hachett, R.I.J. 151, 161

Haghia Sophia (Ayasofya) 9, 65–6
Halbwachs, M. 65, 77
Hale, W.M. 67, 77
Hallaq, W. 25, 37
Hanioglu, M.Ş. 64, 77
Hartz, L. 165–74, 178
Hasrat, B.J. 122, 140
Hausner, S. 137, 140
Hayes, R.P. 25, 37
Hefner, R.W. 88, 94
Hegel, F.W. 20, 31, 36–7, 54
Herr, R.S. 26–7, 37
Hinduism
    and common good 7, 23–4
    and equality of human beings 27
    in Nepal, *see* Nepal and Hinduism
    and pluralism 33
    and political culture 33
Hoelzl, M. 5, 16
Holston, J. 168, 179
Honneth, A. 26, 37
human rights 35, 39, 64, 67, 73, 91, 93, 97,
    99, 100–102, 107–108, 110, 122,
    125–31, 133, 136
Human Rights Document of the Russian
    Orthodox Church, *see* Russian
    Orthodox Church and human rights
Huntington, S.P. 18–19, 37

Il'in, V. 80, 94
immanent frame 4, 92, 113
India 20, 88, 91, 93, 115, 122, 125, 134,
    137, 143, 163, 173
Inglehart, R. 98, 113
Interpenetration 4, 9, 16, 76
Iran
    and Islamic veiling 8, 45, 49, 51–2, 59
    and public sphere 8–9, 41–60
    religious authoritarianism 45
    and Turkey, *see* Turkey and Iran
Isin, E.F. 70, 77
Islam
    Alevis 44, 67, 69, 78
    and coffeehouses 8, 44, 49–50
    and common good 7
    and consent 25
    and consumption 9, 47–9, 54–5, 57, 60
    and equality of human beings 27

and gender-relations 50, 52–3
and holiday sites 44, 48, 50, 59
and individuality 28, 34
and Islamic politics 47, 75
and life-styles 9, 53
and pluralism 2, 9, 24–6, 42, 65, 68
and priority of rights 30, 34
and public space 41–60
and secular life-styles 9, 41–60
Shiite 44, 46, 53, 58
Sufi 50
Sunni 8, 25, 44, 46, 64, 67, 69, 73–4
and veiling 41–60
and westernization 41, 81
Islamism 8, 43–4, 46–7, 51, 54, 59
Itçaina, X. 97, 112

Jakelević, S. 5, 16
Jakobsen, J. 118, 140
Jaspers, K. 7, 17, 20, 37
Jedan, C. 4, 15
Jenkins, G. 144, 161
Jenkins, P. 62, 77, 144, 161
Judah, T. 57, 60
Judaism
    and pluralism 25
Juergensmeyer, M. 1, 6, 15, 12, 117, 139

Kalmanson, L. 27, 36
Kalu, O. 145, 148, 153, 157, 161
Karagiannis, N. 176, 178
Karasipahi, S. 68–9, 77
Kateb, G. 22, 28, 37
Kattel, S. 121, 140
Katzenstein, P.J. 97, 105, 113
Kaul, V. 6, 16
Kemalism, *see* secularism, Kemalist
Keyman, E.F. 75, 77
Kieser, H.-L. 69, 77
Knöbl, W. 103–104, 113
Knott, K. 4, 8, 16, 65
Kömeçoglu, U. 2, 8–9, 41, 47, 49, 60, 70, 77
Kong, L. 65, 77
Kostjuk, K. 99, 113
Kratochwil, F. 109, 113
Krog, Antjie 175, 179

Kumari, *see* Nepal and living goddess Kumari
Kupperman, J. 28, 37
Kyrlezhev, A. 92, 94
Kyuman, K. 6, 16

Lane, C. 90, 94
Lanternari, V. 156, 161
Larrain, J. 171, 179
Lassander, M. 6, 16
Laurent, J.P. 156, 161
Lawless, E.J. 151, 161
Lecomte-Tilouine, M. 125, 140
Leontiev, K. 81
Lerner, D. 68, 77
Letizia, C. 11–13, 115, 122, 132, 140
Leve, L. 120, 140
Levingston, J. 87, 94
Lewis, B. 68, 77
liberalism
    criticism of 107
    and democracy, *see* democracy
    and religious claims 99
Lienhard, S. 122, 140
linguistic turn 164
Lijphart, A. 34–5, 37
Lipton, M. 175, 179
Lotman, Y. 80, 95

Machiavelli, N. 32, 34, 37
Madan, T.N. 117, 140
Maharjan Pun Devi 126–9, 130–33, 136, 140
Mahmood, S. 118, 140
March, A. 28, 37
Mardin, Ş. 62, 70, 77
Margalit, A. 26, 37
Markham, I.S. 73, 77
Marshall-Fratani, R. 144, 158
Martin, D. 87, 95, 117, 140
Martin, M.L. 156, 161
Marx, K. 31, 70, 82–4
Mary, A. 156, 161
Mbembe, A. 172, 179
Meeker, M.E. 62, 68, 77
Mendieta, E. 16, 94–5, 105, 109, 113

Metropolitan Kirill of Smolensk and
    Kaliningrad, *see* Patriarch Kirill of
    Moscow
Metz, J. 87, 95
Meyer, B. 152, 160–62
Michaels, A. 122, 125, 136, 141
Milbank, J. 87, 95
Miller, D.E. 149, 162
Moaven, N. 122, 141
modernity
    and human agency 164–5, 167, 169–70
    implicit 11, 85, 91–2
    interpretative space of 164, 169–71
    and new societies 165–70, 172
    Western program of, *see* Western
      modernity
modernization
    Bolshevik 10, 80–81
    classical theories of 117, 143, 160,
      163–6
    and religion, *see* religious traditions
      and modernization
Mokoko Gampiot, A. 156, 162
Molendijk, A.L. 4, 15, 118, 141
Montesquieu, C.L. 23, 33, 37
Mota, A. 164, 171, 179
Müller, O. 98, 113
Mulmi, A.R. 132, 141
multiple modernities
    criticism of 103–104, 163–6
    definition 97, 102, 107–108, 110–11,
      143, 160
    and local modernities 163, 165–6,
      170
    and multiple democracies 17–40
    and postsecular society, *see* postsecular
      (society) and multiple modernities
    and religious traditions 100–104, 109,
      143, 160
Murti, T.R.V. 25, 38

Nattrass, N. 176, 179
Navaro-Yashin, Y. 63, 77
Nepal
    and Buddhism 120–23, 129–31, 135,
      139
    and Hinduism 115–16, 120–23, 125,
      130–31, 134–8
    and living goddess Kumari 116, 121,
      122–33, 135–8
    and multiple modernities 119–20, 138
    and postsecular society 138
    and religious minorities 120–21, 134,
      138
    and secularism 115–17, 119–22, 126,
      130, 132–5, 137–8
Neumann, I.B. 111, 113
Nietzsche, F. 84
Nigeria
    and modernization 143–5, 157–8
    and multiple modernities 145, 160–61
    and Pentecostalism, *see* Pentecostalism
    religious diversity in 147
normativity, *see* postsecular (society),
    normative and empirical
    dimensions
Norris, P. 98, 113
Nursi, S. 70, 73, 77
Nynäs, P. 6, 16

Offe, C. 176, 179
Ojo, M. 149–50, 156, 158–9, 162
Okur, Ö. 49, 60
Olajubu, O. 151, 162
Omenyo, C.N. 149, 162
Ortega, F. 171, 179
Orthodox Christianity, *see* Christian
    orthodoxy
Özal, T. 61, 67, 70
Özdalga, E. 69, 70, 77
Özdemir, A. 69, 78
Özyürek, E. 62–3, 78

Pace, V. 2, 13–14, 144–5, 149–50, 162
Pamuk, O. 69, 81
Panarin, A. 94
Parla, T. 62, 68–9, 78
Pase, A. 146, 154, 162
Patriarch Kirill of Moscow 99, 101,
    102–104, 107, 113
Paz, O. 81
Peel, J.D.Y. 157, 162
Pellegrini, A. 118, 140
Pentecostalism
    and empowerment and communication
      149, 151

and indigenous religious traditions 145,
147–8, 157, 160
and modernization 145, 149, 157, 159
and pastoral leadership 144–5, 148–51,
153–5, 157
and sacred space 145, 150–51, 154,
158, 160
and women pastors 150–51
and young generations 151, 158
Peter the Great 80
Pirim, S.B. 73, 77
Plato 21
Poe, M. 80, 95
postsecular (society)
and co-existence 4–6
and complementary learning process
3–6, 8–9, 71–4, 106, 108
definition 3–6, 8, 70–75, 105–106,
108–109, 118
and de-privatization of religions 5–6
global postsecular society 109
and multiple modernities 98, 104–105,
107–10, 118
and mutual translation 108
normative and empirical dimensions
106, 108–10
and public sphere, *see* public sphere
and postsecular society
and reflectivity 4–6, 9–12, 71–3, 106,
119
and religious pluralism 98, 100–101,
106, 109, 111
and the sacred 5–6, 74
sanctuaries 65
social practices 8–9, 72–5
principled distance 12, 134
protestantism, *see* Western modernity and
protestantism
public reason 4, 28, 38
public sphere
multifaceted 8, 41, 43, 45
and neutrality 47
and postsecular society 68, 73–4, 92,
98, 106, 119
and religions 3–5, 8–9, 41–59, 61–8,
91, 133–5
Putnam, R. 145, 155, 162

Ramet, S.P. 98, 113
Ramirez, P. 125, 141
Rasmussen, D. 6, 16, 31–8
Rawls, J. 23–4, 34, 36, 38, 68, 91, 95, 105,
113
reflectivity
and axial civilizations 4
and religious traditions 4, 6, 71–3, 106,
119
and Western modernity 106, 109–10,
119
religious pluralism, *see* postsecular
(society) and religious pluralism
religious traditions
and authoritarianism 45
collectivistic 5, 16
and de-privatization 119
distinction between religion and culture
127–8, 132–3
freedom of 24, 27, 68–9, 73, 100, 120,
130, 134
and modernization 2, 7, 11, 13–15,
41–60, 61–75, 88, 99–100, 102,
109, 116, 118, 120, 131, 143, 160
and principled tolerance 4, 72
and public reason 4, 122
and reflectivity, *see* reflectivity and
religious traditions
and secular forms of life 100, 144
and secularization (of religion) 4–6, 10,
55, 74, 105, 107, 116–18, 127, 143
and Western liberal democracy 23, 29
Riedel, J. 143, 162
Robertson, R. 90, 95
Robson, R. 89, 95
Rosati, M. 1, 2, 8–9, 14, 119, 141
Rousseau, J.J. 23, 38
Rousselet, K. 90, 93
Roy, O. 73, 78
Russia
and modernization 80–82, 107
and multiple modernities 88, 111, 163
and postsecular society 90–92, 100,
104, 107, 111
and secularization 86, 98
and Western European modernity 98–9,
102–103, 111
Russian Orthodox Church

and cultural tradition 102, 110
and human rights 99–102, 104,
    106–108, 110
and modernization 87, 98–100, 103,
    105–108, 111
and nationalism 98, 104
and Old Believers 89
and secularism 98–101, 103, 107–108
the bases of the social teaching of the
    99–100, 104, 106–107

Sachsenmeier, D. 143, 162
sacred (the)
    eclipse of 5
    immanent and heteronomous 6
    and postsecular society 6, 55, 65, 74
Sadiki, L. 22, 38
Sadria, M. 58, 60
sanctuaries, *see* postsecular sanctuaries
Schluchter, W. 102, 112
Schmidt, L.P. 99, 113
secularism
    assertive and passive 9, 12, 64, 68–9,
        77
    and authoritarianism 45
    contextual 134–5
    and immanent frame 4, 92
    Kemalist 8, 63, 66, 68–9
    and life-styles 9, 53
    multiple secularisms 118–21
    and reflectivity 4–6, 71–3, 119
    and religious symbols 47, 66
    and Western modernity 98, 118
secularization, classical theories of 3, 8,
        10, 17, 41, 69, 71, 73, 79, 117–19,
        134
Seekings, J. 176, 179
Seligman, A.B. 4, 6, 14, 16, 25, 30, 38, 71
settler societies, *see* modernity and new
        societies
Shakman Hurd, E. 118, 139
Shakya, R. 122, 141
Shankland, D. 69, 78
Sharma, S. 115, 141
Shils, E. 62, 78
Shootill, J.E. 151, 162
Simmel, G. 33, 38
Slavophiles 81, 89

Slusser, M.S. 122
Smith, J. 164, 179
Smith, K.E. 2, 15
social doctrine, *see* Russian Orthodox
        Church, the bases of the social
        teaching of the
Sorkin, D. 86–87, 95
Soroush, A. 30, 38
Soviet Union 82, 89–90, 99, 163
South Africa 14–15, 163, 165–9, 173–8
Spohn, W. 97, 102, 113
Shrestha, J. 129, 141
Stoeckl, K. 10–11, 14, 99, 114
Suny, R. 80, 95

Taha, M.M. 27, 38
Tasie, G.O.M. 156, 162
Taylor, C. 4, 16, 26, 31, 32, 38, 68, 75, 78,
        88, 92, 95, 118, 168–9, 179
Tepe, S. 67, 78
Therborn, G. 88, 95
Thesing, J. 107, 114
Thiebaut, C. 74, 78
Thomassen, B. 20, 39
Thurman, R. 29, 39
Toffin, G. 122, 141
Tohidi, N. 46, 60
Tocqueville, A. 26, 39, 171, 176
Torpey, J. 6, 16
Touraine, A. 58, 60
Tschannen, O. 154, 162
Tu, W. 25, 39
Tuğal, C. 70, 78
Turgenev, I. 81
Turkey
    and Armenians 64, 67
    and Ergenekon 64
    and Iran 41–60
    and Islamic veiling 45–51
    and Kemalism 41–60, 62–77
    and modernization 41–3, 57, 61, 69,
        70–1, 79
    and multiple modernities 41–59, 61–75
    and postsecular society 41–60, 61–75
    and public space 9, 44–5, 47, 49–55,
        61, 63–4, 66–8
    and secularism 41–59, 61–75
    and secular nationalism 64

and social memory 49, 63–7
symbolic value system 62
and Western European modernity 42,
61
Turner, B.S. 3, 16

Uertz, R. 99, 107, 114
Ukah, A.K. 159, 162
United States of America 165–6, 168–70,
172–3
Upreti, M. 127, 141
Uspensky, B. 80, 95
Utriainen, T. 6, 16

Vajracharya, C. 128–9, 141
Van Beek, M. 118, 136, 139
Van Dijk, R. 157, 162
Van Antwerpen, J. 1, 6, 12, 15–16, 95, 117,
139
Vlahov, G. 2, 15
Voegelin, H. 20, 36, 39
Voltaire 24

Wagner, P. 14–15, 104, 114, 163, 169, 174,
179
Währisch-Oblau, C. 144, 162
Walitsky, A. 81, 95
Walzer, M. 19, 20, 25, 39, 105, 114
Ward, G. 5, 16
Wariboko, N. 156, 162

Warner, S. 86, 96
Weber, A. 17
Weber, M. 7, 9, 17–18, 20, 22, 31, 38–9,
83, 86, 155
Western modernity
and cultural hegemony 109, 117, 164
cultural program of 98, 101–102, 105,
109, 116–18, 143, 164–7, 172, 177
and democracy 17–35, 177
and inner tensions 105, 109–10, 164,
177
and priority of rights 30–32
and Protestantism 7, 17–18, 22–3, 118,
164–5, 167
and religious individualism 5, 13, 119
and reflectivity, *see* reflectivity and
Western modernity
and secularization 2, 4, 8, 15, 41, 73,
87, 97–8, 105, 110, 143
selective appropriation of 100–101,
138, 177
Wittrock, B. 2, 3, 15
Woodiwiss, T. 32, 39

Yamanori, T. 149, 162
Yavuz, M.H. 63, 67–70, 78
Yitik, A.İ. 24, 39

Zaman, M.Q. 23, 39
Zhuk, S. 89, 96